REPETITION

Hay House Titles of Related Interest

YOU CAN HEAL YOUR LIFE, the movie,
starring Louise L. Hay & Friends
(available as a 1-DVD program and an expanded 2-DVD set)
Watch the trailer at: **www.LouiseHayMovie.com**

EVERYTHING YOU NEED TO KNOW TO FEEL GO(O)D,
by Candace B. Pert, Ph.D., with Nancy Marriott

*HEALING YOUR FAMILY HISTORY: 5 Steps to Break Free
of Destructive Patterns,* by Rebecca Linder Hintze

*MESSAGES FROM SPIRIT: The Extraordinary Power of Oracles,
Omens, and Signs,* by Colette Baron-Reid

THE MIRACLES OF ARCHANGEL MICHAEL, by Doreen Virtue

PAST LIVES, PRESENT MIRACLES, by Denise Linn

*REGRESSION TO TIMES AND PLACES,
SPIRITUAL PROGRESS THROUGH REGRESSION,* and
REGRESSION THROUGH THE MIRRORS OF TIME:
3 CDs by Brian L. Weiss, M.D.

*TEMPLES ON THE OTHER SIDE: How Wisdom from
"Beyond the Veil" Can Help You Right Now,* by Sylvia Browne

*TRANSFORMING FATE INTO DESTINY:
A New Dialogue with Your Soul,* by Robert Ohotto

All of the above are available at your
local bookstore, or may be ordered by visiting:

Hay House USA: **www.hayhouse.com**®
Hay House Australia: **www.hayhouse.com.au**
Hay House UK: **www.hayhouse.co.uk**
Hay House South Africa: **www.hayhouse.co.za**
Hay House India: **www.hayhouse.co.in**

REPETITION

Past Lives, Life, and Rebirth

DORIS ELIANA COHEN, Ph.D.

HAY HOUSE, INC.
Carlsbad, California • New York City
London • Sydney • Johannesburg
Vancouver • Hong Kong • New Delhi

Published and distributed in the United States by: Hay House, Inc.: www.hayhouse.com • *Published and distributed in Australia by:* Hay House Australia Pty. Ltd.: www.hayhouse.com.au • *Published and distributed in the United Kingdom by:* Hay House UK, Ltd.: www.hayhouse.co.uk • *Published and distributed in the Republic of South Africa by:* Hay House SA (Pty), Ltd.: www.hayhouse.co.za • *Distributed in Canada by:* Raincoast: www.raincoast.com • *Published in India by:* Hay House Publishers India: www.hayhouse.co.in

Editorial supervision: Jill Kramer • *Design:* Tricia Breidenthal

Library of Congress Cataloging-in-Publication Data

Cohen, Doris Eliana
  Repetition : past lives, life, and rebirth / Doris Eliana Cohen. -- 1st ed.
    p. cm.

  ISBN-13: 978-1-4019-2021-0 (hardcover)
  ISBN-13: 978-1-4019-2020-3 (tradepaper) 1. Reincarnation therapy. I. Title.
  RC489.R43C64 2008
  616.89'14--dc22   2008005428

Hardcover ISBN: 978-1-4019-2021-0
Tradepaper ISBN: 978-1-4019-2020-03

11 10 09 08   4 3 2 1
1st edition, November 2008

Printed in the United States of America

This book is dedicated with
all of my love and appreciation to:

*The thousands of clients from
whom I have learned so much*

*All of my mentors and teachers who have
lovingly helped and supported me over the years*

*My Spirit Guides and Angels who
have tirelessly and patiently inspired,
loved, and instructed me for decades*

*And to all of you who read this book—
may you embrace the Light that dwells
within you and change your world*

Author's Note: The beliefs in this book are strictly mine and have evolved from my work as a clinical psychologist, past-life-regression hypnotherapist, psychic reader, dream analyst, Reiki healer, and exorcist for more than three decades, with many thousands of clients. The spiritual inspiration for this work comes from my Angels and Spirit Guides, who channel their wisdom to me. Thus, the information provided is the result of what I have learned, experienced, and channeled throughout the course of my extensive and comprehensive practice.

I deliberately did not discuss in detail, nor did I annotate, the vast body of research and data mentioned herein that I and others have done or gathered throughout the years. My intent in writing this book is not to have it viewed as an academic work, but rather as a teaching aid for those interested in better understanding how repetition works in their lives.

Some of the stories are graphic and may disturb some readers. I have included them because it's important to understand that many of our repetitions began with serious emotional, physical, and psychological trauma in this lifetime or in a past life—and yet, if one uses the four techniques explained in this book, significant healing is always possible.

My clients' names, professions, locations, and other specific details have been changed to protect their privacy.

CONTENTS

FOREWORD

You hold in your hands an illuminating and practical guide for making the most of your life right now. *Repetition* can teach you how to identify and change patterns that originated before you were born. This knowledge is brought to you by clinical psychologist Doris Cohen, Ph.D., with the purest intentions and from a place of both nurturing and self-empowerment. And it can set you free. It has certainly helped me! All you need do is open your mind and heart to the truth that is written here. Savor the wisdom and lessons this book has to offer. In return, you'll gain insights that can set you free from the past—so that you can live your life more fully and joyfully.

Doris makes it crystal clear why so-called bad things happen to good people—and even why good things happen to so-called bad people! Moreover, she presents this information in riveting story form, with case histories that help you apply it to your own life, right now. Peace and healing are the result. At the same time, of course, this knowledge doesn't preclude you from doing your best to compassionately alleviate suffering—both your own and that of others—whenever possible.

Although I've long believed in reincarnation and past lives, it is a very rare individual who is able to help put this information into a context that is immediately relevant and helpful to daily life in the present. Doris is just such an individual. Believe me—I've been a student of this type of information for years, so I know a treasure such as she when I find one!

Here's a little background: When I was 13 years old, I read the classic book *Many Mansions: The Edgar Cayce Story on Reincarnation*, about the famous sleeping prophet Edgar Cayce. This man, who would be called a medical intuitive these days, had the ability to diagnose the causes of many illnesses that mystified the doctors of his day. Very often he made reference to past-life conditions that were precursors to the current ones. Frequently, his advice (when followed) cured the patient.

According to Cayce, his ability to "read" people came from a lifetime in which he was lying on a battlefield, mortally wounded and in great pain. Before dying, he managed to free his consciousness from the confines of his physical self. This gave him access to all kinds of knowledge about others that simply wasn't available when he was trapped in a painful body. He was born into a subsequent life (as Edgar Cayce) with the extraordinary ability to know things about others that can't be explained logically.

When I first came upon Cayce's material on reincarnation and past lives, it made perfect sense to me. *Yes, of course,* I thought. *This feels absolutely correct. I already knew this.* Knowing that we are old souls at birth—and not just blank slates—has provided me with a great deal of peace and comfort, both as an individual and as a doctor who has had to make sense of all kinds of pain and suffering, such as stillbirths, infertility, and premature death. Doris's work has added considerably to this peace and comfort.

Rather than seeing illness as a random event that strikes unfortunate people with bad luck or poor genes, I know deep in my bones that our life circumstances, including our state of health, are strongly correlated with our unique thoughts, beliefs, and constitutions—all of which comprise our "soul qualities." How else can we explain the genius of a Mozart . . . or the fact that at the age of three, I begged my parents to let me play the harp—even though I'd never seen one before? Doris's information also helped me have a greater appreciation for, and understanding of, my mother and the legacy she has provided for me. My mother,

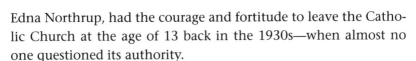

Edna Northrup, had the courage and fortitude to leave the Catholic Church at the age of 13 back in the 1930s—when almost no one questioned its authority.

During the Depression, Edna worked at a Catholic girls' school to pay her way. When the mother superior wrongly accused her of painting the Virgin Mary's toenails, she left the church and never returned. Although blameless, my mom was never given the chance to prove her innocence. When she had a reading with Doris, Edna was told that in a past life she had been a man living in Salem, Massachusetts, who was in love with a woman who had been wrongly accused of being a witch. He stood up for that woman, and both were burned at the stake. That couple—with genders reversed—became my parents in this life.

This information put so much in perspective. It's why my parents had the courage to sign my little brother out of the hospital against medical advice—knowing that if they left him there, he would die. Their conviction literally saved his life. And that same backbone has allowed me to redefine women's health and stand up for what I believe—even in the face of considerable ridicule and professional censure, especially in the early days.

As with my family and me, you'll also find that Doris's work will help you see your life and your challenges in the broadest possible context—and as a continuation of many lifetimes. This approach is light-years ahead of the conventional victim mentality of our culture, which posits death and disease as an enemy completely outside of ourselves that can strike out of the blue. This attitude doesn't encompass the whole truth, and it leads to a feeling of helplessness and hopelessness. All meaning is removed from our suffering. Worse yet, it simply prolongs it by favoring the victim role.

Thankfully, Doris provides us all with a better way to look at our challenges. She not only confirms the reality of past lives and their present influence on individuals, but she also provides us with concrete and practical advice for removing ourselves from the wheel of karma and repetition. She educates us, helping us update our perspectives so that we may finally break free and experience the health and happiness that are our birthright!

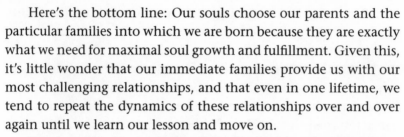

Here's the bottom line: Our souls choose our parents and the particular families into which we are born because they are exactly what we need for maximal soul growth and fulfillment. Given this, it's little wonder that our immediate families provide us with our most challenging relationships, and that even in one lifetime, we tend to repeat the dynamics of these relationships over and over again until we learn our lesson and move on.

For example, if you had a difficult mother whose love you didn't feel fully, you will undoubtedly re-create that same relationship with others (such as a spouse or a boss), until you heal the part of you that feels unlovable as a result of that primary relationship. But as Doris so brilliantly points out, the relationship with your difficult mother didn't begin with your birth either: You are, indeed, old friends. And you're now back doing the same old relationship in another body. A friend of mine once described this as "same doll, different dress." All kidding aside, in dealing with difficult people whose influence I can't seem to get rid of, I've often prayed the following: *Please let me know my role in perpetuating this conflict so that I don't have to come back and have that person as my mother.*

On the other hand, I also know that we are each gifted in this lifetime with the presence of individuals who have loved us and saved our lives in the past and who are now with us to continue providing us with their considerable gifts. My assistant and good friend Diane—who is a blessing to me in every way—is in that category.

One of the things that is most delightful—and helpful—about Doris's approach is the fact that in addition to being able to see the continuing influence of a particular past life on a present situation, she also has a Ph.D. in clinical psychology and is absolutely grounded in Western psychology. She isn't some flighty psychic, but instead is a very astute professional who works only for the highest good of all concerned—without judgment and without making "dire" predictions that can scare a client. Doris's years of compassionate and intelligent service to the highest purpose of all concerned inform every page of this book.

Doris brings something else to her work that makes it very special indeed: She has access to a group of enlightened Guides and Angels who provide her (and her clients—and now you) with a crystal clear picture of why things are happening as they are . . . and better yet, a unique and practical seven-step process to help you change your destiny and get off "automatic pilot." How comforting to know that all of us have Angels and Guides available to help us at all times. All we have to do is call upon them for direction and assistance.

Over the past two years, I've worked with Doris on a wide variety of issues, both personal and professional. I've also referred every member of my family, plus many friends and colleagues. In every case, the person has been touched and helped by the life-changing information that Doris and her Guides and Angels have provided. What I also love about her is that she has absolutely no ego attached to this healing work. She is as uplifted and touched by the quality of her Guides and Angels' messages as her clients are!

It thrills me that through this book people everywhere will find hope; healing; guidance; and most important, the tools they need to rediscover the health, happiness, and peace of mind that are our birthright—regardless of the past.

— **Christiane Northrup, M.D.**

PREFACE

Having been a clinical psychologist and psychotherapist in private practice, Reiki healer and teacher, psychic reader, past-life-regression hypnotherapist, and dream analyst for more than three decades, I felt compelled to write a book on repetition that is based on my broad-ranging experiences, along with the Divine inspiration I received while working with my clients. My intention here is to provide self-help tools for healing in the present lifetime and to give you, the reader, hope that healing can swiftly be achieved if these tools are carefully used.

The essence of *Repetition: Past Lives, Life, and Rebirth* is two-fold: (1) God gave us the gift of free choice, which is the most important message in this book; and (2) we can change ourselves and our world by taking personal responsibility for our stories. The goal is to shift our consciousness: to move away from the mentality of the perpetrator and the victim, the accuser and the accused, the judge and the one who is being judged. The Divine doesn't judge us, and we shouldn't judge ourselves or each other. We must simply open our hearts, see with clarity, and accept that it's up to us to tell our life stories in ways that promote our healing and growth. Only then can we begin the process of making lasting changes in our lives.

Unconsciously, we repeat the stories of our current lives and our previous ones because we're trying to heal from past traumas.

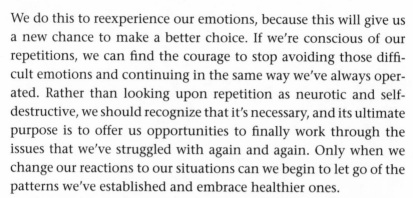

We do this to reexperience our emotions, because this will give us a new chance to make a better choice. If we're conscious of our repetitions, we can find the courage to stop avoiding those difficult emotions and continuing in the same way we've always operated. Rather than looking upon repetition as neurotic and self-destructive, we should recognize that it's necessary, and its ultimate purpose is to offer us opportunities to finally work through the issues that we've struggled with again and again. Only when we change our reactions to our situations can we begin to let go of the patterns we've established and embrace healthier ones.

Acceptance without judgment is vital not only for owning our story, but also for healing ourselves. There are many forms of judgment, including self-criticism, diagnoses that are handed down or imposed upon us by ourselves or others, and self-punishment and denigration. No matter how crazy or self-destructive our behavior may seem, we should let go of our negative judgments and look at its potential to help us heal ourselves physically, emotionally, and spiritually. Blame is distorting. Karma isn't punishment—it is consequence. It functions to help us advance to the next level of consciousness.

We need to stop thinking of ourselves as victims, because then we keep seeing the world through the eyes of our child self—the self that is fearful, unhealed, and incapable of making new choices that will lead to healing. The victim stance prevents us from exploring our spirituality and our relationship to God, the Angels, and our loved ones.

This isn't just a self-help book; it's a guide to understanding how to change. It's about creating a shift in our individual consciousness, and by extension, in humanity at large. Our victim mentality causes us to point a finger at others when we should be looking to ourselves and saying, "What can I do to make changes for the better in my life and in the world?" Change can't happen when we're pointing fingers. Our job while we're here in our human existence is to grow, evolve, unfold, become enlightened, and share our wisdom with others. For too long we've been perceiving ourselves to be victims, and as a result, we've become stuck in our patterns of repetition. It's time for us to stop pointing fingers and begin to heal our own issues.

Repetition takes a unique approach to breaking destructive life patterns and releasing the guilt associated with them. This is the first book to explain why we repeat the stories of our present and relevant past lives and how inevitable and necessary these repetitions are for healing ourselves of the traumas that wounded us not just in the current lifetime, but in our previous ones. My goal is to inspire and guide you in changing your reactions to the repetitions you create so that you can at last heal yourself of these wounds that continue to cause you to suffer.

This work also provides an alternative and less-restrictive way of looking at your life. Instead of wondering why you have all the "bad luck" while others have it so much easier, you'll gain insight into how to accept responsibility for your choices and understand the process of self-healing. You'll learn to move from being a victim to being a creator, from reactor to initiator, and from the child to the adult mode. You'll experience a profound shift in consciousness as you start to recognize that each of us is in charge of our own life.

This book offers a route to freedom and positive change not only for ourselves but also for our world. My ultimate aim is to challenge the way we perceive our lives and help bring about a shift in consciousness in all of humanity. Only when we own our God-given gift of free choice and take responsibility for our stories can we change them, empower ourselves, and transform ourselves from being victims to being co-creators.

PART I

REPETITION

INTRODUCTION

Very often, we feel trapped in a situation and think there's no way out, as if "history is repeating itself" over and over. Actually, it's not history that's repeating itself, but rather, *we* are repeating our stories; history does nothing on its own. Each time we attempt to break a pattern and fail to do so, we begin to feel powerless. We may not even recognize that we're trapped in the cycle of repetition, because we've become deeply entrenched in it. Eventually, frustration and discouragement set in, and the patterns or repetitions seem to run our lives. Most spiritual disciplines teach that God gave us the gift of free choice, which each and every soul exercises moment by moment, both consciously and unconsciously. When we're caught in our patterns, we lose sight of our ability to exercise free choice and thus we feel victimized.

I've heard the same themes over and over again for many years from thousands of clients. These recurring themes are expressed as current- and past-life patterns and traumas. By exploring our present-life stories as well as those of past lifetimes, by identifying the repetitions within these stories, and by acknowledging and completely owning our painful life patterns, we'll begin to recognize the lessons we need to learn—and learn them at last.

At an unconscious level, we repeat patterns, playing out themes in various ways so that we can experience the emotions attached to those patterns again and again. These are the same emotions that originally arose in us during a specific traumatic event in our childhood or relevant past life.

For instance, if as a child you were repeatedly scolded by an angry, raging adult, you might totally avoid confrontation once you grow up or become an angry, raging adult yourself. The pattern created in childhood becomes unconsciously ingrained as part of your behavior in one way or another, setting you up to experience rage—as the angry person yourself or as the one who is at the receiving end of someone else's anger—again and again. Therefore, when you encounter confrontation now, whether it's you who's enraged or the other person, the childhood fear is immediately experienced fully and totally in the present time. You feel as if you're in a battle for your life, and you either withdraw or fight with all your might. You may even be aware that you're overreacting but be confused about why you feel so strongly.

Why are we continually drawn into the same scenarios? The emotions generated by trauma can be very uncomfortable, so we consciously avoid feeling them—yet at the same time, our deep-rooted desire to break away from this discomfort actually inspires us to create situations in our lives that force us to face those emotions and heal them at last. This happens at an unconscious level. Once we've healed the emotions connected to our traumas, we can begin to exit our patterns because we've learned what we needed to learn.

Recognizing and accepting our feelings and repetitions is the first step in the healing process. When viewed without judgment or guilt, our emotions serve as indicators of our patterns, giving us the opportunity to recognize that we're back in the same old classroom and have a choice to change our reaction this time so that we may begin to exit the pattern and move on.

The Power of Past Traumas

Each of us experiences repeated traumas during our lifetime. All such events are fear producing. During a trauma, we experience

tremendous stress and often, some sort of personal loss. Our traumas have a major effect on how we view and respond to life.

Traumatic experiences during early childhood are typically the most defining and have the deepest long-term effect, because as children we don't have the maturity to even begin to process them. These events may be seemingly inconsequential from our adult perspective. It may seem that being teased at school, being chased by a dog, or getting temporarily lost in a store and not knowing where our parents are wouldn't significantly influence us, but children may experience these events as terrifying and horrific.

On the other hand, some of our traumas may have been major, such as dealing with the death of a parent or sibling; overcoming a life-threatening disease; or being subjected to physical, emotional, or sexual abuse. *Any* event that children perceive as threatening their survival in any way leaves an indelible imprint on the brain and affects their behavior patterns, setting them up for repetition of the situation that caused the original wound.

The experience of trauma triggers the same physical reactions in the body and brain whether the threat is great or small; what matters is our *perception* that we're being threatened. The brain secretes chemicals, adrenaline rushes through the body, the heart races, and the experience is stamped into the brain and memory as terrifying. The effects of trauma are so profound and pervasive that they hurt us both emotionally and physically. Stress hormones damage and kill brain cells in the hippocampus, the part of the brain where memory is located, which is why we're forgetful when under stress.

The story we tell about who we are and why we experience life the way we do locks us into our patterns, which we reinforce each time we tell it. The woman who keeps saying, "I always seem to pick the wrong man" is revealing a set of emotional patterns of fear and victimization. She believes this statement to be true about her past, present, and future, so she leaves herself no way out of the pattern. Lacking the belief that it can change, she continues to behave as she always has, yielding the same unhappy results. Her feelings of despair, disappointment, rejection, and abandonment at the end of each relationship reflect the essence of repetition.

She may believe that the "problem"—the source of her pattern—lies in the men she dates, but other people are merely the instruments that push her emotional buttons, which, in turn, trigger reactions and responses that are rooted in her unconscious. Although she probably doesn't realize it, the pattern of behavior is within her, and she's drawn to men who fit into it, so she's not attracted to those who don't match up with it.

Without realizing it, we repeat events and situations again and again because that's what we know. Our behaviors, even when seemingly destructive or self-defeating, feel not just familiar but comfortable in a way, and we're lulled back into that feeling of familiarity and the behaviors attached to it.

Your pattern may be the same as that of your parents, grandparents, and siblings. As you become acquainted with your personal life story, you'll begin to notice recurring themes in other people's lives as well, and even in world events.

The essence of repetition is a profound universal law. It is one of several that guide our human experience.

The Universal Laws

The more I learn, the more I'm amazed by how simple the laws of the universe are; how profound they are; and how applicable they are to the leaves of the trees, to the heart of the deer that runs through the forest, to the thoughts of my clients and their feelings, to my own story and theirs, and to all of us. These same principles apply to everything in us and in the universe.

God's laws are the same everywhere, and the Divine teaches us about them in myriad ways. This redundancy exists because the Creator knows that we humans often do not learn what we're meant to learn the first time we hear it. The laws of the universe are expressed in mathematics, nature, biology, and physiology . . . as well as through spirituality, religion, food, our skin, our mind,

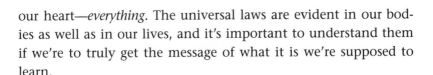

our heart—*everything*. The universal laws are evident in our bodies as well as in our lives, and it's important to understand them if we're to truly get the message of what it is we're supposed to learn.

The Universal Law of Repetition

The body and its functions follow the same laws of repetition that affect human behavior. For instance, when we experience a reaction of pain or phantom pain, our bodies have been conditioned to react in a particular way, whether the physical cells are there or not, because the conditioning has taken place in the brain. The brain engages in certain biochemical-electrical responses that are repeatable and become habitual. Long after a finger has been lost in an accident, the nervous system continues to feel pain in that missing digit because it's repeating the pattern of responding to stimulus that is no longer there.

Similarly, many postmenopausal women experience mood and hormonal changes that are comparable to those they had during their menses years before. The brain, through repetition and habit, continues to reexperience the mood and hormonal changes that affected the body long ago, even though its physical state is different.

In our own lives, we continue to react in the way we've been conditioned to react. As a result, we have "core issues," or themes of repetition, in our lives.

Common Themes of Repetition

We typically have at least three themes that become core issues in our lives, repeating themselves in our relationships with others at home, at work, at school, and in myriad situations. Here are some common ones:

- Feeling inadequate or "not good enough"
- Choosing what seems to be the wrong romantic partner
- Being abused emotionally, physically, and/or sexually
- Feeling victimized
- Feeling helpless and powerless
- Fear of loss, commitment, intimacy, or being alone
- Feeling abandoned
- Lacking money, health, love, or friendship
- Being unacknowledged for one's gifts or contributions
- Feeling misunderstood by everyone
- Feeling unworthy; experiencing low self-esteem
- Being overlooked for advancement
- Being unheard and ignored
- Having personal boundaries violated and disrespected
- Not fitting in
- Being angry; having difficulty managing anger

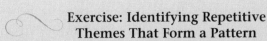

Exercise: Identifying Repetitive Themes That Form a Pattern

What are the recurring themes in your life? What patterns are you continually repeating? The following questions will help you identify repetitive themes that form patterns for you:

- Keeping in mind that your feelings may not be rational but always make sense, in what situations do you experience each of the preceding common themes of repetition?

- Which themes seem to appear in your life frequently?

- In what situations have you felt, *This seems familiar to me?* Which of the common themes of repetition were at play in those circumstances?

- In what situations do you feel victimized and powerless?

- How do you respond to situations in which you feel victimized and powerless—do you do so quickly and automatically? Do you overreact? Do you manifest physical symptoms of stress, such as a headache, racing pulse, or stomachache? Do you feel anxious and angry?

- Do you find yourself obsessing and having trouble moving beyond certain types of distressing situations? What themes are at play in these situations?

- Are you unable to distance yourself from particular events and gain perspective on them? Again, what themes are at play in these situations?

Just as our nervous system becomes conditioned to experience physical sensations, we also become conditioned to experience particular emotions. We grow so accustomed to our feelings of unhappiness or anger that we become addicted to them. Our daily outburst of rage or sense of despair is so familiar and comforting that we start to crave it and indulge in that emotion. Whether it's a large battle or just a small conflict, we react with the same old emotion. Our anger might be directed at a child, our spouse, the world, the government, terrorists, or others—if there's no one or nothing to be angry at, we'll find a target to justify our anger so that we can have that familiar feeling.

Why are we designed to continue to cause suffering for ourselves? On average, every seven years each cell in the body has been replaced with a new one. Why is it that even though we refresh and renew our physical selves every seven years, we're not completely youthful? Why don't we program the new cells to work with each other in a different way so that we can break the old patterns—so that arthritic joints and angry reactions can be left in the past?

The answer is: *Because we're meant to repeat our patterns, reexperiencing our traumas so that we can learn their lessons at last by working through our emotional and psychological issues.* Our bodies will continue creating symptoms, and worsen them, in order to draw the conscious mind's attention to what our unconscious mind knows.

We repeat the stories of our current and relevant past lives because we're trying to heal from past trauma—trauma that leads to anger, fear, rage, or avoidance. Just as the cells in our brains are replicated, so do we repeat the stories of our lives. The continual reenactment of the same emotions makes our behavior patterns more dramatic. The drama, like a nightmare, tugs at us strongly enough to make us pay attention and choose to change our reaction.

The Universal Law of Conservation of Energy

Why do young children yearn to hear the same story over and over again? When we offer variations to the story, they want it read exactly, word for word, as it has always been read. At the same time, research in child psychology shows that young children are continually seeking new experiences. One of their primary motivators is curiosity. This seeming dichotomy presented a challenge to me, and one day it dawned on me what the explanation could be.

Our physical cells at birth, in a sense, present a clean slate. Nothing has been written on them; nothing has been learned, except what went on in the mother's womb. Physiologically and neurologically, billions of brain cells that are fresh and new begin to develop, creating new connections with each other. They do so by communicating across synapses from one cell to the next, in chains that affect millions of cells. Because of the continual repetition of the identical material over and over, the cells create neuropathways in the brain. The communication between and among cells, chemically and electrically, becomes the basis of defining and developing the brain.

For example, if only one neuron (brain cell) communicates with another, we have one tiny connection. However, if that communication is repeated a hundred or a thousand times, the connection then grows much stronger and more definitive. This process of creating a neural connection becomes automatic, and it takes less energy for the cells to communicate along the same old pathway than it does for them to create a new one. This is an example of the universal law of conservation of energy: It is easier to do what's been done before than to invent a new way to operate.

This law is also evident in our dreams and in our behavior as adults. The more neural pathways we create, the more the brain goes on automatic, because it needs very little energy or effort to maintain that connection. If a thought or behavior conserves energy, it doesn't involve decision making or engage the upper regions of the brain: the frontal lobes.

The brain always works as efficiently as possible, which is reflected in repetition that produces automatic, habitual responses. The brain uses the habits that we've repeated hundreds and thousands of times, "clicking" into those behaviors swiftly. Even when we're tired, we find ourselves automatically driving the correct route home without thinking about it. Children may seek novel experiences, but that desire to learn is balanced by the brain having been wired to seek reinforcement of the neural connections it already has. The same old story is comforting, just as the same old route home is comforting.

The conservation of energy enables us to use the rest of the brain and its functioning to attend to whatever crises may arise, ensuring our survival. Imagine that we've built and established a new city. We now find it necessary to construct several additional roads in order to create a better flow of traffic. One day soon after they have been completed, we get the news that our child was in a terrible accident on the other side of town. What is the quickest route to get us across town? *We're going to use the roads that we already know because they're familiar.* Although the new ones might be more direct, we may be unsure as to all the twists and turns, and we can't afford to get lost now. We instantly and unconsciously make the decision to drive very fast on the familiar roads so that we can get to our child. When in crisis, the brain will seek to conserve energy.

The Universal Law of Survival

Survival is another universal principle and the most powerful motivation for behavior. Everything in us is geared to survive. If we don't survive, we don't live and have experiences. If we don't live and have experiences, we don't change. If we don't change, the soul doesn't grow. If the soul doesn't grow, it doesn't do what it came here to do . . . and then the whole purpose of coming to Earth and living in a human body becomes irrelevant.

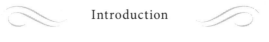

The brain is "wired" to go on automatic at times of crisis so that we can immediately act in ways that ensure our survival. The amygdala is a small organ in the hypothalamus, the emotional area of the midbrain. It's immediately activated to respond extremely swiftly—in a fraction of a millisecond—for fight or flight, allowing us to battle whatever is threatening us or quickly run away from it. When we activate the frontal lobes of the brain where we think and make decisions, consciously reasoning, *I'm not actually in danger in this situation—that was just my immediate perception,* we pull ourselves out of the automatic fight-or-flight survival response that occurs in the amygdala.

Judy is in therapy to learn how to handle her temper. She has acquired new tools to adjust her thinking so that she can make better decisions. She may have used these new tools only 5 times and expressed her old behavior at least 5,000 times. When a crisis arises, even one that doesn't truly threaten her survival, her brain will immediately go back to the old behavior, enabling the rest of the brain to deal with the current emergency. This illustrates the universal principle of conservation of energy. Judy's pattern is to respond automatically by becoming angry at the slightest infraction—she gets furious at everyone from the checkout clerk at the grocery store to her husband to her brother-in-law to the government. Anger, anger, and more anger—this is her habit.

My focus as a therapist is to teach Judy to call upon her new tools to deal with each situation as it arises—to counteract the brain's old habits of repetition and conservation of energy and use her conscious mind to create new habits and disconnect that automatic fight-or-flight response. Part of the therapeutic approach is to: (1) help her stop perceiving that she's in danger when she isn't, and (2) help her stop telling herself the same old story that she's a victim of circumstances and other people's behavior. Only through repeated use and practice of the new tools will she begin to alter and exit the pattern of constant anger and rage and take responsibility for her story of victimhood.

The Universal Law of the Pendulum

How our themes play out in our life stories can vary widely. If we're struggling with the issue of anger, we may become very angry people or we may become terrified of and bullied by others who are angry. We go from one lifetime to another, from one extreme to another, with intensity and swiftness, just as a pendulum swings back and forth, always with the intention of balancing somewhere in the center. As we're carried from one extreme to another, we build up momentum. Were we to move in small increments, a little at a time, it would be more laborious and take longer to reach center. However, when the pendulum swings from one extreme to another, the increased momentum and intensity of movement brings it there more quickly and with less expenditure of energy.

The soul continually seeks balance. This concept is universal: It appears in all spiritual disciplines and approaches. Thus, if Judy doesn't learn to moderate her angry response and let go of her pattern of perceiving herself as a victim and lashing out at everyone and everything, in her next life she may swing to the opposite extreme and become someone who can't express anger in any situation and is continually treated unfairly. Her lesson, to balance her anger and learn to be assertive instead of a bully or victim, is one her soul will try to master in this life or the next . . . or the next. Her soul knows that the most efficient way to get to the center—to stop behaving in extreme ways and repeating an issue—is to experience the issue first from one extreme and then the other.

Similarly, a man who is cruel and self-centered may well choose in his next life to be born to parents who are cruel and self-centered. The themes of suffering and cruelty stop being issues when his soul reaches a middle ground, living a life in which he's neither victimized nor persecuting anyone else. Between lifetimes, his soul chooses to be born into a situation where it's likely that he'll act in these extreme ways so that he can feel the intense emotions and have the impetus to deal with them at last.

The Universal Law of Relationships

Our sense of urgency to connect with others stems from the universal law of relationships, which says that we're meant to form relationships rather than go through life disconnected or isolated from other people. To corroborate this principle, a study was done with college students in which participants were divided into two groups, each of whom ate a meal in the cafeteria. In one group, the students sat at a table and ate in the company of others. In the other group, each student sat and ate alone. Blood was drawn from every individual before and after the meal. Blood tests showed that participants who sat and ate alone didn't digest their food as well as those who sat in the presence of others even when those others were strangers.

This study was very simple yet profound. The urge to connect is basic to and necessary for human beings, not just emotionally but physiologically. It's essential for survival that we connect. Studies have shown that people who live alone and have limited relationships with others don't recover from surgery as well as those who live with a spouse or family and have supportive relationships with friends, relatives, and neighbors. If we don't love each other and perpetuate the race, we humans will become extinct. And if we don't survive, we won't remain on Earth long enough to learn whatever lessons we came here to learn.

The Universal Law of the Wave

The wave, or bell-shaped curve, illustrates how we learn, how matter moves, how the cycles of the seasons change, and many other phenomena in our experience. If we were to graph the amount of greenery in the natural world, the top of the bell curve would represent the time of the year when the land is the most lush, when everything is in bloom. As the fall season begins, the amount of greenery decreases and the curve slopes downward, reaching the baseline at winter when all is barren and rising again in the spring when the first grasses and buds begin to appear.

Water moves in waves as well. The water of the ocean builds, crescendos, and breaks, mirroring the shape of the bell curve. Our own bodies experience the wave pattern of water: As Masaru Emoto explains in his book *The Hidden Messages in Water,* we start life as fetuses with very little water content; and the amount of this substance in our bodies peaks when we're babies, then diminishes as we get older and the wave begins to come back down.

The template of the wave also applies to the functioning of the brain. Brain waves are patterns of electrical energy that can be measured. An equally important organ in our system is the heart, whose energy is also measured in waves. Sound travels in waves, as does light and electrical energy.

Invariably, the template of the wave, found in nature and in our bodies, is reflected in our behavior and in how we learn. When we're at the beginning of a learning curve, there is much we have yet to know. We work hard, improve, do much better, start to reach the peak of our knowledge, and finally achieve mastery. Then we experience setbacks, we plateau, we have problems or conflicts, and we realize that we have to learn something new in order to get back to being a master. After a respite or break, we begin to learn anew, and we ascend the bell curve again.

Nothing occurs in a straight line. This is important to remember when we want to change, when we're in therapy, when we learn a language, and when we're in a relationship. If we expect everything to go, go, go . . . be perfect, perfect, perfect, we may well move in a line of upward momentum. But then—boom!—glitches occur. We think that we've conquered our tendency to cringe and feel ashamed of ourselves when we're criticized, and then one day someone delivers a particularly brutal rebuke, and we're devastated and shocked to learn that we haven't "fixed" ourselves after all.

When we expect continuous improvement with no setbacks, it behooves us to remember that progress will take place very nicely and significantly up to a point. There will be peaks and then there will be valleys, which is why it takes many repetitions to finally exit a pattern. When we're experiencing the dip in the

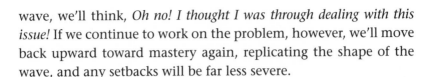

wave, we'll think, *Oh no! I thought I was through dealing with this issue!* If we continue to work on the problem, however, we'll move back upward toward mastery again, replicating the shape of the wave, and any setbacks will be far less severe.

The Universal Law of Homeostasis

The template of the wave is related to homeostasis, yet another universal law—one that states that every system seeks balance. This law's effect on every internal system in human beings can be observed. For example, a very well-known side effect of anti-depressant usage is increased and intensified dreaming. These drugs diminish the libido—at least while we're awake—and flatten the emotions. On antidepressants, we experience less passion and less intensity, sexually and otherwise. Colors aren't as brilliant. Joy isn't as sweet. As we sleep, the body will try to bring us back to a state of homeostasis by creating nightmares and vivid dreams that we recall upon waking. The intensity that's missing in our waking life gets enacted in our sleeping one.

Judy's choice to become involved in situations that make her angry happens at an unconscious level. Deep down, we all have a powerful urge to heal ourselves and to create homeostasis—to bring ourselves back into balance. Why, then, would Judy be attracted to intensely upsetting situations again and again? The reason is that unconsciously, she knows the only the way to achieve homeostasis is to confront the issue of anger and start working with it.

When we reincarnate, we'll often choose to be born into a family and circumstances that will allow us to experience one of our core issues from a different angle. Unconsciously, we know what we must do in order to bring ourselves back into balance.

Let's say you went through life raging, blaming, and accusing others. Your soul may well decide to experience a lifetime in which *you* are raged at, blamed, and unjustly accused. Similarly, in your present life, if your father was always furious and directed his anger at you and your siblings, you might unconsciously choose situations in which you're not the victim of someone's rage, but rather the one who's angrily lashing out at others.

When you experience the issue of anger from a new angle, it may be easier for you to start letting go of your judgments about others and yourself. As you catch yourself giving in to fury, you feel the same fear and powerlessness that led your father to rage at people, and you understand that his behavior toward you was rooted in his fears and insecurities. Then you can start to let go of your judgment of him as a bad or cruel father and see him simply as someone wrestling with the issue of anger. Letting go of judgments allows you to move toward a state of balance, where you're not experiencing the extremes of anger (raging and being raged at).

The Necessity of Repetition

Typically, professional therapists, psychologists, psychiatrists, social workers, and counselors are trained to understand and view repetitive behavior as "neurotic repetition." This is a judgment and implies that the healthy thing to do is to end the repeated "neurotic" behavior. If we look upon repetition as neurotic at its mildest level and crazy at its extreme, we'll think of it as bad and something that must be stopped. However, if we stop the pattern, we're totally dismissing this important vehicle for change. In fact, repetition is the *only* vehicle that enables us to change significantly.

Annie, the daughter of an alcoholic, starts out by choosing an alcoholic for a mate. As she gets healthier, she finally has enough strength to leave him. She next selects a drug addict and leaves him, too. A gambler is next in line, and she leaves him as well. She then chooses a healthier person who is completely addicted to his work. The repetition of addiction is obvious even though it appears with slight variations. With the last partner it's much gentler because Annie finally worked her way to a healthier and somewhat gentler relationship.

By judging, diagnosing, and labeling as "neurotic" her behavior of getting involved with men with addictive personalities, we lose sight of how repetition is actually *necessary* for achieving significant healing. When Annie has healed completely, she'll have the capacity to maintain a relationship with a partner who has far fewer, and healthier, addictions: an addiction to walking, to lively and positive conversation, or to a certain type of music, for example. Our positive addictions bring us back into balance, which is why we don't feel quite right if we don't have a chance to indulge in them.

Often my clients will say, "Why do I keep being drawn to abusive partners?" or "Why does it feel like no matter what job I'm in, people start taking advantage of me?" They wonder whether they're cursed in some way, since the same situations seem to repeat themselves in their lives. I tell them that it's not because they're cursed, but because the Divine Creator wants them to pay attention to something they're overlooking and ignoring. Our highest self, which is connected to the wisdom of the Divine Creator, will present us with challenging situation after challenging situation in order to wake us up.

We can be slow learners, so the Creator unconditionally supports us on our journey and in our need to awaken by helping us create repetitions. Our repetitive messages even occur at the level of the body.

If your liver function is sluggish, your physical self will reveal this in many ways. If you go to an iridologist, he will peer into your eyes, analyze the pattern of the flecks, and say, "Your liver is out of balance." If you visit an acupuncturist, she will hold your wrist, feel your pulse, and announce, "Your liver isn't working right." A Western physician will look at your blood tests and say, "I can see that your liver function is sluggish."

You have many opportunities to get the message to attend to the health of your liver. In the same way, you'll have many opportunities to get the message to attend to the health of your heart and soul. There's no reason to judge yourself as foolish or helpless if you find yourself once again in a situation that feels familiar but is making you unhappy or uncomfortable. It's only natural that your soul, working with the Divine, has created yet another chance for you to learn what you came here to learn.

Unpeeling the Onion

Edgar Cayce, the amazing and famed American psychic who lived in the first half of the 20th century and delivered more than 14,000 readings for clients, used the metaphor of the onion to describe the process of healing. He taught that we are like onions, and each of our layers looks very much like the one before. But as we peel the onion, we get closer and closer to the center: to the heart of the matter, the core themes that are pervasive in our lives.

Just as our behavior is a repetition of earlier reactions, so, too, does each layer resemble the previous one. We don't always see this, because we're so focused on our current drama, but our unconscious mind may tug at us, whispering, *Does this feel familiar? It should!* If we heed its message, we can begin the process of peeling back another layer and uncovering the memory of a painful trauma that requires healing.

When we finally do heal the trauma, we will create new, healthier layers as we behave in a healed way again and again and again. Just as the body will mend a cut in our skin by creating first one thin layer of skin, then another atop that, then another, and another, we can heal our trauma by reinforcing our new, healthier behavior. The more we respond to a minor conflict by consciously choosing not to give in to rage, opting instead to let go of the thoughts that reinforce our feeling that we've been victimized, the easier it will be to do so the next time we find ourselves in a conflict.

If you have a deep wound and take the time to address it, layer after layer, it eventually will heal. It may leave a mark, but it *will* heal—if not in this lifetime, then in the next. You can start by attending to your emotions, your early childhood experiences, your heart, and your mind, peeling back the layers of the onion and facing the painful inner core. Then, by letting go of any self-judgment and simply choosing to transform your thoughts, feelings, and behaviors, you can begin the healing process.

The Child Mode

To heal, we must exit the child mode and perceive with the eyes of an adult. When we're stuck in a repetition of a pattern, we behave like the frightened children we were when we originally experienced the trauma. We operate from the unconscious. Only when we feel like adults, capable and in control, can we *consciously* make a different choice than we did before, regardless of how painful it is to do so. This requires us to allow our conscious mind to access the unconscious's repressed memories of traumas in this life and relevant past lives.

However, we all need to be patient with ourselves and others and temper our expectations of getting "fixed" once and for all. If we can own and understand our story, which we repeat again and again in this lifetime and perhaps even carry into another, we can stop making unconscious choices and replace them with conscious ones. We can move from the child mode into the adult mode. We'll then be able to change our reactions, embrace the process of healing, and learn our lessons.

About This Book

The client stories I present will help you identify your own life stories and the patterns you have created and continually repeat. However, drawing from my extensive experience, I've developed a seven-step approach to help exit destructive patterns and accompanying anxieties and distress. I found that these steps yield exceptional results, dramatically changing my clients' lives. The 7 Steps of Rebirth (which I will explain in Chapter 3), used with the 4 Steps of Joy and combined with the tools of writing and then rewriting your story (presented in Part III), show you the way to set yourself free from self-defeating patterns.

As I mentioned in the Preface, my strong desire to share these life-enhancing techniques with as many people as possible was the motivating factor for writing this book. By changing ourselves, we create an important shift in consciousness that will affect all humanity.

CHAPTER ONE

PAST LIVES

I was raised in the Middle East by Jewish parents who taught me to believe that after we die, we go to heaven or hell. I was always trying to be good and kind to ensure that I earned a place in heaven. However, when I was young, I worried very seriously about dying because the notion of ending up in hell forevermore was completely terrifying to me. I wondered, *What if at the time of reckoning, no matter how hard I've tried, I miss getting into heaven by a single point? Does that mean I'll go to hell forever?* As I grew older, I thought it didn't make any sense that a loving, compassionate God would somehow be so judgmental that He would banish my soul to hell for eternity simply because I missed the accounting by one point!

Reincarnation

I began to read about death and dying in the 1970s and finally came across a book about the life of Edgar Cayce, the American psychic I mentioned in the Introduction who was referred to as "the sleeping prophet." Cayce would lie down, enter a trance, and give amazing psychic readings about the health of his clients, providing recommendations to bring them balance in this lifetime, as well as healing their emotional wounds that had been created by traumas in other lifetimes. He talked about past lives and reincarnation. Reincarnation seemed to contradict his Christian beliefs, but because this information kept reappearing in his trances during the readings, he finally began to trust that it actually occurs. He continued to believe in the concept of Christ consciousness: of love and light that transcends all religions, races, and cultural differences.

Since that time, I've explored the idea of past lives and reincarnation in depth. Because I'm Jewish, I felt comforted when I discovered that mystical Judaism—Kabbalah—not only incorporates this concept but also identifies it as *Gilgul Neshamot,* the cycle of souls. Finally, I could begin to let go of my fears of eternal banishment to hell. A far more loving and gentle concept is the view that, in fact, each soul comes to this life incarnating as a man or a woman, African, Asian, Native American, Caucasian, Hispanic, or Eskimo, depending on the work the soul has chosen to do while on Earth. Other religions, such as Hinduism, also recognize reincarnation that occurs for the purpose of learning and healing.

If you think of your soul as choosing to come to a school that specializes in the specific discipline on which you need to work, many things begin to fall into place. For example, if you wanted to learn physics, you wouldn't enroll in a famous art school. You would choose the best setting for this lesson, which might be esteemed universities such as Stanford or MIT. Likewise, if a soul wants to learn the lesson of trust, it will be born into a family where the themes of betrayal and loss are played out again and again.

Depending on how we've learned our lessons and whether we've passed our courses, our soul may choose to return to Earth and take an advanced-level course. Or, it might decide to take another subject altogether and return at some later point to repeat the course that it has "failed." By using this metaphor of going to school and studying one semester at a time, one subject at a time, the concept of past lives not only makes sense but can be extremely helpful in order to understand life in the present. The value of accessing former lives is only to clarify the present and bring healing and a release of the past that may be holding us back now.

Essentially, we do past-life regressions so that we can review the origins of our repetitions. According to most spiritual disciplines, God created each soul as an individual spark of light. He gave us the gift of free choice to act, react, create, and be co-creators with the Divine. If we stumble and fall, we can always come back, try again, and (hopefully) succeed in learning our lessons. In Kabbalah, this is referred to as *Tikkun,* which means "correction."

All souls have the intention to return home to God someday. Since we have the gift as well as the responsibility of free choice, when we're in between lifetimes, we assess which school to attend—that is, what life situation we would like to experience in the next incarnation so that we may learn the lessons we need to master. This assessment is done in consultation with our Angels and Spirit Guides.

I've come to have faith that a gracious and compassionate God doesn't judge us, but rather, always loves us unconditionally. I know that my past, current, and future lives are expressions of my choices and my desires. By shedding the fear of "damnation forever by just one point," I was able to live more freely and richly because I'd come to accept the inevitability of death, and I no longer feared it.

My Story

I decided to familiarize myself with the process of accessing past lives by discovering my own relevant ones. I began this endeavor almost 30 years ago. For a year and a half, I attended three psychotherapy/hypnosis sessions a week, each lasting two to three hours. This intense work resulted in my developing a great deal of understanding about the nature of my relationships with the people in my life, including my siblings, and even my ex-husband.

This memory came to me in the very first session when I began to delve into my own past lives:

> *I am hanging on to the sails with all my might. We are somewhere in the Indian Ocean in the A.D. 900s. A sudden storm rages, and the seas have become tumultuous with little warning. My pantaloons are a second skin as the waves crash over me and the pounding rain slashes at me.*
>
> *Unable to maneuver the boat to safety alone, I beg the princess, my mistress, to help with the sails. She adamantly refuses, shouting, "How insolent can you be?! You are just my servant! Don't ask me to participate in something so demeaning!"*
>
> *As the storm grows angrier, I go reeling over the side of the boat, cursing the princess for her arrogance. The powerful pull of the waves instantly swallows me up, and I drown.*

I discovered that the person sitting in that boat was one of my siblings in my current lifetime. Having two sisters who are older, I was often asked to bring them a glass of water or fetch something from another room. Interestingly, I always resisted helping my sister whose soul was that of the princess in the lifetime in which I was her servant. I would inevitably say to her, completely spontaneously and without any conscious awareness, "I am not your servant! Go get the glass of water yourself!" She also happened to be the sister with whom I had the most repetitive pattern of conflict and disagreements, which were steeped in ongoing sibling rivalry. That wasn't the case, however, with my other sister.

After the regression was completed and I'd cried intensely during the experience of dying so frightfully, I recalled that this sister who had been so cruel to me in a previous lifetime had almost drowned in the Mediterranean Sea in Tel Aviv in our current lifetime when she and I were 19 and 15 years old, respectively. She didn't know how to swim, and going into the ocean, she got caught in a whirlpool and began to wave her hands and cry for help. I couldn't swim either but felt compelled to follow her in and pull her out, only to be caught up in the whirlpool myself.

Luckily, we were both rescued by a lifeguard who dragged us onto the beach, gave us mouth-to-mouth resuscitation, and saved our lives.

The core of this repetition became clear: Unconsciously, my sister and I are, in essence, repeating the stories of our current and relevant past lives because we're trying to heal from past trauma. This time, when we re-created the scene of a possible drowning, she was the one in danger and *I* was the one in the position of potential rescuer. On this occasion, rather than re-creating our dynamic of two rivals who are so spiteful that one lets the other drown, I made a different choice—I sought to help my adversary so that we could stop repeating our deadly rivalry in lifetime after lifetime.

I went from being the reactor to being the initiator, from damning her for putting me in mortal danger and not risking her life to save me to risking my own life to save hers. My choice brought us closer in to balance, lessening the dramatic swings of the pendulum. Now it's true that our rivalry would continue to be played out in this lifetime and probably in future ones, but it would do so in a much gentler fashion than it had in the past.

My relationship with my sister improved significantly. Once I was conscious of the origin of my resentment toward her, I could let go of that feeling. At last, I was able to experience genuine love and forgiveness in my heart for what had happened in the past and apply it to the present. My sister and I were then able to enjoy trust and closeness. Of course, we still had our differences, but the quality and nature of our relationship changed so that we could now open our hearts to each other.

I was able to reach out and get past any feelings of hurt or resentment because I'd come to realize that on an unconscious level, we were both working for the same goal: freedom from suffering. We didn't actually want to hurt each other—we wanted to help each other *heal!* To this day, although my sister and I argue and tend to compete with one another, I see this for what it is, and I consciously choose to work on healing our rivalry even further.

The healing power of this regression made such an impression on me that I began to use these techniques in the context of psychotherapy with my clients. The experience I had with George, the first client of mine who was willing to do hypnosis and permitted me to direct him in a relevant past life, became the basis of my conviction that past-life regressions can be amazing, and more important, extremely helpful for understanding and addressing current-life problems.

For many years, I'd used a number of techniques I'd learned in my traditional, scientific behavioral and clinical training as a psychologist and psychotherapist. As I continued my training beyond my doctorate, I found that regression into past lives offers a powerful source of clarification and healing. Ultimately, healing depends on whether individuals will choose to apply the insights gained during the sessions to their current lives. Regression into earlier events in the present lifetime has proved to be very effective, dramatic, and healing for my clients as well. Trauma experienced in early childhood is often buried in the unconscious. Regression hypnotherapy brings these traumas to the surface so that healing can begin.

The dramatic recovery and responsiveness of my client George convinced me of the value, effectiveness, and healing associated with exploring relevant past lifetimes.

George's Story

George came to me because of insurmountable problems with his two ex-wives that had led to both divorces. Forty years old, George was down-to-earth, plain, and lacking in imagination—a very left-brained, logical man who worked as an accountant. While I'd found past-life regression therapy very helpful for myself, I didn't think this type of therapy would work for him. I thought that his rational mind would block his soul's memories from coming to the surface—but I was proved wrong.

George told me that whenever he'd had sexual intercourse with his former wives, he couldn't maintain an erection. No matter what position, additional stimulation, or preparation he tried, the outcome was always the same. After he'd experimented with a wide variety of behavioral techniques I'd suggested (I was also trained as a sex therapist), he began to relax and experience some desensitization of his fears and anxieties. (This was years before Viagra.) He made a little improvement and left therapy after a few months. However, three months later, George returned to therapy. He now had a girlfriend but was still unable to complete intercourse and ejaculate. He admitted, "I feel better, but the real problem hasn't been solved."

At this point, I suggested that perhaps he might be willing to explore other lifetimes, which could potentially give him a broader perspective on the situation. Looking at the bigger picture might finally lead us to the source of his problem so that he could resolve his sexual and emotional difficulties.

Accessing George's relevant past lives took three sessions. In the first one, he was regressed to a lifetime in 16th-century France when he was a gambler and womanizer who took gross advantage of everyone around him. Interestingly, in his current life, he was a man of relatively modest means and worked with money, but the large funds that he handled weren't his. George expressed regret that he had greatly abused women as well as money in that first lifetime.

In the second lifetime George accessed, he was extremely rich but ended up a pauper, having lost his money as well as all his friends. This raised the issue of trust: How could he really trust people, opening up and giving of himself, when all his friends had betrayed him?

I pointed out the contrast between the two lifetimes and the lessons that he'd learned. He went from one extreme to another: from being the womanizer and the user to being the one who had been taken advantage of and abused. It was a perfect example of the universal law of the pendulum. George began to see the startling choices that we make in selecting our stories in order to move beyond our painful experiences. (Again, we always do this with the intention and the hope of healing and recovery.) The profound issues to be addressed were trust, intimacy, and relationships with

women. These were complex pieces that together added up to the whole picture.

In George's case, he seemed to be working through his issues about money by having access to large sums that didn't belong to him. Would he meet the challenge of being able to work with money without stealing it or abusing it? If he could, he would resolve that karmic issue at last. His issues with women and abandonment, however, were still playing out in this lifetime, and I suspected that his sexual dysfunction was related to them.

The two sessions we'd had together were very valuable, but what was revealed about those previous lives still didn't bring us to the crux of the issue: Why was George having sexual problems with his partners? George dug a little deeper during the third session, and then—boom!—it came. (The awareness always comes when we're ready to face and experience it, so George may have needed to access other lifetimes before he could tolerate the pain of confronting the traumatic one he was about to recall.)

In a dirty, isolated cabin in the woods in 19th-century Colorado, George is slumped over, sitting at the edge of his bed. His head is cradled in his left hand, and a bottle of rum is loosely dangling from the fingers of his right hand. He is miserable, alone, and guilt ridden. Emaciated and drunk, George crumbles to the floor and dies. . . .

One evening six years earlier, George had gotten all spruced up to go down into the valley for the monthly village dance. He lived alone in a cabin he built in the woods on a mountaintop. The view was spectacular and the land lush and fertile, but he yearned for female companionship. As soon as George arrived at the dance, his eyes fell upon the most beautiful and delicate young woman he'd ever seen. She had black curly hair and wore a long yellow dress with tiny orange rosebuds printed on it. George and the young woman danced all night and fell madly in love. His feelings for her were intense, and his heart was fully open to her. They soon married, and he took her up to his mountaintop cabin.

Nine months later, George and his pregnant beloved were walking hand in hand in the clearing in front of their cabin. Without warning, leaving no time to summon help, she gave birth to a baby girl, bled profusely, and died immediately thereafter. George was too grief stricken to take care of the baby, who was a painful reminder of the loss of his beloved. He gave the newborn to friends who lived in the valley.

Five years later, George was sitting in his bedroom, crying and drunk. In a deep depression, he was finding little comfort in the bottle. His pain overwhelmed him as his thoughts constantly drifted toward suicide. Finally, having stopped eating, he died of starvation.

When George came out of the regression, we engaged in what I call a *debriefing*. This is an important part of the past-life-regressive work that I do, because it helps clients make the connection between the events of a previous lifetime and their current situation in order to ascertain which lessons were learned and which ones still need to be addressed. Why was George feeling so guilty? What was he feeling so terrible about that had led to such a tragic ending in that lifetime?

George immediately responded that his greatest distress stemmed from impregnating his beloved. Had she not become pregnant, she wouldn't have died in childbirth. Unconsciously, in *this* lifetime he was avoiding this tragic outcome by preventing himself from getting another woman pregnant. His inability to keep an erection and ejaculate into a woman ensured that he would never again suffer a similar fate. In other words, if his partner didn't get pregnant, she wouldn't die. Understanding at last the source of his sexual dysfunction, George began to use the 7 Steps of Rebirth (which I'll explain later) to recover from his trauma, as well as breathing exercises and other techniques to help him forgive himself for his past actions.

In our fourth and final session, George came in saying, "My fiancée thanks you, and I thank you!" After a couple of weeks, the effect of the regressions was so freeing that he was finally able to

have full and satisfying sexual relations with his present girlfriend . . . whom he was now engaged to.

When I experienced my own regressions, I was engulfed in tremendously rich and highly detailed past lives. Having a great deal of imagination and a gift for being able to visualize easily, I initially thought that it was easier for me to readily access past lives than it was for others to do so. However, George taught me otherwise. He wasn't a very imaginative, creative person; yet with a little guidance and some simple techniques, he was able to access vivid past-life memories.

I began to believe that anyone might be able to use these techniques effectively, and in fact—over the years, with many different clients of varying personalities—I found that the process was superior to the many methods I'd been formally trained in and was using: behavioral therapy, cognitive therapy, and so on. My clients had always made progress in resolving their problems, but no one changed in a dramatic way until I used my regression technique.

I believe that this approach is extremely helpful primarily because it delves into the unconscious, where our entire history resides. It allows people to do healing work at a much deeper level—at the core of the onion, so to speak.

In accessing past lives, a professional and experienced therapist should guide the way. If we only use CDs or tapes to explore our past lives, we won't obtain much relevant information or get very far in our quest for healing. Although we may journey and discover who we were, where we lived, and what we did during several lifetimes, this knowledge can't help us unless we explore what we learned, what we have yet to learn, and what our traumas were.

Our traumas are so painful that very often our conscious mind won't allow us to remember them—it's only when we dive deep into the unconscious that we discover our most painful and significant wounds. If we do begin opening up to traumatic events, our unconscious will protect us; we'll immediately disconnect or move on to a gentler, safer memory of that life. We're unlikely to allow ourselves to face the depth of our pain without a professionally trained therapist there to support us, guide us, and extricate us from the intense suffering that such memories re-create in us. Our unconscious mind knows that to go exploring these hidden traumas without someone alongside us is like wandering into the rain forests of the Amazon alone with no guide, map, or tools to help us, so it prevents us from making that dangerous journey alone.

I've always considered myself to be an excellent travel guide who can safely bring people deep into the unconscious, past lives, and dreams. I'm well trained and have traveled the path thousands of times with my clients. I'm also trustworthy because I never work alone—I can always call upon my Angels and Spirit Guides because they're there at all times to give me insights. I'm knowledgeable about protection, safety, and how to get myself and the client out of the jungle every time.

If you go to the "jungle" of the unconscious alone and see a metaphorical tiger, you'll react like a child and panic. In fact, you'll *over*react and probably stay stuck in the child mode. You won't remain in the hypnotic state you entered in order to access the memories buried in your unconscious. You may even re-traumatize yourself because you don't know how to exit the feeling of panic, how to breathe your way out, and how to recognize the lessons you need to learn.

I've discovered that we can't just talk about our history and say, "Oh, whatever happened, happened." Rather, we must look at the present, procure some tools for healing, and learn how to change. If we don't experience our past traumas with an emotional charge, we'll never release them . . . so while we mustn't venture into the jungle alone with no guide, we must have resources to help us as we explore its edges.

You'll learn later in this book about the tools my clients have found useful for helping themselves reexperience the emotions associated with past traumas in order to work through their issues. Whatever *your* trauma, you must speak of it, experience it, feel it, and then learn to move beyond it—now.

In relevant past lives, 95 percent of the time we're accessing traumatic events. Once in a great while, if we want to tap into a life that was particularly pleasant, we can ask for an uplifting experience to present itself. But the majority of the time, the experiences that come forward during hypnotic regression are painful and emotionally charged. We become aware of these emotions and experiences and then release them. The process of recovery can then begin, and it will deepen when we make conscious decisions in the current lifetime that promote our healing.

Reincarnating in Families and Groups

We tend to reincarnate with family members because energetically there's much similarity and familiarity with these souls, so we're drawn to repeat our interactions with them. A soul that was our brother in a previous life may now be our husband, our father may now be our daughter, and so on. Reincarnating in families is very efficient, because it gives us the opportunity to resolve "old business" with the people we were involved with originally.

Your current family has probably already experienced your unbalanced emotions regarding issues in a relevant past lifetime. Because in your former life it was your father who pressed your buttons about authority issues, in your current one he may be your child and *you* may be the authority figure. The lessons will be learned more easily and efficiently because the theme and energy are familiar.

Incarnating in families or groups conserves energy, allowing us to repeat the story, although we may be playing a different role this time. The probability of the same issues arising among related people is high. We don't have to leave our family and go out into the world to find someone who can help us work through our issue of betrayal, because our family members will have the same issue.

Because I know so much about my own family and *our* stories, I'll describe an incarnation that reveals one of our shared issues:

My sisters, my father, my mother, and I are Jewish slaves during the Exodus from Egypt more than 3,000 years ago. We are headed for the Promised Land together. I am in love with an Egyptian soldier, who is the enemy at the time. He cares for me deeply and says, "Stay with me. I'll marry you. You'll no longer be a slave."

Because I love him so very much, the decision to leave him and join my parents and sisters is devastatingly hard. However, my family takes precedence. I leave with them, and we wander in the desert for 40 years. We all die before we reach the Promised Land.

The Egyptian soldier in that lifetime was a long-standing boyfriend of mine in my current lifetime. When we met, it felt like magic because our attraction was very powerful. I accessed relevant past lifetimes to discover my whole story with him, and it turns out that our relationship always ended in separation, whether he played the role of son, wife, husband, or lover. Our relationship in each accessed past lifetime, as well as in the current one, was never fully completed or resolved.

My family relived the repetition of the Wandering Jew, changing countries again and again before ending up in Israel. Transition and finding our place in the world were issues for all of us. In fact, one of my sisters decided that she'd had enough of wandering and settled down, vowing never to relocate to another country again—but her grown children moved away to various countries, repeating the pattern established in my family many generations ago!

It's fascinating when we access the story in the present and realize the threads we've carried over from previous lifetimes. In this way, we can recognize the clues that point to a shared connection going back to prior incarnations. My client Mary Lou was able to access a relevant past lifetime that explained her relationships and her issues in this one.

Mary Lou's Story

Mary Lou, 43, was married with two children, both of whom were in college. She'd been a surgical nurse in hospitals for 20 years before being promoted to a supervisor on the surgical floor. While she loved this work, she became very stressed from the pressures of the job and was diagnosed with fibromyalgia—a condition that can cause fatigue, sleep deprivation, difficulty focusing, muscle pain and spasms, and irritability. Her doctor advised her to stop doing whatever was causing the excessive stress.

Mary Lou realized that the sense of urgency and emergency that's inherent to a medical setting was almost surely aggravating her condition. Therefore, she left the hospital and found a job with a private company as a visiting nurse, working with the elderly and disabled in their homes. Her stress began to diminish significantly, and her fibromyalgia symptoms decreased. She started a low-impact exercise program and began doing yoga. She was happier and healthier in all aspects of her life.

It seemed that Mary Lou had solved her problems, but repetition was at work, helping her face her unresolved issues. The company she was working for got a contract to do home visitations for the parents of school-age children in a district with many blue-collar workers who had very little money and many social problems, including drug and alcohol abuse and unemployment. Many of the students were truants, and when they did come to class, they were often either hungry or unfocused. As a visiting nurse, Mary Lou was expected to find out what was going on at home that might be causing the children's problematic behaviors. The job seemed like a perfect fit for her, since visiting nurses are experienced in and familiar with going into people's homes and assessing the family for the presence of problems, medical conditions, and social disturbances.

She thought that this work would simply be an extension of what she was currently doing. To her surprise, within three weeks she started having anxiety attacks for the first time, which occurred every morning before visiting the students' homes.

Her symptoms of fibromyalgia also returned, and her blood pressure was elevated, so Mary Lou went back to her doctor, who prescribed antianxiety medication. After taking the drugs for two months, she began to feel a little better. However, she knew that there had to be an underlying problem because she was having nightmares. She decided to seek therapy in order to learn stress-management techniques so that she might lessen the severity of her symptoms or get rid of them altogether.

Mary Lou told me that she was the oldest of five children from a very poor family who had lived in the hills of West Virginia. Her mother worked nights in a factory; and her father, a drunk, was unreliable, irresponsible, and often depressed. As a little girl, Mary Lou felt she had no choice but to take care of her younger siblings. It was clear that her childhood was similar to those of many of the students she was visiting. The experience of dealing with children from troubled homes was causing the same anxiety and stress she'd confronted while growing up.

In the initial part of the therapy, I taught her stress-management and breathing techniques, which immediately began to relieve her tension and anxiety. I then taught her the 7 Steps of Rebirth (which I'll explain in detail in a later chapter). One of the steps required Mary Lou to quickly think of a number—4 and 7 immediately came to her mind. Knowing that these seemingly random numbers had great significance for her, I asked her to tell me what had happened to her when she was four and seven years old.

Mary Lou told me that when she was four, her third sibling, Jimmy, had been born with severe physical and mental impairments, requiring extra help and support from everyone in the family. Since her mother wasn't home nights and her father was unreliable and distant, the main responsibility of taking care of Jimmy fell onto Mary Lou. The fear and anger stemming from having all that responsibility and all those burdens placed on her came through and revealed themselves with a vengeance. The little four-year-old was filled with resentment. When Mary Lou was seven, the fourth sibling was born, which heaped even more obligations upon her. She was utterly bitter and angry at that point and more conscious of her emotions than she'd been when she was four.

Mary Lou was now able to identify the reasons for the return of her fibromyalgia when she visited the blue-collar families: She was reliving the feelings she'd experienced as a child and had left unresolved. As she used the 7 Steps of Rebirth, she started working through those feelings and soon felt significantly better, both physically and emotionally, so she terminated therapy after three months.

Six months later, however, Mary Lou returned to therapy because she was having intense anxiety attacks again. I asked her when they were occurring, and she said that it was when she visited one home in particular. She knew that the attacks must be a sign of underlying issues that still needed to be addressed. We then decided to explore her relevant past lives.

The lifetime that Mary Lou accessed occurred in the 1700s in the hills of West Virginia. Mary Lou was Lightning Feather, a Native American warrior who had been given that name because he was as fast as lightning and so light on his horse that no one heard him coming. Lightning Feather's tribe was experiencing chaos and tremendous distress. The French and British were trying to take over their land. The tribe was in a constant state of tension and readiness, uncertainty and war.

Lightning Feather, riding bareback on his roan horse, Wind Chaser, races through the mountains to reach his sister tribe. Their village is about to be attacked, and Lightning Feather must warn them. Known for his courage, stealth, and silent movements, Lightning Feather is determined to get to the tribe in time to save his allies.

As Lightning Feather gets closer to the tribal village, he slows down and quietly approaches. Not a footstep, not a sound, not a breath must be heard, because the enemy is near. As he enters the village, he sees that the entire tribe is gathered around the chief, listening to his wisdom. The medicine man speaks, warning his people of terrible losses and longtime suffering.

Lightning Feather comes forward, and all welcome him with a nod of their heads. They are already aware of the danger lurking in the air, but Lightning Feather explains what is going to happen. "Your tribe will be caught in the middle of a great battle between the British and the French. You will be destroyed. You must listen and do as I say."

Lightning Feather's own tribe will be spared because of their location, but the sister tribe must escape—quickly. He tells them to flee and lets them know the routes of the advancing armies. After spending a few hours with the tribe and sharing a meal with them, he gets on Wind Chaser and rides off into the night, quietly and swiftly.

Lightning Feather loves to ride Wind Chaser at night in the peace of the forest. He is intimately familiar with every sound, with every movement. He always knows when a rabbit is surprised out of sleep, a squirrel is pushed from its perch, a snake is shedding its skin, or a bear is silently searching for food. Lightning Feather loves the forest: the animals, the sounds, the smells, the feel, the air. The forest is his home away from his tribe.

Lightning Feather finally arrives on the outskirts of his own village. As he noiselessly approaches, he doesn't hear a sound. When he sees the tribal encampment, he dismounts and falls to his knees sobbing, beating his chest, and then pounding the ground helplessly. His people have been brutally massacred in the French and British attack! Crawling to his collapsed wigwam, he sees the bodies of his sister, mother, and grandfather. Their throats have been cut, and their heads are barely attached to their bodies.

Enraged, devastated, and overwhelmed, Lightning Feather mounts Wind Chaser and flees to the secret cave that he has been going to for solace since he was five years old. Sitting cross-legged, he barely recognizes the echoing sound he hears: It is that of his own sobbing as his whole body shakes with grief and disbelief. All the warriors have been killed, his family has been slaughtered, and no one in the tribe has survived . . . except him. He doesn't know what to do next.

In the midst of grieving, a horrifying thought comes to him: He now realizes that Red Heron, his cousin who had married

*a French woman, betrayed him. It was Red Heron who sent
Lightning Feather to warn the tribe of the movements and plans
of the French and British, lying about their strategies. Lightning Feather realizes that he has unknowingly passed along
this false information to his sister tribe, and now they, too, will
be massacred.*

*Lightning Feather leaps onto Wind Chaser's back, and they
race along the mountain paths through the forest, hurrying to
reach the other tribe before it's too late. As he gets closer, he
slows, moving silently so as not to endanger them or himself.*

*When he reaches the village, he is immobile with shock,
unable to make a sound, avert his eyes, or flee: The entire tribe
has been slaughtered. He is too late! Bodies are strewn everywhere. The men and women have had their throats slit; babies
have been sliced in half. The women's clothes are ripped to
shreds, and he knows they must have been raped before being
killed. Lightning Feather, shocked and enraged that he has been
the instrument for such death and destruction, pledges to dedi-
cate the rest of his life to destroying Red Heron and everyone
in his family. He will wreak his anger on Red Heron by taking
vengeance with his own hands.*

*Meanwhile Red Heron, knowing that Lightning Feather will
kill him when the warrior realizes he's been betrayed, stays on
the move with his family. It takes Lightning Feather more than
a year to finally track down his people's betrayer.*

*One early spring morning, Lightning Feather spots Red
Heron's oldest daughter, Hummingbird, a beautiful 16-year-old
maiden with shiny black hair, dark eyes, and tawny skin. She is
bathing in a small stream. Lightning Feather hides behind the
bushes, waiting for Hummingbird to come out of the water. He
jumps out, puts an ax to her throat, and cuts off her head in the
midst of her terrified scream.*

*Lightning Feather finds Red Heron and decapitates him in
the presence of his two youngest children. He then plunges a
knife in the belly of the little four-year-old boy before turning
to the five-year-old girl. Red Heron's wife, paralyzed with grief*

and horror, watches the last of her family being killed before her eyes. Lightning Feather can taste the bitterness of his intense vengeance and rage. He allows Red Heron's wife to live—by doing so, he will inflict pain that is even worse.

With no family, tribe, or land to go back to, Lightning Feather retreats into the forest and lives out the rest of his life isolated and angry. He survives on herbs, berries, plants, and small animals. Within two years, he gets very sick and realizes, too late, that he has eaten poisonous berries. He had been so preoccupied with his anger and loneliness that he didn't notice that the berry he was eating was of a slightly darker shade than the variety that is safe to consume.

Doubled over with cramps and pain, Lightning Feather suffers in agony until he collapses in death, draped over Wind Chaser. Finally, his tortured soul leaves his body.

When Mary Lou described Lightning Feather's death, she said that she kept seeing him hovering over the areas where the French and British were camped and over both of the tribal villages. I began to work with her to aid the soul that was the brave warrior Lightning Feather. We allowed that part of her to finally leave and go into the Light, to rest and be at peace.

When Mary Lou came out of the regression, she was crying hard for having caused so much pain and yet having lost so much herself. After doing some deep breathing, releasing the past through imagery work, and returning to the present, she decided to tell me about a few of her hobbies she hadn't disclosed earlier.

Mary Lou had always loved horses—roan ones were her favorite—and as an adult, she had finally been able to afford riding lessons. Riding through the woods seemed to comfort her, yet she would feel restless on her way back home. She was always fascinated with herbs, Native American flute music, and drumming, which seemed strange to her since no one around her shared in any of these interests. She participated in drumming circles at least once a year and felt unusually connected to the change of seasons, particularly during the winter and spring solstices. Winter was

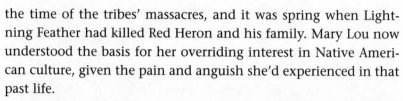

the time of the tribes' massacres, and it was spring when Lightning Feather had killed Red Heron and his family. Mary Lou now understood the basis for her overriding interest in Native American culture, given the pain and anguish she'd experienced in that past life.

We then clarified the connections between her previous reincarnation and her current one. The soul goes from one extreme to the other—from one lifetime to another—like a pendulum, always seeking balance somewhere in the center. When Mary Lou was the warrior Lightning Feather, she had been healthy, vibrant, and strong but still ended up as a vengeful killer. Her soul was devastated by the slaughter of the tribes and the guilt over feeling responsible. In her current lifetime, Mary Lou was raised in the hills of West Virginia, the same area where the tribes had lived 200 years before. She came to this life having made a clear decision, albeit unconsciously, to become a healer and a helper—the other end of the continuum, or pendulum, from being a warrior and killer.

Becoming a surgical nurse was an unconscious repetition of seeing cut-open and slaughtered bodies in the past life. In her current life, she observed ones that were cut open in surgery, but they were sutured and the people brought back to health. At an unconscious level, this was precisely what she needed to see and experience after having witnessed the massacre of her people and then killing Red Heron and his family.

In order to help poor and troubled families, Mary Lou was required to report to the school system any signs of neglect or abuse that she saw—just as she'd brought alarming information to her sister tribe in that past lifetime. Since this created a repetition of being the bearer of bad news, she reacted by having anxiety attacks. Unconsciously, she had stimulated her soul's memories of the anguish, pain, and horror of seeing the massacres and causing the deaths of Red Heron and his family. Mary Lou was fascinated to see the connection, as well as details of the past life and their relevance and meaning in her choices, both conscious and unconscious, in the present.

Mary Lou then made more connections between the past and present lifetimes. Her current father, with whom she was always angry, was the same soul that had been her cousin Red Heron. Both drank, were irresponsible and unreliable, and ultimately betrayed their families. Hummingbird, Red Heron's 16-year-old daughter in that past lifetime, was now Mary Lou's husband. Mary Lou deeply loved her husband even though she found out that he'd had extramarital affairs on three separate occasions. Just as Lightning Feather had betrayed his cousin Hummingbird by killing her, now Mary Lou's husband (Hummingbird) was betraying Mary Lou (Lightning Feather). The healing of their souls would take place when both of them transcended the past, opened their hearts and minds, and moved beyond the pain of the old story.

After exploring, understanding, forgiving, and healing the aspect of herself that was the warrior in the past, Mary Lou found that her anxiety attacks subsided. She continued to practice the 7 Steps of Rebirth to work on both healing herself and her soul as Lightning Feather.

How We Forgive Ourselves and Others

Ultimately, we need to forgive everyone, but to do so because we're "supposed to" isn't really forgiveness. We must first recognize how we've cast ourselves in the role of victim, and then we must own our part in the story and do something to change it. Forgiveness alone doesn't alter the feelings attached to the story. We need to experience the emotional charge that occurs when we reenact what took place in our past, whether the event happened in this lifetime or in a relevant previous one. The intensity of this charge propels us to become aware of past experiences and events.

When we say, "I'm so angry at my boss—he's acting just like my mother used to . . ." we're able to recall our interactions with our mother vividly. When we forgive out of love, without understanding how we contributed to the story we've lived, we don't experience an emotional charge. We simply put the issue aside. We may address it in another lifetime, and that's fine; we've helped ourselves and others for now, in a small way, preventing ourselves and them from repeating the story and creating strong feelings of anger, betrayal, resentment, and so on. This type of forgiveness isn't worthless, but it's never enough to allow us to fully release the story.

In order to forgive someone on a deeper level, we must experience the anger attached to the story, work on it, and transform it. Then and only then will true forgiveness be achieved. The process is often very painful because we're forced to reexperience difficult emotions, but we emerge from it knowing that we can finally say good-bye to the old stories that continually created suffering for ourselves and others.

The way to truly forgive someone, as you'll learn, is through using the 7 Steps of Rebirth. But first, I want you to understand some very important aspects of how we incarnate.

CHAPTER TWO

INCARNATION AND BIRTH

We come into this world wanting only to love and rejoice, to play and to gurgle. We're open and trusting because we don't consciously remember the choice we made in the in-between time to experience suffering in the hopes of healing our karma. Each of us incarnates into a body that's extremely likely to face situations that will repeat the patterns of our past and re-create painful emotions in us. As souls not yet taking on human form for a new incarnation, we observe the mother and the circumstances surrounding her pregnancy and say, *Yes, <u>there's</u> the perfect parent for me to be born to, the perfect set of conditions for me to experience if I am to overcome my karma.* Then we make a contract with our mother to be born from her womb.

Our chosen mother isn't consciously aware of the contract we make with her; it's her *un*conscious mind that enters into an agreement with us. She, too, sees that the interaction between her soul and ours will bring her opportunities for healing her own issues.

According to Kabbalah, the soul visits the fetus while it's *in utero.* It inhabits the body, hangs out for a while, checks things out, and then leaves. Once the fetus is fully formed and ready to be born, the soul occupies the body (although sometimes it doesn't do so fully until two or three days after birth), ready to experience life in this realm.

As babies, we're blissfully unaware of the suffering we'll face in our lives because we have no conscious memory of the decision we made before we were born to come into this world for the purpose of experiencing repetition. The memories of the traumas we suffered in our past incarnations become deeply buried in our unconscious.

The birth process is a traumatic one for all of us. We lose our sense of connection to the Divine as we begin to experience our humanness, and our memories become lodged in our unconscious. We're pushed—or pulled—out of the warm, secure environment of the womb and subjected to cold air and harsh lights. Although on Earth we mourn death and celebrate birth, on the other side—in the in-between life—it's just the opposite: Souls are saddened when they see another begin the suffering that is inevitable in a human incarnation . . . and joyous when they see one detach from its human form and rejoin them in the timeless realm where there's no pain.

Immediately after birth, we begin to attach to our caregivers —usually, our parents. We start to experience feelings of love that are intense and profound. In fact, this parental bond begins even before we're born. In neonatal experiments, researchers have reported that a baby recognizes its father's voice immediately upon delivery, distinguishing it from those of other males (even so, the infant's dependence on the mother and attachment to her exceed all other relationships).

The mother's feelings and reactions deeply influence both the fetus and the newborn. The soul that intends to become permanently attached to the fetus's growing body has consciousness, and experiences its mother's fears and anxieties, primarily absorbing them through the placenta. All emotions, all chemicals, as well as all the shifts in energy, are transmitted by the mother, mostly through this structure that connects her with the baby, who absorbs everything. Because the soul floats in and out of the developing fetus—attaching and then detaching itself, yet always staying close by—it's also aware of what the mother is saying and doing.

Abortion and Adoption

As I said, according to Kabbalah, the soul doesn't inhabit the body permanently while the fetus is in the womb, so Kabbalists don't consider aborting the fetus to save the mother to be abhorrent. The soul that intends to incarnate in the body of the baby is aware of the mother's choices, and if she decides to terminate the pregnancy, it accepts her decision without anger or resentment. It feels somewhat sad that its contract with the mother has been canceled, but it knows that there will be other opportunities for being born into human life.

If the mother gives the baby up for adoption, the infant will develop very strong issues of abandonment and rejection. But while the birth mother may feel tremendous guilt over her decision, the soul of the baby benefits from the choice she has made because it has a chance to work through its issues. It has unconsciously chosen to be born to this mother, at this time and place. The soul is aware that it will be given up for adoption and will suffer rejection and abandonment as a result, but it also knows that this is an opportunity for it to heal its abandonment issues by reexperiencing the trauma of rejection.

A baby has no sense of awareness of where it stops and "Mother" begins. While in the womb, it ate whatever she ate, felt whatever she felt, and sensed her thoughts. There's no sense of separation, even after the umbilical cord is cut. The newborn baby doesn't perceive that it's a being apart from its mother. Its feeling is: *Everything is me, me, me. The world is me. My mother is me. I am my mother.* The sense of separation doesn't begin until a baby starts to crawl, and it peaks again when it starts walking, because the baby recognizes, *If I can propel myself away from Mother, that means she can propel herself away from me . . .* and that's a very frightening thought.

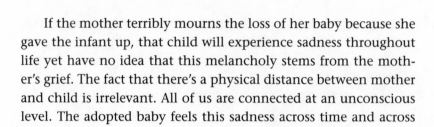
If the mother terribly mourns the loss of her baby because she gave the infant up, that child will experience sadness throughout life yet have no idea that this melancholy stems from the mother's grief. The fact that there's a physical distance between mother and child is irrelevant. All of us are connected at an unconscious level. The adopted baby feels this sadness across time and across continents.

The adoptive parent may be very loving, supportive, and nurturing, but the blueprint of rejection has already been stamped in the brain of the child. If the source of these very deep-rooted feelings, which most adoptees are unaware of, aren't addressed, they may never get resolved. Although many children feel happy with their adoptive parents and have no interest in meeting their birth mother or father or exploring the circumstances of their adoption, it's always important that they address this early, deep wounding and work on healing it. Otherwise, they'll unconsciously choose to repeat the trauma of abandonment and rejection again and again in this lifetime and future ones.

In no way do I mean to suggest that I oppose adoption. On the contrary, saving babies, saving lives, and offering children wonderful opportunities and love is a genuine expression of one human being reaching out to another. I believe that love heals and transcends all. An adoptive family is likely to provide an environment in which the child can work through issues of abandonment and rejection. For instance, the adoptive parents may be deeply religious and insist that their child accept their beliefs or else they will cut off contact. A gentler repetition might be a set of parents who, despite their best efforts on a conscious level, can never quite accept that their adopted child is different from them. If children seize upon the opportunity such parents provide, they may end up doing much healing of the original wounding caused by being given up for adoption.

The Birth Experience

The fetus completely absorbs its mother's emotions, anxiet-ies, joys, and fears. It also takes on the responsibility for whatever she's feeling, because it feels that Mother's emotions are its own. Often, my clients who have been regressed to their birth experi-ence report a sense of being responsible for the pain on the part of the mother during labor and become anxious at the thought that they caused her so much physical trauma that she risked death. The baby's feeling about the traumatic birth experience is: *If it weren't for me, Mama wouldn't be so depressed and frightened.*

By regressing to the birth experience through hypnosis, a person can reexperience the trauma, re-create the painful emo-tions, and achieve healing. When I help clients relive their birth, I then guide them through it again but with an entirely different script. In essence, I retell the story, changing the details so that the unconscious mind can let go of the old story of jeopardizing the mother's life and causing her suffering, and accept a new one in which the baby was the source of great happiness during a safe, easy, gentle, and joyous birth process.

With just about everything in life, we're on a two-way street. We can get help and be saved, or we can ignore our problems and suffer. We can put on weight or lose it. We can even have out-of-body, near-death experiences yet still come back. We have a choice between this decision or that one. However, the birth experience is the only action that takes place in just one direction: If we want to live, we don't have the choice to remain in the womb indefi-nitely. We have no alternative but to move forward, even though we know that we're going to be born into a world where suffering is inevitable. We choose to do so because we choose to work on our issues and heal them.

No matter how loving our parents were, all of us have aban-donment issues that stem from the experience of being born and being separated from the Divine. In fact, according to individu-als who have been regressed to their past lives as well as to their birth experiences, by all accounts being born is one of the most

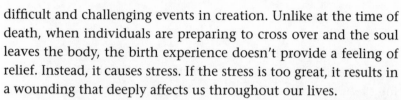

difficult and challenging events in creation. Unlike at the time of death, when individuals are preparing to cross over and the soul leaves the body, the birth experience doesn't provide a feeling of relief. Instead, it causes stress. If the stress is too great, it results in a wounding that deeply affects us throughout our lives.

Our unconscious memories of our experiences in the womb and during the process of birth can reveal themselves during a past-life regression, but sometimes I'll have a hunch that my clients' issues have something to do with their birth, and I'll deliberately bring them back to when they were in the womb and are about to be born.

John's Story

John, an attorney in his 30s, came to me because of his inexplicable and insistent fear of heights that he felt was holding him back. He also spoke of being afraid to "move up the ladder" or "rise too high" in his work. My intuition told me to regress him to his birth experience with his mother, Joan:

> *Joan, fully pregnant at nine months, is in her glory. Participating in a singing contest at the county fair, she loves nothing better than to be onstage and to "let it rip," basking in the thrill of performing. Joan's voice, both powerful and enchanting, fills the tent, enthralling her audience.*
>
> *In the middle of her song, while adding a few dance movements, she falls off the stage, immediately goes into labor, and is rushed to the hospital. The anxiety, panic, and all-consuming fear stemming from the possibility of losing her baby are agonizing and pervasive. Arriving at the hospital just in time, Joan gives birth to a perfectly healthy baby boy. Both mother and son are well and safe.*

Joan's intense anxiety and fear at the time of her fall and during John's delivery immediately imprinted onto the fetus's consciousness. From that moment on, John was never able to explain his phobia of heights. After John was regressed to his birth experience, his fear was clarified and he was able to begin the healing process. To recover from that trauma, he had to reexperience his birth in a completely new way. We rewrote the script of this event. I helped him enter a trancelike state and guided him with my words.

In the story that I talked him through, his mother was able to complete her song at the fair, win the contest, feel a few twinges as labor began, and then calmly and comfortably ask her husband to escort her to the hospital. Joan, eager and excited about having a baby, could transmit a message of safety as well as a sense of adventure to her son rather than transferring fear and panic to him.

Emotionally experiencing this new script while in a trancelike state, John was able to transform his reactions and transcend his phobia of heights. Afterward, he was able to walk out onto a balcony and eventually, onto a terrace of a ten-story building. Within a year, he took pictures of himself standing at the top of a cliff in the Rockies! His newfound confidence caused him to scale new heights in another way, too: He applied for a higher position in his firm, and he got the job.

Overcoming his fear of heights and releasing the conflict at the source—namely, the events around the labor and delivery—offered John tremendous relief. It enabled him to begin to transform himself without suffering the paralyzing fears that once plagued him.

Eileen's Story

When Eileen sat down in my office, the first words out of her mouth were: "I'm here because it always seems as though I'm looking out at the world through a glass door with my nose pressed against it." She was a bright woman in her 30s, but she would get to a certain point in professional and personal endeavors and then just stop. She yearned to finish college and progress in her career, but she'd dropped out of school and couldn't explain exactly why. She was married and wanted to have children; however, for some reason, she was unable to carry any pregnancy to term, experiencing several miscarriages. She felt that she simply couldn't complete anything she attempted.

I pointed out to Eileen that her expression about looking through a glass door sounded as if she were in a womb, so it might be a good idea for her to regress to her birth experience and discover what her unconscious knew and was hiding from her.

Baby Eileen is working very hard to exit the birth canal. She tries again and again to push through but keeps bumping up against something at the exit point. She's stuck and can't get out.

After I'd regressed Eileen to her birth experience in her current lifetime, she spoke to her mother about what had happened during the delivery process and discovered that her mom had developed a large tumor that completely blocked the birth canal. It initially went unseen and unrecognized by her gynecologist. (This was in the late 1940s when ultrasound wasn't available.) Rather than exiting the birth canal and meeting life with its problems and its joys, Eileen encountered this large tumor that blocked her. Eventually, the problem was identified, a quick incision was made, and the obstruction was removed. Both baby and mother suffered tremendous stress and anxiety going through this trauma, wondering whether one or both would actually die.

While reliving her birth and experiencing her consciousness as a fetus, Eileen exclaimed, "I feel terrified! I know if I don't get out of here, I'm going to die." The motivation of survival is, bar none, the strongest instinct in human beings. We want to live at any cost.

During the regression, while she was in a gentle trance, we rewrote the script of her birth. I directed her to go through every contraction during the labor as if she were performing a dance. In synchronization with her mother's contractions, she moved her shoulders and head, edging her way farther down and out of the birth canal. Upon her exit, rather than being grabbed and placed on a cold table or being slapped on her behind beneath harsh lights, with loud noises all around her, she experienced her birth as a gentle, loving, quiet, and momentous event. She was welcomed by strong, nurturing hands in a room with low lights and soft music playing. Next, she was placed on her mother's chest and was able to continue to hear and feel her mother's heartbeat. This helped the two of them have a healthy bonding and allowed Eileen to feel safe, eager, and excited about her new journey into this life.

Eileen felt a tremendous relief at the end of the regression. Within a year, she became pregnant. This time, she was able to complete the pregnancy and deliver a healthy baby boy. Three years later, she reported to me that she'd gone back to college and was about to graduate with a degree in her chosen field of communications.

The regression to her birth experience—accompanied by understanding her story at last and releasing it to be replaced by a more gentle and nurturing story—resulted in a genuine and significant transformation that led to a happier and more productive life for Eileen. She chose to act on the changes that were taking place in her mind and heart. She was now the proactive adult making healthy choices, rather than remaining "stuck" in the past as she was that momentous day of her birth.

Leroy's Story

Leroy was a single 28-year-old African-American engineer. His parents, an accountant and a nurse, were attentive, loving, and hardworking; and he got along with his two sisters. Although bright, educated, and much loved, he was entrenched in depression, withdrawal, and isolation. He always felt left out and different. He had difficulty with authority figures and resented being told what to do. He couldn't understand why he felt so unhappy,

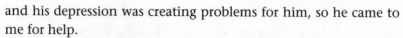

and his depression was creating problems for him, so he came to me for help.

Leroy's first words when he came to see me were: "I feel like I'm in a dark cave. I want you to pry me out of this depression." I immediately picked up on the fact that his description of the cave matched up with the image of being inside a uterus. Thus, I immediately regressed him to his birth experience.

Leroy's mother was nine days late in giving birth. After 20 hours of labor, the midwife picked up an instrument and literally pried him out of the birth canal, rudely yanking him from the gentle, dark place where he wanted to remain just a little longer.

After the regression, I helped Leroy rewrite the script of his birth. I created a new story of how he was born, featuring a gentle emergence from his mother's womb when he was ready to enter the world and not a moment before. Then I asked Leroy to listen to the tape of this story for 40 consecutive days. If he missed a day, he was to start over and begin again at day one.

> *As Baby easily moves through the birth canal, Mother and Son create a sweet harmony and synchronous rhythm. Gentle, strong, warm hands now firmly ease Baby out. Lights are low; and soft, soothing music is playing. Baby is born right on time, when he's ready to come out.*
>
> *Mother and Father are brimming with joy as Baby is placed on Mother's chest. He hears his heart beat in unison with hers. Mother smiles and baby gurgles. They both drift off to sleep.*

Leroy was amazed that based on his description of being stuck in a cave, I was able to discern that he was living with the consequences of a birth trauma. I explained that I'd listened to him with my "third ear"—that is, I was paying attention to the symbolism in what he said.

Just as when we think back to a dream we had and suddenly recognize the meaning of one of its images, we can use our "third ear" and discover the symbols in our waking lives. Waking-life symbols can include words or phrases we say, illnesses we suffer, gestures we tend to make, or objects that we feel strongly about. Had I only done cognitive behavior therapy and followed typical psychological-protocol procedures for discerning the causes of Leroy's depression, I would have completely missed the origin of his issues.

In working further with Leroy and helping him access a relevant past life, I discovered that his depression was also related to a previous lifetime in Peru:

Huancayo, a gifted and intuitive high priest of the Inca, lives in ancient Machu Picchu. He has so much power that no one dares question him. Although very committed to his calling, he begins to abuse his position by sexually exploiting others. He selects either a man or a woman who has come to him for worship and proceeds to seduce the person. So power hungry is Huancayo that he is totally indiscriminate as to the gender or age of his victims. Coerced into secrecy, those he has abused are terrified. Huancayo continues his behavior for 13 years until one of his victims discreetly questions others who have come before Huancayo and the secret finally comes out.

Huancayo is forced to stand before the tribunal and is confronted with his transgressions. As he vehemently denies the charges, the injured slowly begin to step forward and tell their stories of seduction, betrayal, suffering, and fear. Some of them sob and shake, explaining that they were so terrified they'd be cursed or killed that they remained silent until now.

Huancayo is found guilty.

The large mountains in Machu Picchu are lush with greenery. At the top of the highest peak, there's a small opening with bars where prisoners were once housed. Now it's vacant, frightening, desolate, and isolated.

Huancayo is imprisoned there and allowed only minimal food and no human contact. He falls into utter despair. Since he's akin to a sorcerer, his powers remain potent, and he soon begins to use them. He lifts his spirit out of his body and hovers around the area; however, his body remains in prison, in isolation.

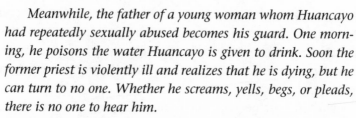

Meanwhile, the father of a young woman whom Huancayo had repeatedly sexually abused becomes his guard. One morning, he poisons the water Huancayo is given to drink. Soon the former priest is violently ill and realizes that he is dying, but he can turn to no one. Whether he screams, yells, begs, or pleads, there is no one to hear him.

Huancayo dies slowly, painfully, desperately, and totally alone.

Being trapped in such a small space caused Leroy's soul to experience a tremendous wound of isolation, and it formed the basis of the repetition of being trapped in his mother's womb in this lifetime.

The experience of being alone and depressed was repeated later on as well. In Leroy's current life, he felt that "no one ever heard" him; in that Incan lifetime, no one was around to hear his screams. Although Leroy had attentive and supportive parents in the present, he still felt alone, isolated, and unheard. The past incarnation in Peru was responsible for his depression, as well as the experience of the womb as a cave or prison. Unconsciously, he'd chosen to remain inside and to reexperience feeling alone and trapped.

Leroy began to practice deep-breathing techniques to release the fear and pain of his birth. His depression gradually lifted, and he no longer felt as though he were in a dark cave.

I saw Leroy for only three sessions. The first consisted of my interviewing him to establish his history and identify the source of his depression. I regressed him to his birth experience, and we rewrote the story of this trauma and taped the script so that he could listen to it. His second session included the relevant past-life regression in Peru. The third and final session was a review of the independent work he'd done for 40 days. At that time, he handed me an unsolicited outline detailing his impressions of the first two sessions, as well as his independent work and the healing benefits he'd derived from it.

He wrote:

1. Opening up a lot of suppressed feelings—anger, impatience, lack of motivation, depression—but now I have the confidence that I can do something about them.

"Opening up a lot of suppressed feelings" was the result of reliving his birth experience and rewriting the script. Leroy was first transported to the place of pain; then, by working for 40 days on the new script, he was able to begin healing himself. His unconscious mind (and now his conscious one as well) still held the memories of his past traumas, but they were tempered because he'd rewritten his story and was training his brain to believe it.

Imagine, for instance, that you hate to drive a car because when you were learning to do so you had an accident, and every time you get behind the wheel, you feel anxious and uncomfortable. The more you drive the car safely, the more you start to overcome that anxiety and discomfort. You don't forget the accident, but it no longer intrudes upon your experience on the road. You've accepted it and now have a new experience of driving, one that's pleasant and even relaxing.

Rewriting your story is transformative. Leroy said that he was depressed on many occasions while going through those 40 days, yet at the same time he felt confidence because he was doing something about his profound sadness. Confidence and action are on the opposite side of the continuum from depression. Act, validate to yourself that you're changing, and depression begins to lift.

Leroy continued his outline:

2. A proactive rather than a reactive outlook.

Instead of feeling that the world was "doing me in," as he called it, and being convinced that he had to react to whatever was happening, Leroy now felt empowered to be proactive. He was aware that he could choose how to interpret events and which feelings he wanted to create.

Although our emotions can be very powerful and can arise almost instantaneously, using healing tools (such as the ones that will be explained later in this book) slows down this process. Our emotions become less intense and affect us more gradually so that instead of instant anger or sudden fear, we feel a twinge of irritation or a fleeting sense of apprehension. Rather than going into the reactive, child mode, we can deal with our emotions as adults and actually choose to feel confidence instead of fear or compassion instead of anger. We step out of the melodramas our emotions create.

3. More willingness to do what needs to be done and the confidence that the situation will turn out well.

This statement expresses hope—the opposite of despair, a feeling that's intrinsic in people who are depressed. Leroy's pattern of despair was experienced in the prison in Machu Picchu; when he was trapped in the womb; and in his current life, where he'd felt engulfed in depression.

4. Recognizing patterns and feeling confident that I can correct them, like going from a "battle mode" consciousness to a "dancing" consciousness with my current project.

Leroy was working on a team project at his job that was very difficult and demanding and presented a constant struggle. Now he was able to view it as a dance rather than a battle! I thought it was terrific that he could reinterpret his interactions using this metaphor and then make a point of going out dancing with his co-workers so that he could reinforce the feeling of engaging with them in a cooperative and joyous way. This was quite a change from feeling isolated and embattled.

5. Seeing patterns in others and how I fit into their patterns—like with my girlfriend, who, I suspect, has "unwanted" issues and is ambivalent about being involved with me.

Leroy now realized that his girlfriend had always felt very rejected. He also realized that if this was the case, she may have selected *him* because he was ambivalent and uncommitted.

> *6. Expecting patterns and relationships to change because of the new consciousness, and being open to that change.*

Leroy recognized that without the pull of the repetitive patterns of his past, he might no longer mesh with his girlfriend romantically. He'd no longer be playing the role of the unavailable man because he'd made great progress in working through his issues of isolation and loneliness. His girlfriend hadn't worked through her own issues and might very well become attracted to a different man who would offer her the opportunity to suffer the pain of being rejected—and the opportunity to heal that pattern of rejection at last.

> *7. Identifying staying in my basement one-room apartment as being a way of staying in the womb, and the new apartment as a space where I can be out of the womb, in a new life.*

Leroy used to be so depressed that he would stay in his small, basement apartment much of the time. When he decided to get a new place with windows and sunlight, on an upper floor, this was comparable to exiting the womb and being born to a new life.

> *8. Using the dancing symbolism, I even went dancing the day I completed the 40 days of using the rebirthing tape.*

After only two sessions and the independent work of listening to the tape for 40 days (only a few minutes each day), Leroy felt that he had transformed his life. His total commitment produced a heartwarming and amazing outcome for him. By acting out the metaphor of dancing with life instead of struggling with it, he imprinted on his unconscious a new belief—that he was engaged in a positive interaction with the people around him instead of

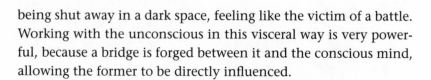

being shut away in a dark space, feeling like the victim of a battle. Working with the unconscious in this visceral way is very powerful, because a bridge is forged between it and the conscious mind, allowing the former to be directly influenced.

Suzanne's Story

Suzanne was an educated and bright 20-year-old who came to me because she was anxious and felt that she didn't have a strong sense of direction in her life. She had an exaggerated fear of being abandoned, and this caused her to be apprehensive about relationships. She would try to become involved with men, but they would stop calling her after the second date, as she seemed too eager and needy. She relayed the following story during a hypnotic regression that transported her immediately to her experience in the womb:

> *My mother is having a huge fight with my father, and my dad angrily slaps her face and walks out of the apartment. My mother is crying, frightened, worried, and anxious about the possibility of being alone trying to support herself and a baby. Mother and I (still in her womb) are very relieved when my father returns home many hours later. They make up and resume their loving and supportive relationship.*

Because Suzanne's mother was still alive, Suzanne was able to verify that the fight, and her father's storming out, had actually occurred. Her mom explained to her:

> We had a third-floor apartment. Your father had just lost his job. I was sitting on the sofa trying to relax after a difficult day at work, and your father came home drunk. I was really angry at him because we were going to have a baby, and he was wasting money on alcohol. While I was yelling at him, he slapped me. I was overwhelmed and frightened because he'd never struck me before.

When he ran off, I was devastated, and worried about how I was going to manage if he left and I would be alone raising you. But he came back and we made up. Everything was fine after that because he soon got a job, and you were born.

Suzanne was amazed that she'd been able to sense her mother's feelings and share them. Those hormones of distress during the fight went right through the placenta and into Suzanne as a fetus. That experience was so defining that it imprinted itself on her consciousness.

She was especially surprised that she could remember her father walking out of the apartment. How could she have possibly known that that had happened when she was in her mother's belly? I explained that, as a soul not yet fully attached to the developing fetus, she was able to float in and out of her mother's womb and could actually see her father leave the apartment and slam the door. This traumatic experience set Suzanne up for feeling anxious about romantic attachments and fearful about the future. Bringing the memory to the surface from her unconscious allowed her to begin healing those feelings created when she was still inside her mother.

Incarnating as an Animal

When a soul has come to the level of incarnating as a human, it usually doesn't choose to go "backward" to an animal incarnation. Animals function at an instinctual level; they don't make choices consciously. They're wired to simply seek food, procreate, secure a living space, protect and train the young, and (sometimes) adjust to life in a group. In other words, animals don't need the kind of training and learning development that we do.

By contrast, human beings have been given the gift of free choice, and they exercise it both consciously and unconsciously. The soul usually needs to reincarnate as a human in order to carry out its legacy and to learn its own personal lessons. However, there are exceptions. It may choose to incarnate as an animal to experience the attribute it seeks to acquire because an animal experiences qualities in a simpler, purer form. A soul that's having difficulty exhibiting a certain trait may elect to come back as an animal so that it can do so.

One of my clients, Richard, had lifetime after lifetime in which he betrayed his spouse, family, country, and tribe. No matter which position he took on the pendulum—the loyal one who's betrayed or the betrayer of one who's loyal—he just wasn't learning the lesson of loyalty and healing himself. His soul was stuck on experiencing payback, so he was unable to exit his pattern. After all that, Richard's soul chose to create an opportunity for healing by incarnating in a past life as a dog (which we discovered during regression) so that he could experience loyalty and faithfulness in a pure form, in the hopes that he could forgive those who had betrayed him and stop betraying others.

Charlene's Story

Charlene, a physician and a workaholic, was very bright, capable, highly educated, and intellectual. One of her past-life regressions revealed that she'd had these qualities before, but in a very different incarnation, as she explained:

> *I'm swimming and diving in the water. I'm holding my breath for a long time underneath the waves. I'm leaping out of the water and having so much fun. I'm with my pod, and we're playing and swimming in the ocean. I feel I'm a dolphin. I am a dolphin!*

What is the essence of a dolphin? It is the experience of joy in being alive. A dolphin rejoices. It plays. It is highly intelligent, curious, and very community oriented, experiencing and rendering much group support. Dolphins are very loving toward each other and toward humans.

In order to understand the significance of Charlene's incarnation as a dolphin, we viewed a panorama of her relevant past lives that most expressed the need to experience these qualities.

In the first accessed lifetime, she'd been notorious for her cruelty and control over everyone around her, especially her husband, who was of one of the Caesars in Rome. In another lifetime, she'd been a nun. Instead of being compassionate, kind, and giving, which would have helped her heal her cruelty, she horribly abused the children in the orphanage where she taught. In the next life, she'd been a wizard, whose power over others was less direct than in her other lifetimes because she was only able to influence people energetically, not actually harming them physically. And yet, Charlene still had been unable to transcend her propensity for cruelty and excessive control.

In the current lifetime, her boss was very hard on her and demanding, just as her father had been. Her mother was kind and gentle yet very strong, a wonderful role model for being powerful without misusing that power. Yet, Charlene hadn't been able to follow her mother's example and was still wrestling with cruelty, although in a gentler form than in previous lifetimes. After all, she was never uncaring to her patients, and her boss and father were harsh but not actually abusive.

Charlene's soul, in order to experience kindness and joy, had chosen a prior lifetime as a dolphin. It was delightful and uplifting to be one of these wonderful creatures. She felt safe because she had no expectations of performance, achievement, or power. As a dolphin, she felt no drive to express control. Her only needs were to live with the pod, love her fellow dolphins, and be loved by them. Clearly, this lifetime had been very healing for her, and tapping into it helped her in her current life.

Now that she'd experienced kindness, intelligence, curiosity, and a sense of community without having any need to wield power over others, Charlene's soul chose to reincarnate this time as a physician: a life of service in which she expresses sensitivity, compassion, and giving. Having experienced the essence of delight, support, and joyousness as a dolphin, at last she was able to carry those feelings and qualities into her human incarnations.

Shortly after Charlene completed therapy, a position opened up in another area of the hospital where she worked, and she immediately knew that she and her new boss would get along well. He was playful, lighthearted, and kind, even when there was a lot of pressure; and now that she'd done so much healing, she was able to consciously choose a situation in which she could work with others in an uplifting, joyous collaboration. This wonderful professional environment was one she hadn't imagined was available to her, but after doing work on her issue of cruelty, her eyes were open to the possibility that a better job would present itself to her—and she found it.

Thomas's Story

Thomas was a 40-year-old married man who came to me because he felt stuck in his life. He was fearful of change and had turned down several offers for far better positions because they would have involved leaving the comfort zone of his current job. I helped him scan various past lives, as if using a remote control on a television. At one point, he told me that he didn't understand what he was experiencing in a particular lifetime he'd accessed, and he kept repeating, "It's like I'm looking through the eyes of a lion."

The essence of a lion is courage. The head of his pride, he sits beneath a tree protecting the lionesses and cubs. If a younger lion encroaches on his territory, he will fight him—and usually, he'll win. He maintains his dominance by fearlessly facing his foes and ensures the strength of the pride by defeating males who aren't as strong as he, whose genes would weaken the gene pool.

I asked Thomas to experience a past life in which courage was a theme for him.

In the first relevant previous incarnation, Thomas was a Roman general. His scouts reported that the enemy was about to attack from behind a nearby hill. Rather than meet his attackers head-on, Thomas, full of anxiety and fear, took no action. The enemy soon surrounded him and his men and slaughtered all the soldiers. Thomas was taken prisoner and dragged off to be tortured before being killed. He was devastated by the consequences of his cowardice. Because he hesitated and didn't express courage, many lives were lost, including his own.

In the next past lifetime, Thomas was a Greek foot soldier. At the first chance of meeting the enemy, he turned and ran away. He had to live with the shame of abandoning his troops and not being "man enough" to fight.

During an in-between lifetime, Thomas's soul said: *This time I'm really going to conquer my fear and access my courage.* He then incarnated as a woman with children, because what's more important to a mother than to follow her maternal instinct to protect her offspring? In this lifetime, Thomas was a mother of three who lived in a small village that was attacked by marauders. She shielded her little ones in her skirts, but as the attackers crashed through the entrance to the hut, they ordered her to release her children. Terrified and sobbing, afraid of being killed, she opened her skirts. The attackers grabbed the children and slew them in front of her.

Thomas experienced horrible loss and devastation because over several lifetimes—as a man or a woman; as a general, soldier, or mother—he still hadn't been able to exhibit courage. The pain, guilt, and shame were so intense that from a soul's vantage point, it was necessary to learn courage by experiencing it in its purest and narrowest possible context; thus, Thomas reincarnated as a lion. In that incarnation, his entire existence dealt with being courageous. His soul knew that it needed to experience courage in its purest form in order to finally break out of his paralyzing fear.

In his current life, after Thomas completed therapy with me, a robber broke into his home and held him, his wife, and his two children captive. The intruder pointed a gun at one of the kids. Thomas stayed back and glared at the man for a few moments, then lunged toward him with fierce determination, despite the risk of being shot himself. Thomas overcame the robber and saved his family. The interim lifetime as a lion had allowed him, finally, to act with courage. When he was confronted with the repetition of having his bravery tested, Thomas, having experienced courage as a lion, was able to access it and act upon it.

Hannah's Story

Hannah, a client of mine who lives in Israel, was distraught over the death of her dog, Charlie, and wanted to find out the cause of his demise. She called me, hoping that given what I know about animal incarnations, I might have some insight into what had happened.

Hannah and her husband had hired a scribe who specialized in scripting the Torah. This is an extremely expensive and laborious task since every dot and every letter have to be written by hand with absolute accuracy. If a single error is made by the scribe, the whole book is considered unusable and is buried in the ground. When the gift of a new Torah scroll is given to the synagogue, it's such a joyous event that everyone in the town gathers in the streets singing and rejoicing, carrying the sacred book from the donor's home to the place of worship on foot. Hannah and her husband were happy to have made the decision to gift their little nearby synagogue with a new Torah.

Charlie, their flat-faced, flat-nosed English bulldog, was sweet, kind, and loving—and fortunate enough to be richly loved by everyone. On the day of the ceremony celebrating the new Torah, Hannah took Charlie to her son's so that he'd be out of the way during the festivities at her home. She tied him up in the shade and left him plenty of water and food.

Once the festivities ended, Hannah went to pick up Charlie only to find him dead. She was extremely upset and confused because he'd had enough water and food and should have been fine, especially given that he was lying comfortably in the shade. How and why did Charlie die?

After I'd listened to Hannah's sorrowful story, my Angels and Spirit Guides told me that Charlie was a human soul incarnating in a dog's body. Charlie had the soul of a man who needed to spend a short time on Earth as an animal in order to complete a particular part of his story. In between human lifetimes, he decided to incarnate as a dog owned by Hannah, who would someday participate in the creation of a new Torah, because this soul knew that when the book was gifted in the presence of so much light and joy and so many prayers and blessings, he would have the opportunity to leave the body in the swiftest manner possible.

I explained to Hannah that very often after people die, their souls have difficulty detaching from the people and places they knew in life. When there's great joy and celebration, it's easier to let go. Apparently, this soul knew that by becoming Hannah's dog, he would be able to ascend to the in-between world swiftly when the time came.

Because the soul possesses the God-given gift of free will, we have the opportunity, and can make the decision, to incarnate in other forms, as well as into the womb of a mother who we know will make choices and have experiences that will allow us to engage in repetition. Our souls have tremendous wisdom, insight, and perspective in the in-between times; and they make excellent decisions about which mother to be born to and what family to be born into. As soon as we enter human (or animal) form and inhabit the physical body, our unconscious memories and decisions become hidden to us. We can only access them by engaging the unconscious through particular techniques that set aside the domineering conscious mind, which fears the emotional pain of discovering this buried knowledge.

In the next chapter, you'll learn how to access the unconscious in an emotionally safe way so that you can begin to heal—and make your repetitions in this lifetime gentle instead of intense and painful.

CHAPTER THREE

THE 7 STEPS OF REBIRTH

I've been very blessed and grateful to have acquired a wealth of experience and knowledge from my thousands of clients, and I'm deeply fortunate to have received spiritual inspiration from my Angels and Spirit Guides throughout my career. Over many years, this combination of insights led me to develop a process called the 7 Steps of Rebirth, a highly effective formula for healing and forgiving ourselves and others.

Although the 7 Steps of Rebirth may appear simplistic at first, they are broad ranged in their impact. They resonate with and influence every aspect of our behavior, our hormonal responses, the functioning of our brain centers, our breathing, our history, and our psychology. Every step, no matter how simple it may seem, is vitally important in this process.

The 7 Steps of Rebirth will help you heal swiftly. In fact, the process takes considerably longer in the telling than in the doing. I'll describe each step here in great detail, but with a little practice, the 7 Steps of Rebirth will only take one minute to execute, and you can do them anytime you choose.

I suggest performing this exercise three to seven times a day until you start to notice a shift in your patterns. You may

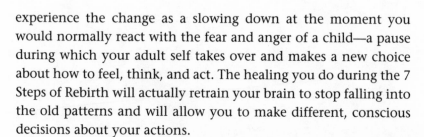

experience the change as a slowing down at the moment you would normally react with the fear and anger of a child—a pause during which your adult self takes over and makes a new choice about how to feel, think, and act. The healing you do during the 7 Steps of Rebirth will actually retrain your brain to stop falling into the old patterns and will allow you to make different, conscious decisions about your actions.

For your convenience, I'll summarize the steps at the end of the chapter, but within each step's explanation, I've italicized the core actions to take.

Step 1: Stop!

Anytime we feel tense, upset, angry, anxious, depressed, threatened, overwhelmed, or frustrated, the child in us, or the child self, has popped out of the unconscious and taken over. We want to stop that automatic reaction we've engaged in maybe hundreds or thousands of times so that we can change the process and respond maturely, as an adult. *When we're re-creating a repetitive pattern, our first step in exiting that pattern is to say "Stop!"*

Say "Stop!" out loud if there's no one around. Think it silently if you're not alone. When you do so, you're consciously choosing to halt your immediate reaction to the situation. *As you say "Stop!" imagine an eight-sided, red stop sign.* This image, which all of us have seen thousands of times, will help reinforce your choice to stop.

The reason why using a visual helps us is because our unconscious expresses itself with images. We dream in pictures and not in sentences. When we mentally create an image, we can tap into the unconscious, where the memory of the original trauma that created our repetitive pattern is kept and where our automatic behavior originates. Therefore, if we access the language of the unconscious by imagining a stop sign, we're directly addressing that part of our awareness.

Whenever we engage in a frequently used, repetitive behavior, the upper regions of the brain, where we think and make decisions, aren't involved. Because the reaction bypasses our rational, analytic brain, it happens quickly. For instance, because we've spoken our native language for years, the brain needs to expend very little energy for us to express ourselves, but if we're attempting to use a language we've just begun to learn, our rational brain gets involved in the process, and it requires more time and effort for us to speak. To retrain the brain takes practice.

Step 2: Breathe

Whenever we're tense, uptight, strained, depressed, angry, frightened, or threatened, we're operating out of the midbrain, or hypothalamus, the region of the brain associated with experiencing emotions. As I mentioned in the Introduction, the amygdala is a small area in the hypothalamus that becomes activated instantaneously as soon as we perceive a threat. It sends signals to the other parts of the body, causing us to have what's called a *fight-or-flight response*, which is designed to allow us to face a threatening situation and "fight" or run from it with great speed, engaging in "flight." It was developed early in human evolution, when we often faced life-threatening situations and needed to respond rapidly in a way that would ensure our survival.

When the body is in fight-or-flight mode, the amygdala sends a message that causes the heart to start racing, the blood pressure to increase, the blood vessels to narrow, increased amounts of oxygen to be pumped into the cells, and glycogen (sugar) absorption to be stepped up. Originally, the fight-or-flight response allowed us, as primitive humans, to escape dangers such as a tiger, a snake, or a warrior from an opposing tribe. Nowadays, we'll enter this mode when we experience any perceived threat, such as someone scolding us. Although our rational mind might tell us that the boss isn't going to fire us just because he's upset about a mistake we made and that our spouse isn't going to leave us simply because he's upset at the moment, our body responds as if our very survival is at risk. The body and the brain react just as they did

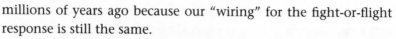

millions of years ago because our "wiring" for the fight-or-flight response is still the same.

When we perceive a threat or feel angry, frustrated, depressed, or overwrought, the heart has to work harder to pump blood throughout our whole system, from the tips of our toes to the top of our head. Everything is go, go, go, and our glands release hormones such as cortisol and adrenaline to prepare us for either facing the enemy or running away—for fight or flight. The part of the nervous system that's involved in this response is referred to as the *sympathetic* nervous system. We also have something called the *parasympathetic* nervous system, which is designed to act as a brake, reversing the wheels of motion that the sympathetic nervous system set spinning.

As soon as the threat to our safety has disappeared, the parasympathetic nervous system sends messages to our body to return it to a state of calm. Our blood vessels expand, our heart rate and blood pressure decrease, our circulation improves, and our system becomes quieter. We also release hormones into our body that promote cellular repair and relaxation.

Unfortunately, in modern times when we experience a stressful situation, our parasympathetic nervous system often doesn't turn on and return us to a state of calm. Although we may come down a little after the experience is over, we rarely do so completely and properly as we're meant to. By remaining in a stressful, fight-or-flight mode, we do damage to our body. Over time, we experience breakdowns of the heart, digestive tract, liver, and brain as a result of being stuck in this mode.

However, with one properly performed breath, we can trigger our parasympathetic nervous system to do its job and return us to our baseline, the state of calm we're meant to experience most of the time. This is a crucial part of the 7 Steps of Rebirth because it actually causes our body to begin the healing process.

When we operate out of the midbrain, we're in the instantaneous stress and reaction mode, behaving like very emotional children. The child doesn't make a conscious choice; it simply reacts automatically. By taking one breath as described below, we quickly cease operating from the midbrain and begin to operate from the neocortex: the upper region of the brain where the functions of conscious choice, decision making, and judgment take place. We are able to move from the overreacting child self to the conscious, mature adult self almost instantly.

There are three parts to this specific breath that brings you from the reactive, child self to the discerning adult self:

1. *First, inhale deeply through your nose, being careful not to raise your shoulders or tighten your muscles.*

2. *Next, hold that breath for a count of four, or about four seconds.*

3. *Then exhale through the mouth, allowing the jaw to drop and making a "Haaaaa" sound to enable the breath to flow out slowly and evenly. The exhale should last longer than the inhale. Be sure not to purse your lips or push the breath out during the exhale, which creates tension around the mouth.*

Throughout the breath, relax your muscles. As you take it, don't cross your arms, legs, or fingers. Crossing your digits or limbs will prevent the natural flow of your body's energy, which is needed for turning on the parasympathetic nervous system.

My Angels and Spirit Guides have told me that it's important to hold the breath for a count of four seconds. According to Eastern wisdom, we have seven major chakras, or energy centers, located in the core of our body from the base of the spine to the top of our head. Four is the number of the heart chakra, which symbolizes balance. The fourth chakra, the central one, has three chakras below it and three above it. The ones below are associated with earth, and those above are associated with spirit. The heart chakra is also associated with loving-kindness, which is how God cares for us: unconditionally and with compassion. Love is the energy that unites us with the Divine. Four also represents balance and the cardinal directions (north, south, east, and west).

Step 3: Acknowledge—"Whoops, There I Go Again!"

Step 3 is to acknowledge and affirm that we are the author of our story. It's difficult for us to do this because our tendency is to blame and judge ourselves and others. We also have trouble owning up to our responsibility because our repetitive behaviors are quite often unconscious. We don't want to believe that we're actually choosing to create situations that are causing us to suffer—but we are. The statement "Whoops, there I go again!" helps us acknowledge our story without judgment.

It may feel as if the world is antagonizing you—that the government is against you, your boss hates you, or your spouse is being cruel to you—but you've chosen the situations you find yourself in. The only way you can heal is by owning your story. This doesn't mean that you must accept blame or judge yourself.

Think of your story as a play. Imagine that you're watching one that you wrote, directed, produced, and are acting in. If you're unhappy with a certain scene, you can change it. If you want to enhance it in some way that will cost more money, you can do so because you're the producer. If there are too many actors onstage and the scene would be more effective with fewer characters, then as director, you can change that, too. The entire story is yours, and you can control it and change it any way you wish. You can do so because you have free choice.

Free choice is always ours. God created souls as individual sparks of light, and according to Kabbalah and other spiritual disciplines, when the Divine made each spark, it was given the gift of free choice. We exercise this choice moment by moment, both consciously and unconsciously. It's very difficult for the majority of us to accept the reality that we have the power to choose to experience traumatic situations. Looking at the bigger picture, we see that the story we create provides us with the opportunity to change our reactions and therefore grow.

This is *our* responsibility. Because we're exercising our free choice, we can't say that God is to blame for our unhappiness. Even conflicts and abuse are the result of decisions that we (and others) make, sometimes consciously and sometimes unconsciously. We don't intend to harm ourselves or others; we're simply aiming to re-create opportunities to grow.

We must own our story by delving into the depths of the psyche and acknowledging that we are the writer, actor, director, and producer. Cognitive behavioral therapy is useful to a point in that it helps us recognize our conscious choices about which thoughts we think, but it doesn't address our *un*conscious choices. Research using MRIs and brain scans has shown that 95 percent of our behavior is determined by our unconscious. If this is true, then why are therapists still doing cognitive behavioral therapy, which is only going to address the remaining 5 percent? Our responsibility, I believe, is to access and affect that 95 percent. When we're able to do so, acknowledging all of our behavior, all of our feelings, and all of our story, then we can make the choice to change it.

We can only fully acknowledge our role in our "play" when we let go of judgment. Saying "Whoops, there I go again!" reminds us that we must own our story rather than accusing others of causing us misery, or feeling guilty about consciously or unconsciously creating our problems. We need to move away from self-criticism and criticism of others. As long as we point an accusing finger at ourselves or those around us, we'll never experience the clarity necessary to look at the bigger picture and see how we can change it. Acknowledging our story is a crucial step for healing.

Step 4: Get a Number

After you've stopped, breathed, and acknowledged your story, *allow the very first number that enters your mind to come right into your awareness. This number is going to be the age (between 0 and 10) of the child whom the adult will be meeting and healing in the next step.*

It's important not to think or try to figure out which number you should come up with; instead, simply allow your unconscious mind to choose the very first one that arises. If the number isn't between 0 and 10—let's say it's 28—that's okay. It may be that at age 28, you went through a very difficult and combative divorce; simply note that period and that age, as you may want to explore that trauma more deeply later on. But the most defining events that leave a significant imprint on you are the ones that take place at an early age, so let go of the thought of 28; do Steps 1, 2, and 3 again; and allow a number between 0 and 10 to come up.

When we were very young, whatever events we faced that were experienced as traumatic left an impression on the brain. That became the blueprint on which the rest of our behavior is based and determined. We can even become stuck at a particular age when a trauma occurred and live the rest of our lives unable to mature into full adulthood.

For example, one of my clients, Stephanie, has a mother in her late 80s. Stephanie always complained that because her mom was too childish and concrete, she could never turn to her for any in-depth advice. I asked my client to tell me her mother's story, how she grew up, and what went on in her life.

When her mother was eight years old, she was put in charge of her sister, who was about five at the time. She didn't watch her younger sibling carefully enough, for she was a child herself. The five-year-old was run over by a carriage in the old country and died. The family never dealt with this trauma.

Although Stephanie's mother is in her 80s, much of the time she operates as an 8-year-old child—one who has been completely in control of her throughout most of her life. While the behavior of being very concrete and childish is normal for an 8-year-old, it's abnormal for a 30-year-old, very unacceptable for a 50-year-old, and downright strange for an 80-plus-year-old. It seems such a terrible waste of a lifetime to be stuck at this young age; and it's heartbreaking because every one of this woman's six children is miserable, unhappy, depressed, and angry. They never experienced their mother as a mature, adult parent.

The first time you use the 7 Steps of Rebirth, once you've gotten a number, you need to *create a magical nature scene in your mind*—"magical" because anything, including healing the worst traumas, is possible with magic. Create a beautiful setting that has trees, flowers, colors, and always a body of water. Water is symbolic of healing, the unconscious, and emotions, so it's a very powerful image. You can choose a waterfall, stream, lake, river, ocean, or pond. It doesn't matter what the body of water is as long as it's not intense or turbulent. It must be crystal clear, calm, and quiet. Make the scene as rich as possible so that this isn't simply an intellectual exercise but one you feel and experience.

Because you learn about the world through your senses, it's important to access all of them when you're imagining this magical nature scene. Choose your favorite nature smell, such as fragrant flowers in full bloom, and imagine that they appear everywhere in your scene. Envision blossoms of every hue, preferably in the sequence of the seven shades of the rainbow, which evoke the colors of the seven chakras or energy centers. Imagine the sounds of birds chirping, leaves rustling, and water trickling or flowing. To engage your sense of touch, feel the gentle breeze that caresses your cheek and revel in the coolness of the water as you dip your toe or hand in it. This magical nature scene should be beautiful, gentle, and mysterious; and it should engage and delight all the senses. Then, place yourself in this scene alone (except for the Angels, if you desire to envision them).

If you believe in Angels, call on them, saying, "The most loving, compassionate, and highest Angels of the Light, please be present in this nature scene to keep me and my child self safe and protected at all times and in all dimensions." If you don't believe in these heavenly beings, that's okay. This magical scene will still create a safe, loving place in which your adult self can meet your child self and provide him or her with comfort and reassurance.

You'll return to this magical nature scene every time you perform the 7 Steps of Rebirth, so take the time to create it carefully, with vivid detail, color, sense, sound, enchantment, and beauty that will touch your very soul. When practicing the 7 Steps of Rebirth, you'll be able to enter this healing place immediately.

Step 5: Meet the Child

In Step 5, your adult self meets the child self. *Keeping in mind what number came to you, imagine yourself as a child at that age, playing in the magical nature space.* Greet this little one; observe what he's wearing and what he looks like. (Note that in this step and the next one, I will alternate the gender of pronouns referring to your child self to avoid awkward "he/she" constructions.) Don't question, push, or pressure the child. Don't ask her to tell you any secrets or to reveal to you any events that may have occurred. *Your only agenda is to express unconditional love toward the child and to provide a sense of safety for her.*

Tell the child, "I have come to be with you. You'll never be alone again. You'll always be accompanied by the power of my love . . ." and if you believe in Angels, add: ". . . and that of the Angels." Only you, as an adult, can promise the child that you will always love him and be with him.

There is a beautiful bench near the water. Invite your child self to come and sit beside you. If she's willing to be seated next to you, put your arm around her little shoulder and hold her close. After a while, invite her to sit on your lap. Hold her, stroke her face and hair, and then begin to rock her back and forth until her heart and yours beat in unison.

If the child is very frightened or angry, he may be standing behind a tree, looking curiously at your adult self, not trusting the adult and unwilling to appear. Your agenda must remain the same. Say, "I've come to be with you, and you'll never be alone again. I love you always. It's okay if you're not ready to come out. I'll keep returning, and I'll be here with you until you're ready." Allow this child to come to you when he is ready.

One of my clients, Natalie, discovered that when she sat on the bench in the magical nature scene, her child self wouldn't emerge because she'd been very traumatized at the age of four. Natalie, who was very imaginative, began to sing softly. When the little four-year-old heard Natalie's song, the sweetness of the sound was so reassuring that she slowly began to move closer to the adult.

Finally, she stood next to the grown-up Natalie and touched her arm. In seeing the adult self's smile of acceptance and love, the child self decided to come and sit on the bench close to her.

The process of meeting your child self may be slow. Don't push it or force it. Merely allow it to happen gently, in its own time. The agenda and process in this step are always the same. The only aspect that may be different is the age of the child self. If you experienced a trauma or perceived threat more than once during your childhood, each of those child selves—for instance, the four-year-old whose father abandoned the family, the frightened five-year-old whose mother scolded her as she left her at school to attend kindergarten, the ten-year-old whose mother remarried that year and had little time for her daughter—must be loved, protected, and healed along with the adult. It's important to meet with each child separately and reassure her that she doesn't have to take on the adult role, that she can remain a child because you, the adult, are in charge.

To use the healing tool of the 7 Steps of Rebirth, you don't need to know the details of the trauma the child suffered. If a particular number comes up for you again and again but you don't know why, don't worry about it. Focus on the healing, and at some point your conscious mind may be able to handle the memory of the trauma you experienced at that age.

Step 6: Separate from the Child

In Step 6, you separate from the child. *Set your child self down and say, "I leave you here in this magical nature scene."*

Reassure him of his safety, saying, "You can jump up and down, play, and climb the trees. This is magic. No harm can come to you. You can chase the butterflies, pick fruit from the trees, and do whatever you want because you're safe here. You can even go into the water and you'll never drown, for this place is magical.

"You can play because I've called Angels especially for you. They can play with you. You can hold hands—even ride on their wings and soar, and they'll bring you right back. You are safe and protected, because I've created this special, magical place for you." (Angels love to be of service, by the way. They always delight in play, and you need only ask them to engage in it. Having created this safe space and met the child who was you, you've created an opportunity for Angels to come in and rejoice, frolic, and protect the child.)

Tell your child self repeatedly that you've created this magical place for him, and then separate from him, promising to come back soon. You as the grown-up are doing the healing: The adult is making the choice, and the adult is creating the safety. Therefore, the separation is healing both for the child and for the adult. Always make certain you assure your child self that you'll come back and visit again. You don't need to specify when, since time doesn't exist in the unconscious; simply say that you'll return at a later date. Go back and visit this child again briefly.

The reason why it's so important to take this sixth step and detach from the child is that if you don't, you'll bring her right back with you into your adult life and let her take charge of your thoughts, feelings, and behaviors. If your child self is now sitting on your shoulders with her little legs wrapped around your neck and her hands over your eyes, you're still looking at the world from her childish perspective instead of with the eyes of an adult. Give the child what she needs—love, safety, and acceptance—and then separate from her, leaving her safe and sound in the magical setting.

One of my clients, Samuel, had experienced such profound abuse as a child and was so full of rage as an adult that when he met the child, he was surprisingly angry and impatient with him. He said, "Get away from me and stop bothering me." This response only intensified the conflict between his adult and child selves. I suggested to Samuel that he begin working with the 7 Steps of Rebirth by meeting one of his pets (he had a cat and a dog) rather than his child self. I reasoned that if he could begin to express his love and reassurance to an animal, then he might soften his reaction when meeting his child self.

A pet is helpless, dependent, loving, and eager for attention and kindness, just as the child is. If you have difficulty with this part of the 7 Steps of Rebirth, you, too, may want to imagine meeting a favorite furry friend in the magical, safe place. After going into the scene and encountering the pet several times, try meeting your child self by calling your animal's name and observing as your child self, not your pet, responds.

Step 7: Return to the Present as an Adult

With the first six steps, you were taking a journey into mystery, magic, your past, and other levels of reality and consciousness. It's now time to return to the present. All that matters is *now. In Step 7, you come back to the present as the adult self after taking a breath as described in Step 2.* Inhale deeply through the nose, relaxing your muscles; hold the breath for a count of four (that is, four seconds); then, exhale slowly through the mouth to the count of four (the exhale should always last longer than the inhale). Allow yourself to return from the magical, timeless nature scene to the present moment.

Ground yourself by affirming your name and current age, the place, and the year, saying, for example, "I, James, come back to the present as a 39-year-old adult in New York City in 2008."

In this way, you return to your conscious, adult self who makes choices from the upper regions of the brain. You're able to emerge from a dreamworld, just as you do when you wake up in the morning while you're on vacation and your mind orients you, thinking, *Oh, that's right—I'm in the bed at the hotel, not my own bed.* When you take the specific breath, you move from the emotional part of the brain, the hypothalamus, representing the child self, to the upper regions of the brain—the mature and decision-making adult.

To return to the present in a centered way, we must orient ourselves to person, place, and time. That means we affirm who we are (name and age), where we are, and the present time. When

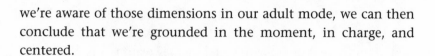

we're aware of those dimensions in our adult mode, we can then conclude that we're grounded in the moment, in charge, and centered.

Concrete Healing Benefits of the 7 Steps of Rebirth

Once you complete the 7 Steps of Rebirth and review whatever event, person, or situation was upsetting to you, you'll be able to make appropriate behavioral choices with a clearer perspective using these new insights. You'll recognize that you—your adult self—haven't been feeling overwhelmed; it was the *child* who felt that way. Now, as the adult, you can affirm that you're capable, mature, and aware.

Over time as you use this process, further insights and understandings will be revealed to your conscious mind as you start to heal and become better able to handle the memories of traumas. The 7 Steps of Rebirth are a powerful tool because they open the door to the unconscious, sending it the message: *It's okay to let me know what you know. I'm ready to heal the pain and stop the repetition of suffering.*

As I mentioned earlier, an integral part of the 7 Steps of Rebirth and their effectiveness is to take responsibility for your story, owning it . . . accepting that you've played the roles of writer, director, actor, and producer. If you don't own your story and work your way through the 7 Steps of Rebirth, you won't access your awareness that you have the choice to *change* the story. Acknowledging your power to exercise your free will makes you feel in control of your life. Your adult self will emerge, feeling calmer and better able to handle whatever life has to offer.

Working with the child self allows you to heal self-defeating patterns by going to the source. When you love, nurture, and recognize this part of you, you begin to heal yourself of past trauma. When you return to the present, leaving the child in the safe and magical scene, you begin to separate your current life from your personal history. This clears the way for you to release the past, embrace the present, and have a cleaner slate for what you want to create in the future, allowing you to begin exiting the pattern of repetition you've established.

As you practice the 7 Steps of Rebirth, you'll start to heal from your traumas, giving you the strength to face, acknowledge, and examine your life stories and themes. Instead of judging yourself or being crippled by shame, you'll be able to let go of any blame and simply notice your patterns and how they repeat in your life.

Use the 7 Steps of Rebirth anytime you notice that you're engaging in repetitious behaviors, thoughts, or feelings. This will help you heal your traumatized child self and operate from your adult self. For example, if you usually withdraw from confrontation and you recognize that you need to go one-on-one with someone, use the 7 Steps of Rebirth several times before speaking up. Allow your adult self to face the conflict head-on, speak up, and remain in the present moment. Afterward ask yourself, *How did this new behavior feel? How effective was it?* It's likely that breaking with your usual pattern and standing up for yourself will feel uncomfortable because it's unfamiliar. You may feel uncertain, self-conscious, and awkward—just as you did when you rode a bike for the first time—but if you have positive results, you'll reinforce the belief that this new behavior feels right for you.

Whenever we make a choice and respond as the adult, the pattern loses its hold over us and begins to recede. Each time we heal and set aside the child self, allowing the adult to be in control, the past will let go of its grip on us and eventually, cease to tug at us. Once the child receives attention, love, and reassurance—which is what was needed all along—this part of us will no longer need to be in charge. The conscious mind doesn't realize it, but in our child mode, we're terrified. Children know that they don't have the maturity to handle a great deal of responsibility. They want to test the waters of their independence, but if they're allowed to have too much power, they'll feel frightened and insecure.

For the sake of the child and the adult, our grown-up self needs to gently but firmly insist that the child be a child and leave the adult in charge. If we give in and let our child self dictate our feelings and actions, we'll remain stuck in repetition, unable to learn and grow. We'll simply react to what's going on around us and create familiar situations again and again. Only the adult has the courage, strength, and wisdom to exit the pattern.

Positive change occurs when we take responsibility for our own lives. With this new awareness that we're in charge of our story and can change it at any point, we'll begin to see the world through new eyes and view our choices as unlimited. At this point, we may even realize that we're participating in a massive shift in human consciousness as people everywhere begin to wake up to the reality that they're the ones writing their own stories and taking part in a larger one. If the storytellers are frightened children, the stories themselves will be repetitive and cause suffering. Only when we write new ones from our adult perspective can we begin to heal ourselves and our world, lessening our suffering as well as that of others.

While the potential for healing is great, keep in mind that when you begin to use the 7 Steps to Rebirth, change will be gradual and progressive. It took you decades—and often, lifetimes—to develop these patterns, so it will take time, effort, and continual use of the 7 Steps of Rebirth to establish new ones. These life repetitions will persist, but as you begin to exit the old patterns, the nature of each one will become gentler. The abandonment, betrayal, or cruelty won't be nearly as dramatic or painful as it was in the past. Remember the universal law of the wave, which was described in the Introduction.

As your awareness increases with the use of the 7 Steps of Rebirth, you'll cease criticizing yourself because you'll recognize that there's no reason to feel ashamed or bad about yourself for unconsciously engaging in repetition. You'll start making better and healthier choices in all areas of your life. Embracing and accepting the inevitable and necessary theme of repetition, you'll feel more empowered, less judgmental toward yourself and others, and infinitely more hopeful.

Summary of the 7 Steps of Rebirth

Using the 7 Steps of Rebirth stops us from automatically reacting to situations as a traumatized, frightened child and instead lets us access our calm, accepting adult self. It allows us to heal by giving us a way to reassure our child self that he or she no longer has to take on an adult role; and empowers our adult self to make better, healthier choices for ourselves.

Step 1: Stop! While saying "Stop," visualize a stop sign.

Step 2: Breathe. Inhale deeply through the nose, hold the breath to a count of four, then exhale slowly through the mouth (the exhale is longer than the inhale). Remember not to cross your arms or legs, and keep your facial muscles relaxed.

Step 3: Acknowledge—"Whoops, there I go again!" Affirm that you're the author of your story. The statement "Whoops, there I go again!" will help you acknowledge your story without judgment.

Step 4: Get a number. Let your unconscious mind reveal to you a significant number that represents your age when a trauma occurred. If it's greater than 10, go ahead and identify what events took place when you were that age, but then repeat Steps 1–3 and allow your unconscious mind to find another number, this time between 0 and 10. This is going to be the age of the child whom the adult will be meeting and healing in the next step.

Step 5: Meet the child. Create a magical nature scene where you meet your child self, giving him or her love and reassurance, remembering to call on loving Angels of the Light.

Step 6: Separate from the child. Reassure the child that he or she is safe, sound, and loved; then detach yourself, leaving him or her in the safety of the magical scene.

**Summary of the
7 Steps of Rebirth (cont'd.)**

Step 7: Return to the present as an adult. State your name, your age, your location, and the year in order to come back to the present and your adult self feeling alert, refreshed, revived, and replenished.

To ensure that the 7 Steps of Rebirth are effective, you must not rush through the process or skip a step. Each one is precise and necessary to create the healing, the separation, and the return to the present.

The 7 Steps of Rebirth should be used on a continual basis. Growth and change take time, patience, and nurturing support. If you repeat the steps three to seven times a day initially, the process will become automatic and will take only a minute. It's important to realize that change is not an overnight process. Because you're reenacting an old theme from your past, you'll become caught up in a repetition of the energy and the emotions you experienced then.

When you feel overwhelmed, stressed, fearful, angry, or upset, practice the 7 Steps of Rebirth and you'll begin to change your reactions, exiting your patterns and responding instead in a mature, proactive, adult mode. This is how you'll heal.

Our stories, experiences, and patterns become grist for the mill of life. Our repetitions provide the lessons that lead us on a path of spiritual awakening and healing.

As we take the responsibility for our lives and all our experiences, we can make the necessary changes using the 7 Steps of Rebirth. We can move away from blaming other people, life in general, or even God for our misfortunes. We often wait for Divine intervention without doing our part to effect positive change. The Creator is with us at all times and loves us unconditionally, but it's up to us to engage in the behaviors and initiate the changes

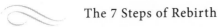
that alter our stories and enable us to heal. With God's love always shining brightly in our hearts and in everyone and everything around us, we'll come to realize that we alone have the power to set ourselves free!

In Part II, you'll see how my clients have set themselves free from destructive patterns and healed specific life issues using the 7 Steps of Rebirth. These case histories will help you recognize and acknowledge your own repetitive patterns so that you, too, can take responsibility for *your* story.

PART 11

LIFE ISSUES

CHAPTER FOUR

RELATIONSHIP ISSUES

Our sense of urgency to connect with others stems from the universal law of relationships, which says that we're meant to form bonds rather than go through life disconnected from other people.

The soul and spirituality have everything to do with connecting to and caring for each other. As I explained in the Introduction, if we don't love and look out for one another and perpetuate the race, we humans will become extinct. And if we don't survive, we won't remain on Earth long enough to learn whatever lessons we came here to learn.

Often clients come to me because they're focused on issues in their romantic partnerships. Because our repetitions play out not only in these, but in every relationship—including those with relatives and friends—and we reincarnate in families and groups, even if we start therapy by exploring the causes behind a divorce or a romantic betrayal, soon we'll come to see that the same themes are occurring in *all* our interactions with others.

Soul Mates

Much as we value all our relationships, most of us fantasize that we'll find our one soul mate, and we place great importance on this relationship. Edgar Cayce said that every soul comes into each incarnation having at least 30 potential soul mates—people with whom we've had a soul connection that was very close at another time, in another place. We've known each other in many different incarnations, and we've had a strong mutual impact. Our relationship in a past life may have been steeped in love and romance or sorrow and pain. We may have been star-crossed lovers; or we may have been parent and child, cousins, or friends. When we reincarnate as romantic partners, we're drawn to each other so that—through repetition—we can resolve all the issues we shared in the past.

The myth or fantasy is: "If I meet my soul mate, everything will be wonderful and we'll love each other forever. We'll feel comfortable and good with each other, and we'll live happily ever after."

First of all, nobody lives "happily ever after." The concept of soul mates, at a deeper level, refers to souls coming together with the specific intent of aiding one another on each soul's journey. The connection is made when partners access their past wounds for the sole purpose of healing them. Essentially, a soul mate is the very one who may have been with you many times before. He or she will, therefore, have more familiarity with your hot buttons and better access to them than anyone else has. Thus, your soul mate may not be a romantic partner.

Sometimes our soul mate is a parent, sibling, or other person who continually upsets us but whom we can't seem to break away from, for whatever reason. It may be the individual who aggravates and infuriates us the most. By pressing our buttons, he or she creates the opportunity for us to work through our issues more swiftly. If we choose to change our reaction, we can heal—but if we don't take advantage of this opportunity to change, we'll only feel that this person is aggravating, nasty, bothersome, or disagreeable.

Your soul mate unconsciously helps you *and* him- or herself by pressuring the two of you to deal with issues that are relevant for both your souls. Of course, this connection may be distasteful to you on a conscious level, but at a deeper one, you're experiencing what you need to experience. Your soul mate didn't only come to "fix" you, but also to *be* "fixed." Each of you has the choice to learn what you came to learn . . . or to miss your chance.

We all have our own journey to take. Before we're born, we make a harmonious agreement with our soul mate: We decide we'll come together at some point and meet in order to press each other's buttons and help each other heal. What we do with this opportunity is completely the expression of our free choice. We can take advantage of it or not. We can react, grow, and learn—or not. It's up to us.

Why Do We Choose the Mates We Do?

While our soul mate doesn't have to be a romantic and sexual partner, often he or she does become one in this lifetime, because when we're in love, the power of our attraction is so strong that we're willing to work on issues that we avoid dealing with in other relationships.

For human beings, romance is exciting, desirable, joyous, and mysterious, so we crave it even when it makes us suffer. It has a potent impact on every area of our lives because it causes us to release many hormones in our brains, hearts, and sexual organs that result in the feeling that we're experiencing something uplifting and even magical.

Pheromones, chemicals that have great power to attract potential mates, are released, altering our scent. This is a powerful attractor because smell is the only sense that has direct access into the hypothalamus, the part of the brain that governs our emotional response. We react primitively, with an immediate and strong emotional response, to the pheromones that we're wired to find attractive. God created these chemicals to draw us to our soul mates and to give us the opportunity to experience an intense relationship.

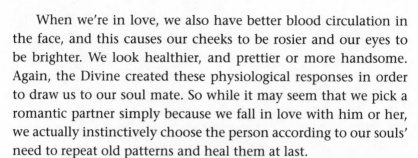

When we're in love, we also have better blood circulation in the face, and this causes our cheeks to be rosier and our eyes to be brighter. We look healthier, and prettier or more handsome. Again, the Divine created these physiological responses in order to draw us to our soul mate. So while it may seem that we pick a romantic partner simply because we fall in love with him or her, we actually instinctively choose the person according to our souls' need to repeat old patterns and heal them at last.

One of my clients, Tony, had a history of failed marriages and relationships. What he didn't realize is that as different as his wives and girlfriends seemed to be, all of them were soul mates for him.

Tony's Story

Tony was a 58-year-old professor of history when he came to see me in hopes of lifting his depression. He wasn't publishing articles, which was a necessary component of being tenured at the university. Although he had ideas and was very capable, he wasn't being productive. First, we discussed his past relationships.

On a dark, rainy night just outside of Memphis, Tony and his fiancée, Ruth, were driving home from their high school prom. They were happy and very much in love. While discussing plans for their upcoming marriage, a car—sliding out of control—came barreling toward them. Tony veered sharply to the right, plowing into a guardrail. Ruth died instantly.

Devastated, heartbroken, and guilt ridden because he'd been the driver and had been unhurt in the accident, Tony left Memphis and moved to San Francisco, where he attended college and established his home. Just before completing his education, he met June. They got married and soon had twin boys. Tony was working as a teacher, had a family he loved, and felt that the pieces of his life were now in place.

Late one evening, Tony came home elated after having a particularly productive day with his students. His five-year-old boys were already in bed. It was a lovely starlit night, and he and June were sipping wine on the patio. Suddenly, June blurted out, "I'm taking our boys and leaving you. I've been having an affair with Don, and we're moving in with each other." Don was Tony's best friend and confidant. Tony, paralyzed from shock and disbelief, was speechless. Within seconds, his whole life had turned upside down and collapsed all around him.

While Tony was going through the process of separation and divorce, he met Vanessa and they immediately hit it off. She had recently transferred to the university where Tony taught and was now one of his colleagues. They shared so many amusing stories about their students that they laughed until they ached. He would say, "I don't crack up like this with anyone but you and my mother."

When her grown daughter had a baby, Vanessa suddenly left town to visit her. The delivery had been difficult, and both mother and infant needed considerable attention. Vanessa's visit lasted much longer than expected. Preoccupied with her daughter and grandchild, Vanessa called Tony only twice during her stay. When she returned, Tony had already put up a wall between them. He was afraid that she, too, had left him. Since he felt that he'd never be able to trust her again, he ended the relationship.

Tony then became interested in Bonnie, a woman who was 25 years younger than he was. She'd been one of his students when he taught high school. They were reacquainted at a coffee shop when he noticed how perplexed she looked while writing a paper and approached her. He soon saw her regularly, helping her with her studies while she attended evening classes at the local college. She needed him and he needed her. It was as if Tony had his children back, because he could act in a paternal way with Bonnie: He took care of her, and she was totally dependent on him.

Tony and Bonnie decided to get married. However, Bonnie became irrationally jealous of his sons and refused to let them visit. Afraid of risking yet another loss, Tony held on to Bonnie so tightly that he made her more important in his life than his own children were. He unconsciously gave away his power to her, and she became very controlling. This was most evident when she

made sex conditional: Whenever they made love, it was all about her and her own agenda and what she wanted to get out of him.

One day, Tony called home and another man answered. When he asked Bonnie about it, she blurted out that the man was her exercise trainer, who had been her lover for years.

After hearing Tony's story, I felt it was no wonder that he was depressed and unproductive. The themes of betrayal and abandonment had pervaded every one of his major relationships with women. We then reviewed his childhood and his relationship with his mother.

His father had left home when Tony was five years old. Afterward, his mother was so distressed and heartbroken that she turned to her son for comfort. Sitting at the kitchen table, Tony's mom would often tell him about her boyfriends. She also talked at length about her feelings of sadness, abandonment, anger, and disappointment, which she'd been experiencing ever since his father left. Tony felt uncomfortable and repeatedly tuned his mother out, his eyes glazing over. Emotionally, he was withdrawing—as a small child, he couldn't handle these discussions. Because of his mother's revelations, the themes of betrayal and abandonment became a part of his life.

Nevertheless, Tony and his mother were close. She played with him, and they laughed together often because she had a great sense of humor. However, her habit of turning to Tony for comfort and relying on him for emotional support was completely inappropriate. Tony was now being held responsible for nurturing her feelings, while at the same time he was disconnecting from her because her behavior felt so threatening to him. Their roles had been reversed: He was the child taking care of the mother, instead of the other way around. His mother's dependence on Tony implied emotional incest.

All of us experience abandonment and loss, literally and physically, beginning at that dramatic moment after we're born when the umbilical cord is cut and we're separated from Mother. (However, as I mentioned, as babies we are totally unconscious of this and have no awareness of where we stop and mother begins, despite the physical separation.) At the spiritual level, we experience this whenever we feel separated from the Divine and wonder if God really exists and cares about us. Ultimately, the issues of abandonment and loss are endemic to us all. For some, however, they become major life themes. This was the case for Tony.

Tony experienced abandonment, loss, and betrayal by his father when he was five years old. His mother emotionally betrayed him because she didn't behave as the authority figure—that is, as the parent he could depend on for comfort, guidance, and support. Instead, she made Tony her confidant and grew emotionally dependent on him.

Tony experienced abandonment and loss again when Ruth, his fiancée and beloved, died. His marriage to June was an expression of total betrayal and abandonment as well. Once again, he lost his cherished partner, but this time he was also deprived of his sons, whom he loved so intensely (and who also lost their father at five years old, just as Tony had), when June took custody of them. He also lost his best friend, Don, who became June's lover.

When Vanessa suddenly left town to help her daughter and grandchild, she had minimal contact with Tony during an extended period of time. Because of his personal history, the issue of abandonment tugged at him, although he was unconscious of this influence. Not recognizing that he was repeating behavior patterns of the past—only this time, as the person who leaves instead of the one who is left—he broke off his relationship with Vanessa. He felt that he was no longer able to trust her and feared that she, too, would leave him.

The persistent control Tony's second wife, Bonnie, exerted over him pressed his buttons; and his fear of loss, betrayal, and abandonment caused him to revert to the frightened five-year-old he'd been. Her continuing jealousy of his sons became so oppressive that Tony, in turn, finally cast aside his own boys and didn't see them for seven years. As he'd feared, Bonnie ultimately did betray and emotionally abandon him by having an affair with her trainer.

Tony came into therapy very depressed and incapacitated. He learned the 7 Steps of Rebirth and practiced them conscientiously.

Within a short time, he began to feel better, his depression lifted, and he became much more productive. Six months later, two of his articles were published. A year later, he mustered enough courage to initiate changes in his life and in his relationships. This was in stark contrast to the reactive stance he'd been in for so much of his life. He decided to diligently work on healing himself.

Here's how Tony used the 7 Steps of Rebirth to heal himself:

Step 1: Stop! Rather than becoming caught up in emotional responses, Tony would simply stop himself, envisioning an octagonal, red stop sign as I'd instructed. This step was certainly easy for Tony because after such agonizing experiences, he'd practically stopped himself from feeling anything, so he was used to cutting off his painful emotions as soon as they arose.

When we don't know what to do next and feel incapacitated, this first step breaks us out of confusion and fear.

Step 2: Breathe. Tony had considerable difficulty committing himself to using the specific breathing technique I taught him for short-circuiting the fight-or-flight response, because the more he would relax, the more his old feelings of pain and loss would resurface. However, the fear of losing his job at the university was so great that he agreed to practice the breathing technique anyway and tolerate those difficult feelings. After a week, he reported that he was beginning to feel calmer and less anxious.

Step 3: Acknowledge—"Whoops, there I go again!" It was very challenging to get Tony to see the relationship between his story and his behavior. Stuck in his perception of himself as the victim, he was unable to own up to his responsibility for co-creating the situations that had caused him pain.

Because we will quickly judge ourselves as inadequate, we often avoid acknowledging that we had the power of free will to choose our situations and relationships and chose ones that caused us to suffer.

Tony would often say that his was a pathetic story, thereby judging himself. Eventually, discussing certain aspects of repetition that were themes in classic novels helped Tony, because he realized that he wasn't the only person in history to make "foolish" choices in relationships. He then began to see the importance and value of owning his story in order to make necessary changes. He identified and acknowledged the repetitions that were so evident in every aspect of his life.

Step 4: Get a number. When practicing this step, Tony often got the number 5, which made sense because, as he'd told me, that was his age when his father walked out on the family. The 58-year-old adult Tony would need to meet the 5-year-old and assure him that he would always be there for him, offering him support and unconditional love.

Tony would also sometimes get the number 7. At this age, he'd moved with his mother to a trailer park because she couldn't afford the apartment they'd been living in. That, too, represented a time of loss and separation, since he had left friends in his old neighborhood.

Step 5: Meet the child. The adult Tony would create a magical nature scene with birds, flowers, and a calm body of water, where he would alternately meet his five- and seven-year-old selves in order to comfort and reassure them that he would always be there for them and wouldn't abandon them.

Tony cried profusely when he worked on Step 5 because he felt so guilty about having abandoned his own children. This also led to a great deal of sobbing and grief about the loss of his beloved Ruth and the guilt he experienced about having been the driver of the car that day. Once again, Tony noted the inevitability of repetition as he grieved over the loss of Ruth, his first love, and over his abandonment of his own children. This all came into his awareness in the context of meeting his child self. Tony still needed to do more work with the five-year-old, because his feelings of rejection were greatest when he was that age.

Step 6: Separate from the child. The adult Tony now needed to reassure the five-year-old (and the seven-year-old, at another time) that no harm would come to him and that he would be safe in the magical nature scene Tony had created. The five-year-old repeatedly refused to approach him and stood aside, crying. Eventually, the five-year-old walked over to him and held his hand, asking him to come along so that he could show him a hole in one of the trees where a squirrel had built its nest. The nest was filled with little baby squirrels.

As Tony described this scene, he was so moved that he sobbed again, realizing the symbolism of the squirrel and the babies. Tony had finally recognized how he'd unconsciously repeated the patterns of his childhood in the abandonment of his own sons.

Step 7: Return to the present as an adult. Taking one breath, holding it for four seconds, and slowly exhaling, Tony affirmed that he was an adult professor and specified his name and age, along with the location and date, grounding himself in the present. The 58-year-old Tony, who had experienced much success as a professor, needed to reaffirm his achievements in order to respond to the world from the vantage point of the adult and not the child.

A particularly serious problem presented itself now that Tony was beginning to face the distress of his marriage to Bonnie. His wife was very resistant to his therapy and the consequent changes in him. She was also very critical of his expression of greater assertiveness. He now insisted on having a more open, close relationship with both of his children.

In having a more interactive relationship with his sons, Paul and Robert, and experiencing the pleasure of bonding with his grandchildren, he was now healing and changing the story of abandonment that had become a generational curse. His father had abandoned him, he'd done the same to his own children, and the probability of their eventually abandoning *their* kids was great. Now that Tony and his sons were able to relate to each other, the grandchildren could feel much more secure. Just as traumas radiate and reverberate across generations, so, too, does the healing.

As a result of his healing, Tony decided that he deserved to be in a healthier relationship. He tried to get Bonnie into therapy as well, but she declined. She hadn't been present in the marriage from the beginning, and she took no responsibility for her part in it. Bonnie also categorically refused to commit to ending the relationship with her trainer. She wouldn't learn the 7 Steps of Rebirth, which Tony wanted to teach her, and he reported to me that she wasn't interested in changing herself or healing the marriage. They divorced soon thereafter.

Tony made the connection with his children and grandchildren a priority in his life, establishing a healthy, joyous, and loving relationship with them. Neither Paul nor Robert were educated—they felt so abandoned and rejected by their father that they didn't want to be like him. Yet, they yearned for their father's closeness.

Within a year after Tony had reestablished a relationship with his sons, Paul—who had a very lucrative factory job—decided to attend college at night. Robert, who had become suicidal due to depression, decided to straighten out his life and join a support group. He was a whiz at electronics and signed up at a technical school to develop and enhance his skills. Tony's healing reverberated across three generations, since it affected his grandchildren's lives as well.

Tony still wanted to know why he had chosen the particular women he'd become involved with and why the relationships had worked out as they had. He was especially puzzled about why he was never able to become seriously committed to Vanessa, whom he'd loved. She was his colleague at the university, and he still saw her often. To clarify some of the issues contributing to their problems and the constraints on their relationship, Tony then explored his relevant past lifetimes with Vanessa.

In the first one that he accessed, Tony was a 21-year-old woman named Jane in England during the 17th century, while Vanessa was Jane's 24-year-old husband, Lawrence:

Jane, Lawrence, and their two children and three dogs are all playing joyously in the gardens of their country home one bright, beautiful summer's day. Laughter and love abound. Jane coyly tilts her head to one side, flutters her long lashes, and seductively winks at Lawrence. Giggling, she runs into the house, up the stairs, and into their bedroom. Lawrence follows close behind.

After an hour of sensual and gentle lovemaking, Jane is overflowing with affection for Lawrence, feeling wonderfully safe and happy. She steps out onto the balcony to inhale the fragrance of their gardens and to admire the beautiful view. She calls Lawrence onto the balcony to join her. Together, they share in the sweetness of their life as they observe their children playing below. Lawrence watches their son, Charles, in particular. He is such a bright light in Lawrence's heart.

Suddenly, Charles, running at full speed, heads straight in front of their horses. In a panic, Lawrence leans over the side of the balcony to warn his son. Extending too far over the edge, he falls onto the brick walkway below and cracks his skull. An hour later, as Jane cradles him in her arms, he dies. . . .

At this point in time, Jane and Lawrence had been married for five years. Three months before his death, Jane found out that he'd been having an affair with her best friend, who lived next door. She was devastated by the news because she loved Lawrence so very much. She withdrew and distanced herself from him—until two weeks before the fatal accident. Lawrence repeatedly apologized and begged for her forgiveness, so finally Jane felt trusting and loving enough to summon him back to her bed and express her love for him. And now, just after they'd shared that magical moment of passion, sensuality, and oneness, tragedy had struck.

Jane blamed herself for the loss of her beloved husband, since she had called him onto the balcony, and the depth of her guilt was indescribable. She never remarried, remaining extremely depressed and isolated until her death 20 years later.

The theme of abandonment, experienced with great intensity in the first relevant past lifetime that Tony accessed, was carrying over into the present—with the same partner.

When a strong energy from a previous life is brought into the current one, the individual is both attracted and repelled at the same time, because of the unconscious recognition that he or she and this partner will, in some form or another, repeat the trauma they shared.

While Tony (Jane) was very much attracted to Vanessa (Lawrence) in the current lifetime, he felt threatened by the possibility of any closeness with her. The guilt of losing his beloved in that past incarnation (Jane blamed herself for calling Lawrence onto the balcony) prevented him from having a meaningful and trusting relationship with Vanessa in the present. Also, at an unconscious level, she triggered memories of the emotional incest with his mother, since they were the only two people with whom he could laugh so freely. This resulted in a double whammy: Too many buttons of guilt and fear were pressed in him, making it next to impossible for him to stay with Vanessa.

Tony felt responsible for his fiancée's death in this life, since he was driving the car at the time of the accident. He felt tremendous guilt about being to blame for his beloved's death not once but twice—in this lifetime, with Ruth, and in that past lifetime, with Lawrence (Vanessa).

Another correlation between Tony's previous life in England and his current one was the issue of marital infidelity. Both of Tony's wives, June and Bonnie, had affairs while married to him. June left Tony for Don, his best friend. In that past life in England, Lawrence had an affair with Jane's best friend.

The repetitions Tony experienced in the current lifetime as well as the past one in England helped him become aware of and understand parts of his history as it related to the bigger picture of his present life. He was beginning to see why he'd been drawn to his romantic partners and why those relationships had ended the way they had.

Tony next accessed a relevant past lifetime with Vanessa in ancient Egypt. She was a 17-year-old girl named Amranel. Tony was a 22-year-old man named Ishtar.

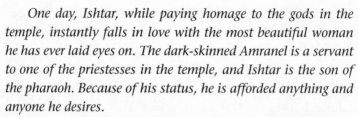
One day, Ishtar, while paying homage to the gods in the temple, instantly falls in love with the most beautiful woman he has ever laid eyes on. The dark-skinned Amranel is a servant to one of the priestesses in the temple, and Ishtar is the son of the pharaoh. Because of his status, he is afforded anything and anyone he desires.

Every time Ishtar visits the temple, he sees Amranel. He often brings offerings to the gods and places them at the feet of their statues. The more he sees her, the more inflamed his passions are and the more enamored of her he becomes. His love for her grows so intense that he begins to look for her outside of the temple. Every time Amranel goes to the edge of the Nile to watch the passing ships and gossip with the girls with whom she works, Ishtar quietly and secretly watches her from behind the bushes. No matter how beautiful the others are, the only maiden who catches his eye is Amranel.

Eventually, Ishtar approaches his father and asks his permission to release Amranel from the temple so that she can become his wife. Ishtar, accustomed to getting what he wants, is surprised and shocked when his father refuses his request. The pharaoh won't challenge the priestess or encourage the wrath of the gods by taking one of the servants from the temple.

Heartbroken and in total despair, unable to envision life without Amranel, Ishtar drinks poison and suffers a painful death.

Tony experienced another traumatic event with the soul that was Vanessa. The intense feelings of despair and desperation culminated in suicide when the soul that was now Tony experienced life as Ishtar. While still in a trance, Tony realized that his suicide had influenced his current-life traumas.

Why the Soul Might Postpone
Dealing with Issues for Many Years

When a human being commits suicide, very often the soul comes back to reexperience loss after loss, hurt after hurt, and challenge after challenge in the current lifetime. Why did the soul that was now Tony return to work on the feelings of intense despair that had led to his suicide nearly 4,000 years before (as Ishtar)? Why did his soul (as Jane) come back to work on the feelings of guilt and depression created 300 years previously?

The reason why we don't necessarily incarnate immediately after death and go straight to work on resolving those issues is because the soul often needs time to handle facing such a severe trauma again.

Imagine that you're studying at a university. You took mathematics your first year, but it was too difficult for you to handle. Now you're in your final year and have yet to complete the class. You determine that now is the perfect time to retake it because your course load is light this semester and you feel ready to tackle it.

Similarly, the feelings of intense despair culminating in suicide are so traumatic that the soul will often choose to delay dealing with that trauma for many years or incarnations until it's finally ready to do so. Suicide has a tremendously strong pull on the soul. A soul, therefore, may choose to come in to meet the challenge of potentially experiencing deep despair in many incarnations. Spiritually, if it's able to confront this feeling and not commit suicide, then it's engaging in the *opposite* of despair: faith.

When we experience faith, we affirm that Divine Energy or the Light is always with us no matter how dark things get, no matter how difficult circumstances are, and no matter how depressing the situation might be.

When Tony made the decision to drink poison in his Egyptian lifetime, the theme of suicide became one he was going to have to contend with in the future. Indeed, he was challenged by it in a number of lifetimes. In his current one, Tony wasn't suicidal himself, even though he'd been very depressed at different times.

However, he faced the horror of suicide when his own beloved son struggled with chronic depression and tried to take his own life. His son's attempted suicide was the worst challenge that Tony ever had to face, but he had to confront the situation in order to heal himself of this issue and exit the pattern.

Visiting and healing relevant past lifetimes offers us a much richer and fuller understanding of traumatic experiences and events in our current lifetime. The repetitions and comparisons experienced in the past and present are fully realized and become transparently clear. We can then change our reactions and exit the patterns we've been repeating.

One common pattern we repeat from lifetime to lifetime is betrayal of our romantic partners. My client Christina learned that while her affairs with married men mirrored her father's infidelities when she was a child, her behavior was actually rooted in a past lifetime.

Christina's Story

Christina, a 35-year-old human-resources director for a large corporation, came to see me for help with relationship issues: For the last seven years, she had found herself playing the role of mistress to several married men. Tall, slender, blonde, and strikingly attractive, she had bright emerald green eyes that drew attention from everyone around her.

Since Christina had been feeling frustrated and depressed because of her choices with men, she thought that therapy would help her. She spoke of two serious relationships she'd had with men who weren't married, back when she was in her late teens and early 20s. Although she was successful and a high achiever, she was unhappy and extremely dissatisfied.

Christina reported that her father, a brilliant physicist who was also charming and funny, had carried on affairs with women as far back as she could remember. Her mother was lovely, kind, and nurturing but consistently seemed to turn a blind eye to her husband's philandering. On the surface, Christina's mother seemed accepting of her situation, but the dark family secret of her husband's betrayals devastated her emotionally, and at one point she even attempted suicide.

Christina admired her father's success and hoped to emulate him in that way—not realizing that unconsciously, in order to be more like him, she was choosing to have affairs as well. Much as she'd hated knowing that her father was cheating on her mother, here Christina was, having to admit that she, too, was sleeping with partners whose wives, like Christina's mother, might be suffering due to the adultery. Deeply uncomfortable with this reality, Christina was living her emotional life in hiding, just as her father had done, without feeling any sense of fulfillment or openness in her relationships.

In order to heal the issues that were driving her to have these affairs with married men, she began working with the 7 Steps of Rebirth and underwent a regression to access a relevant lifetime, one that took place in Egypt in the first half of the 20th century, when her name was Layla.

Layla is a healthy and attractive young woman who loves learning. A brilliant student, she's immediately accepted into the most prestigious university in Egypt. She has such an outstanding mind for detail and a retentive memory that she ends up studying law. Upon graduating, she is to work with her uncle, who is also an attorney. She is eager to start her job in eight weeks, after taking some time to rest from the grueling routine of study.

Meanwhile, Layla's parents insist that she marry. They arrange a marriage with Fouad, a wealthy businessman 20 years her senior. Although Layla doesn't love him at the time, she complies with their wishes. They marry six weeks later.

Layla, now eagerly preparing to begin her exciting career, is to start work in a few days. Fouad, infuriated that she still intends to be a lawyer, insists that her only profession from now on be wife and eventually, mother to their children. Layla is heartbroken. Her desire to express herself and work in her profession is totally squelched as she obediently but resentfully goes along with her husband's demands.

Layla becomes pregnant and has a baby, and as she and Fouad begin to raise a family, she gradually falls in love with him even though he is emotionally distant and rarely at home. They end up having three children, and Layla never works in her chosen profession.

Feeling oppressed, alone, and unfulfilled, Layla begins to experience bouts of depression and isolation. She is unable to be assertive or speak up about her desire for self-reliance, independence, and self-expression. Fouad has complete control over her and never really hears her.

When Layla is 42, she finds out that Fouad has been having a longtime affair with a woman who has borne him two children. This throws Layla into the depths of depression. She never leaves the house after that, nor does she ever leave her marriage. Five years later, while Fouad is at work and the children are at school, Layla dies of a broken heart, alone in her home.

In the current lifetime, neither Christina's father nor mother were interested in her deepest feelings and thoughts—she received no feedback, encouragement, or validation. Her mother, who always felt unfulfilled, participated very little in Christina's life and was emotionally distant. She suffered from depression, and her husband's affairs led her to attempt suicide. Similarly, Christina, in her incarnation as Layla, was depressed and, after learning of her husband's infidelity, died of a broken heart. Pining away was a gentler form of suicide, but this theme would come up again for Christina in future lifetimes because it wasn't completely healed.

As I mentioned in Chapter 2, as souls between lifetimes, we pick the families we are born into, deliberately choosing those that will give us the opportunity to work through our issues. Christina had felt unheard by her husband in her lifetime as Layla, and in this one, she chose a father who was emotionally unavailable. This same father had affairs with women other than her mother; her husband in the Egyptian lifetime had a longtime affair with a woman with whom he had two children. In the current lifetime, Christina reenacted this dramatic experience by repeating the theme of becoming involved with married men. In the incarnation in Egypt, after Layla found out about Fouad's lover and their children, she never left him and was heartbroken. This was an exact repetition of Christina's mother's inability to leave her husband in the current lifetime.

My Angels and Spirit Guides don't judge extramarital affairs as being either right or wrong. However, they point out that because an illicit relationship is secretive, it is necessarily uncomfortable in that it involves lying, deception, and cover-up—unhealthy behaviors that cause wounds. Essentially, my Angels and Spirit Guides say, if we choose to have an affair, then it's our responsibility to assess the consequences.

Christina wanted to exit her pattern of affairs so that she could experience relationships free from secrecy, betrayal, and pain, so she began to use the 7 Steps of Rebirth.

Step 1: Stop. Christina worked 10- to 12-hour days, so it was difficult for her to stop, as well as to comprehend the importance of doing so. However, after repeated attempts, she was able to utter the word *Stop!* and imagine a stop sign. She found it especially helpful to use this step at the end of the day when she was feeling exhausted and particularly vulnerable, or when she was sad and weeping into her pillow at night.

Step 2: Breathe. Christina was immediately relieved, and delighted by the swift, successful effects of taking the special breath (inhaling deeply, holding it for four seconds, and exhaling for longer than she inhaled), which she began to practice, especially in the evening. Every once in a while, she would force herself to stop and take a few deep breaths at work. By the end of therapy

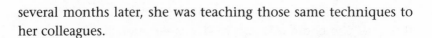

several months later, she was teaching those same techniques to her colleagues.

Step 3: Acknowledge—"Whoops, there I go again!" Christina had always been convinced that it was just "bad luck" that she never seemed to meet the right man. Only when she began to own her story of repeated affairs and recognize the repetition of pain and sadness that this pattern caused in her life—whether it was the sorrow she experienced in a past life or in this one when her depressed mother or preoccupied father emotionally neglected her—did she finally make the decision to change her behavior. Prior to this, she had perceived that she had no control over her attraction to married men or her choice to get involved with them. She realized that as someone who seemed to be very much in charge of her professional life, something else was preventing her from taking control of her relationships: the unconscious decision to engage in repetition.

It was clear why Christina was so afraid to enter into a viable relationship in which she could experience loyalty, intimacy, honesty, and commitment. Unconsciously, she was so frightened of being abandoned and hurt that she chose married men as her lovers. These partners, who were unavailable to engage in a relationship that met her needs, mirrored her father's unavailability to his family.

Christina's feelings of abandonment created the repetition of being in a relationship where she was consistently abandoned, because she wasn't her lover's priority. Secrecy was also a theme in her life: Her mother's suicide attempt was never discussed, and neither were her father's extramarital affairs. Christina's own affairs were secretive as well.

Christina now felt that with her new insights and the tool of the 7 Steps of Rebirth, she could exercise conscious choice and control in her personal life and stop engaging in short-term, dissatisfying, clandestine affairs. She admitted that, deep down, she really wanted to marry and eventually have children, and now she could make decisions that would send her on that path.

Step 4: Get a number. When accessing her unconscious, Christina found that the numbers 4 and 6 often popped up. She had moved with her family to a different city when she was four years old, and her father was busier than ever at his new job. Her mother became more depressed and withdrawn.

Christina remembered that one night when she was four, she woke up and heard her mother accusing her father of having an affair with one of his colleagues. Although she was too young to truly understand what was going on, Christina was devastated when she heard her father say angrily, "I'm not about to end it. You can either accept it or leave!" She was terrified, wondering whether her mother would go away, frightened that she would lose one parent or the other.

Christina also recalled that at age six, she came home from school one day to find her mother slumped over the kitchen table. She tried to awaken her but couldn't. Hysterical and frightened, Christina called a neighbor, and her mom was rushed to the hospital—she had taken an overdose of sleeping pills in a suicide attempt. Already very bright and sensitive, six-year-old Christina understood the depth of her mother's unhappiness. Because she was just a child and the trauma was overwhelming, she'd blocked the memory from her conscious mind. This experience bubbled to the surface from her unconscious for the first time when she met her six-year-old child self.

As young children, when an event such as this occurs, we feel totally helpless and powerless. Assuming that we're responsible, we wonder: *Am I doing something terrible? Am I making my mother so unhappy? Does she want to die because of me?*

Because her parents never discussed her mother's attempted suicide with her, Christina felt guilty about the event. Experiencing this trauma through the eyes of a child, she felt that she was somehow to blame for her mother's act.

Step 5: Meet the child. The 35-year-old Christina created a beautiful and magical nature scene with trees; fragrant flowers; and a gentle, babbling brook. Her adult self alternately met her four- and six-year-old selves. The adult Christina needed to reassure the six-year-old, in particular, that she would always be protected and that her loved ones would never leave her—and neither would Christina. In a different session, the adult met the four-year-old and assured her that she, too, was safe. Given the nature of the trauma that both little ones had experienced, the themes of abandonment and separation were very strong and therefore Christina had been unconsciously choosing to repeat them in her life.

Step 6: Separate from the child. The adult Christina could now separate from the four-year-old, and at another time, from the six-year-old. She reassured the little ones of her love and told them that she would always be there for them. Eventually, the six-year-old burst into tears in Christina's arms, sobbing hysterically and asking for both her mother and her father. She kept saying that she never wanted to be alone but was afraid she would end up that way.

After some comforting and reassurance, the six-year-old eventually calmed down. Holding her hand, the adult Christina took her for a walk through the flowers by the babbling brook. When Christina separated from her child self, she told her that she would come back to visit and reassured the child that she could cry if she wanted to, and chase the butterflies and climb the trees, and that no harm would ever come to her in this magical garden.

Step 7: Return to the present as an adult. The adult Christina affirmed coming back to the present as a 35-year-old, capable, confident professional who could now continue to do the work of healing herself, her mind, her heart, and her history.

Three months later, Christina met Rick, a physician from South Africa who had come to do research at a major hospital in her city. They met at a conference and immediately fell in love. Both single, they dated in earnest. Rick, like Christina, was ambitious, a high achiever, and very successful. He was also a very hard worker and committed to his profession.

However, Rick had an all-consuming passion for soccer that

took up a considerable amount of his leisure time. His preoccupation with the sport aroused feelings of abandonment in Christina, but the repetition of unavailability was now much gentler than it had been in her past relationships, so she was making progress. Christina continued working with her child self in order to detach from her anxiety every time soccer games took precedence over her plans to spend time with Rick. By visiting her child self again and again, she was now able to be more present in the relationship and more accepting of Rick's soccer passion.

Eight months later, Christina and Rick were married in a beautiful early-spring ceremony.

The "Generational Curse"

Practicing the 7 Steps of Rebirth also heals "generational curses" that run in families—issues that are handed down through the generations from parent to children to grandchildren to great-grandchildren. These themes play out in various ways in accordance with the universal principles discussed in the Introduction. If your father cheats on your mother, as Christina's did, the family issue of infidelity will be passed to you, and you're likely to be unfaithful to your partners or be attracted to ones who are unfaithful to you or to *their* spouses. Your children will repeat the patterns in their own way, and their children will continue the repetition.

Maria's Story

Often we overlook these repetitions because we're thinking too literally or because we don't realize that we're simply playing a different role in the same old scenario. That was the case with a client named Maria, who had grown terribly frustrated trying to teach her daughter, Karen, to read. Karen was a bright girl, but unlike her older brothers, she was struggling with mastering this important skill.

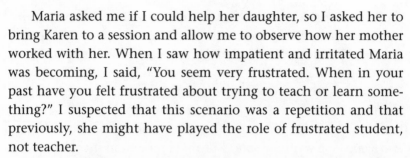

Maria asked me if I could help her daughter, so I asked her to bring Karen to a session and allow me to observe how her mother worked with her. When I saw how impatient and irritated Maria was becoming, I said, "You seem very frustrated. When in your past have you felt frustrated about trying to teach or learn something?" I suspected that this scenario was a repetition and that previously, she might have played the role of frustrated student, not teacher.

"I remember feeling like this when I was 12 years old," Maria replied. "My mother sat with me when I was trying to learn English, and she was very impatient. It was so awful that I thought, *That's it. I'm not going to study English.*"

The consequences of that decision were that Maria came to the United States with very poor English skills. She categorically refused to take a language course, which limited her in many areas of her life: She was unable to get a job in her area of expertise; she could only socialize with Spanish speakers; and although she would have liked to move from her neighborhood, none of the other communities had enough Spanish speakers for Maria to feel confident that she could shop, bank, and get around without becoming confused by the language barrier.

Rosa, Maria's mother and Karen's grandmother, lived nearby, and I asked Maria to bring her mom to our next session. I expressed to Rosa what Maria had told me about her experience learning English with her mother trying to coach her. I asked Rosa, "When in your life have you felt as Maria did when she was attempting to learn English?"

She said, "I remember when I was four years old and I was left-handed. My mother was sitting next to me. She'd bound my left hand behind my back, and I was forced to write with my right one. I felt terrible and so frustrated because I just couldn't do it." Mother and daughter, mother and daughter, mother and daughter—right down the line, they'd experienced exactly the same repetition of frustration and learning difficulties. It had become a generational curse in their family.

I said to Maria, "Let me help you work on your issues by teaching you the 7 Steps of Rebirth. If you stop this generational curse, your daughter won't have to unconsciously participate in this repetition. As you heal *your* patterns, she'll also heal."

Maria was unconsciously helping Rosa resolve the frustration she'd experienced as a girl by repeating the same behavior with her daughter, Karen—who, in turn, was helping her own mother as well. It was as if each daughter was saying to her mom, "Mother, I love you so much that I will play the role of the person to whom you can express your impatience so that you can reexperience the frustration of sitting down to write or learn—only from a different angle. Through this repetition, you can now have the opportunity to change your reaction to being in this stressful, painful situation."

Each daughter also grew up to reenact the repetition with her own daughter because on an unconscious level, she knew that she had to reconnect with the strong emotion of frustration in order to face the situation and resolve it. Maria used the 7 Steps of Rebirth earnestly for three months, and to her amazement, her daughter's reading began to improve. As Maria became more relaxed and was less critical and demanding of Karen, her daughter's reading abilities improved dramatically. The generational curse could now be broken.

It's important to remember that these generational curses are very often carried out unconsciously. For instance, Christina knew of her father's philandering and was consciously aware that there might have been some connection between his behavior with his wife and her own pattern of getting involved with married men, but many times children never learn of their parents' infidelities even though they are repeating them.

This is why in therapy, I will question clients about *their* pattern of behavior and relationships, but I'll also inquire about those of their parents. I know that the unconscious mind may be aware of the clues that all was not as it seemed. If I ask questions about how their parents interacted and about their family life as children, I

can bring to the surface issues that are part of an intergenerational pattern of repetition.

By using the 7 Steps of Rebirth and the other tools that will be presented in these pages—writing your story, rewriting your story, and the 4 Steps of Joy—you can start to not just recognize, but actually *heal*, your generational curses. You can learn to own your story, accept responsibility for your choices, and do your own healing work rather than blaming your parents for your issues or projecting your expectations onto your children and trying to "fix" them. As you heal yourself, your children will easily change along with you, because by breaking a generational curse, you free them from having to participate in the pattern of repetition.

CHAPTER FIVE

HEALTH ISSUES

When we experience prolonged depression, chronic emotional pain, uncontrolled anger, or psychological trauma, our physical bodies are often affected. In fact, any emotional trauma may eventually manifest itself physically if we don't heal ourselves at the core of our being. The ailment may be so frightening or troublesome that we finally face our issues.

Robert's Story

Robert, a 43-year-old plumber, came to me initially because he was experiencing persistent, pernicious headaches that couldn't be treated with strong medication because the side effects would have been too dangerous given his many other medical problems. Robert decided to engage in a past-life regression because he could no longer live with the pain and the excessive pressure he was experiencing in every area of his life. When I asked him what his headaches felt like, he cried, "I'm going crazy! It feels like someone's taking an ax to my head."

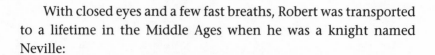

With closed eyes and a few fast breaths, Robert was transported to a lifetime in the Middle Ages when he was a knight named Neville:

Clad in heavy armor, perched high and solid atop his steed, Neville fixes his eyes on Perceval, his opponent. Their lances are raised, and they're ready for the joust. Little do the tournament spectators know that Neville and Perceval are vying for the same woman, making this their personal battle—a duel—for the hand of their beloved. With horses galloping head-on and eyes blazing, the two knights face off. Perceval fells Neville with one swift blow, decapitating him.

As soon as Robert experienced this past lifetime and the drama of the joust, with its disastrous outcome, he began to breathe more slowly and calmly, releasing the emotional charge he'd just experienced. He commented that he felt "dazed and a little buzzed, but my head doesn't hurt as it did before." By the time he left my office, his headache was completely gone, never to return.

During therapy, we also explored Robert's commitment issues, and the connections between his past-life trauma and his patterns in this life again came to the surface. In the current lifetime, Robert had been engaged to three women during a ten-year period but had broken up with each of his fiancées only a few months prior to the wedding. He commented, "I always fall so deeply in love that I'm afraid of losing my head."

Was he at an unconscious level avoiding commitment with females because in that past life he'd literally lost his head over his beloved? In that lifetime, he was very handsome and trim and cut a dashing figure as a knight. In the current one, he was plain and riddled with many medical conditions that were disabling. Because, as I've said, we tend to go from one extreme to the other, from one lifetime to another like a pendulum, always unconsciously seeking balance somewhere in center, he may have come into this incarnation fearing intimacy with a woman. His soul may have chosen a body that would be unattractive and afflicted with illnesses.

Robert's relevant past lifetime set the scene and the tone for the creation of issues of commitment and intimacy and feelings of conflict and distress in the current one. When Robert became an adult, he was unable to fully commit to a relationship that would lead to marriage.

Traumas leave indelible impressions on our conscious and unconscious minds. If death occurs immediately upon our experiencing such an event, as happened with Robert, the probability of that experience being instantly buried in the psyche is very great. His unconscious kept tugging at him so he would become aware of the story, own it, change his reaction, and then finally let it go. He unconsciously chose to experience headaches in order to alert himself to the unresolved trauma from a previous lifetime.

The point of regression hypnotherapy—whether we're transported to early childhood in this lifetime or to previous lifetimes—is to reexperience the emotions, know the story of the past, own it, and then release it in our current experience. When we do so, we often heal physical ailments that we don't realize are caused by our patterns of repetition. Applying the 7 Steps of Rebirth after the release allows us to rewrite the ending of that story, both in the conscious and unconscious. In other words, only by changing our reaction can the movement toward finally exiting that pattern become possible. When we begin to do so, we'll often find that our physical ailments start to clear up, because their underlying cause was the original trauma.

Joyce's Story

Often the origin of a chronic physical condition or sudden persistent pain is based in a past life. Joyce had been diagnosed with an ovarian cyst that was the size of a grapefruit. A recent college graduate in her early 20s, she'd just become engaged when she got hit with this terrible news. She was scheduled for surgery in two weeks.

During those two weeks, Joyce tried every holistic and alternative treatment available to her, including body realignment,

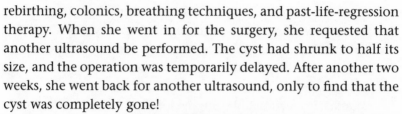

rebirthing, colonics, breathing techniques, and past-life-regression therapy. When she went in for the surgery, she requested that another ultrasound be performed. The cyst had shrunk to half its size, and the operation was temporarily delayed. After another two weeks, she went back for another ultrasound, only to find that the cyst was completely gone!

Joyce, who was very skeptical and always rational, said to me, "It really took an amazing experience for me to say, 'This too shall pass and I'll be well again.' My faith has been restored. Once I accepted this, it was like a load was lifted from me. I knew I could live through it, get through it, and I would be fine. I just had to accept the fact that I would be okay and could deal with it."

Joyce is a perfect example of someone who truly came to accept and believe in the healing benefits of holistic work. By working intensely and in a focused fashion, she ended up with an astonishing outcome.

One of Joyce's regressions was to a relevant past lifetime that took place during the Holocaust, when her current mother was her sister. Both innocent, gentle, and loving girls, she and her sister—ages seven and nine—were overcome with pain, agony, and despair as they died in the gas chambers. In that previous lifetime, a Nazi guard had struck Joyce in the abdomen with the butt of a gun, and in this life, she developed a tumor in that area of her body. Being diagnosed with an ovarian cyst once again aroused pain, agony, and a sense of despair; hence, the repetition. This time, however, Joyce would be able to change her reaction—and she did.

In that past lifetime, Joyce was small, frail, helpless, and powerless. In the current one, she was strong, healthy, and vibrant—and an adult who had options. Having experienced the intensity of those emotions in the past life, she was now able to release them and let them go. Because Joyce took the responsibility for owning her story and facing her difficult emotions, and because she had the courage to make a shift in her beliefs and engage in healing practices, she was able to experience an extraordinary healing. This story has a wonderfully happy ending because Joyce eventually got married, had two children, and now leads a very rich and full life. Today, 13 years later, she's healthy: The ovarian cyst hasn't recurred.

God gives us multiple avenues for reexperiencing our traumas and healing them, just as He created many fruits for us to eat and sources of water for us to drink from. We don't have to use only one method of recovery. Joyce used a number of holistic approaches, although she said that the past-life-regression work was the most significant factor in her recovery.

Sergio's Story

When Sergio came to see me, he was 33 years old, well educated, very handsome, and HIV positive. His current partner, Frank, was also well educated and good-looking. A top marketing executive for a brand-name company, Frank was very much in love with Sergio and totally loyal to him. He was kind and gentle and was always thoughtful and considerate, according to my client. Sergio felt that he was lucky to have such a partner, and that he should be able to return Frank's unwavering fidelity—but he couldn't.

Sergio came for therapy to understand why he was attracted to having affairs with abusive men even though he had a loving partner, and why he'd felt compelled to have unprotected sex with them—behavior that had led him to acquire the AIDS virus. Contracting HIV had been deeply upsetting to Sergio, yet he was still having one-night stands—encounters that were, as he described them, "strictly physical." He wanted to understand why he continually gravitated toward these sexual experiences, and he hoped to address his low self-esteem.

Often, we'll judge our behavior as neurotic and feel bad about ourselves because we can't seem to act in a healthier way. Even when we suffer negative consequences for our choices and cause ourselves to suffer health problems, we continue in the same old behaviors because of our unconscious desire to reexperience a

trauma that needs healing. It doesn't matter what the unhealthy form of repetition is—overeating, smoking, drug use, avoiding doctors, or whatever. The consequences are often not powerful enough to prevent the repetition, because what we really need to do is heal ourselves by reexperiencing the trauma that set the pattern in place.

Knowing that the reasons for Sergio's behavior lay hidden in his unconscious mind, I helped him enter a trancelike state and then recover a memory from his current life:

> *Sergio, a scrawny six-year-old boy, is shaking uncontrollably and vomiting in the fort that his older brother built. His 13-year-old brother has just walked out, turning his back on Sergio, seeming not to care about the little one's distress. He has just raped him anally.*
>
> *With feces smeared on his body and his clothes, Sergio's shame and pain are overwhelming. He is terrified of his brother and horrified by these occasional assaults. Sergio never knows when his brother will turn on him next. He lives in fear and trepidation.*

While we were reviewing the part of Sergio's history of which he was consciously aware, he revealed that he was sexually abused by his uncle starting at the age of nine. He also said that his brother had molested him for ten years, since the age of six.

For years, Sergio had engaged in harsh and swift sex with partners who were strangers, and he continually put himself at risk because he rarely used condoms. Although he always practiced safe sex with Frank, who continued to be free from HIV, Sergio was inconsistent in doing so with his secret, anonymous partners, acting self-destructively.

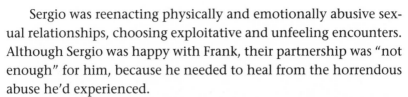

Sergio was reenacting physically and emotionally abusive sexual relationships, choosing exploitative and unfeeling encounters. Although Sergio was happy with Frank, their partnership was "not enough" for him, because he needed to heal from the horrendous abuse he'd experienced.

Understanding the source of his behavior, Sergio practiced the 7 Steps of Rebirth conscientiously, wrote his story, and rewrote it the way he would have liked it to have unfolded in his life (this writing/rewriting exercise is fully described in Part III of this book). After diligently working through these processes, Sergio was able to begin changing his reactions. Whenever he'd get the urge to pick up a man for a rough sexual encounter, he would stop himself and immediately practice the 7 Steps of Rebirth. This instantly transported him to the conscientious, mature adult who could make a different choice and exit the pattern.

Of course, as a child, Sergio had had no choice but to submit to the trauma—after all, he'd been raped by people who were bigger than he was. Also, he understood that if he told anyone what had happened to him, it might break up his family, which is an utterly frightening thought for a young person. Would his mother forgive him for telling her something terrible about his brother and his uncle? Would she believe him? Would she actually blame *him* for the encounters? All these thoughts were so deeply upsetting that as a child, Sergio had remained silent and tried to believe that the rapes would stop.

As an adult using the 7 Steps of Rebirth, Sergio had the power to reassure his child self that he didn't have to suffer any more sexual or physical abuse or carry the burden of keeping his family from knowing the painful truth of what was happening when they weren't looking. The 7 Steps of Rebirth were incredibly healing for him. Once he was able to consciously change his reactions to potentially abusive situations, he then exited his patterns of repetition, layer by layer. He wasn't able to be completely faithful to Frank, but instead of having two or three random sexual episodes a week, Sergio was now having only an occasional encounter once every few months, and the sex was less harsh and always involved a condom.

Stress and Survival

Stress and its consequences have now been recognized to be the primary contributor to most chronic illnesses and diseases.

The most powerful motivation in human beings is survival. Every part of our body and brain and every cell is designed to help the organism survive. When we perceive a situation as threatening or unsettling, emotions such as fear or rage stimulate the sympathetic nervous system and produce the chemically induced fight-or-flight response, preparing us to deal with whatever is at hand.

As a child, the fight-or-flight pattern may have served to help us survive under extremely difficult circumstances. In our present adult life, however, when a challenging situation triggers old emotions that haven't been resolved, we tend to overreact, generally out of fear or anger. As I mentioned before, the amygdala, a small organ in the emotional part of the brain, is activated and moves us right into the automatic fight-or-flight response to ensure survival. We react, then, in much the same manner as a very young child would—from the vantage point of our needs and wants. The experience of fear or trauma bypasses the connections to the analytical upper regions of the brain, as we operate from our primitive brain, which is focused on survival.

Repeated stress and trauma damage the body in many ways, affecting us at a cellular level and eventually causing physical illness. In fact, recent research has shown that toward the end of their lives, Alzheimer's patients have a damaged and shrunken hippocampus, a critical area of the brain that's involved in memory and emotion management. Could chronic stress and unexpressed emotions lead to such a drastic outcome?

When it goes untreated, stress can have devastating physical effects. Fortunately, our new understanding of it often leads people to seek relief before physical symptoms become too serious. For one of my clients, however, being in a continual state of fight or flight was wreaking havoc on his body.

Philip's Story

Philip, 29, had been in the U.S. Army in Iraq and was now suffering from post-traumatic stress disorder (PTSD), which was causing him not just emotional suffering but also typical physical symptoms of PTSD: stomachaches and gut problems, headaches, rashes, and insomnia. A physician had prescribed a cream for his rash and diagnosed him with irritable bowel syndrome, but Philip felt that I could help him address what was behind all of these ailments. As part of therapy, I hypnotically regressed Philip to the trauma he experienced while in Iraq:

> *Philip has been in Iraq for only three days when two men and a little boy in a beat-up car stop right in front of his tank. His three buddies jump onto the hood of the tank to investigate the situation. The deafening explosion that follows rips through the streets of Baghdad and into Philip's psyche.*
>
> *Philip realizes that the suicide bombers have killed themselves and his friends, leaving him dripping in blood and bits of flesh. Screaming, Philip finds himself alone, frightened, and traumatized.*
>
> *Totally devastated, and incapacitated by intense reactions, he's no longer fit to continue his tour of duty. He is a danger not only to himself but also to his fellow soldiers. Three months later, Philip receives a medical discharge and is sent home.*

About a year after arriving home from Iraq, Philip sought my help for PTSD. Even though he was eligible for free care through the Veterans Administration, he chose to pay for my services because he was impressed by the changes that had come about in his older sister after she had worked with me a few years earlier.

Philip was having anxiety attacks, recurring nightmares, temper flare-ups, and sudden crying jags during the day. He was constantly fighting with his wife and had very little patience with his two children. He was unable to remain focused long enough to return to his trade as a computer analyst or to maintain his employment at other jobs.

During our sessions, Philip told me that he was ashamed about coming home from Iraq without finishing his tour of duty. He felt he wasn't man enough to handle being in the Army and the stress associated with it. Having always had a sense of not being good enough or measuring up, Philip also felt that he had let his buddies down.

In reviewing Philip's personal history, he revealed that his three older sisters teased him mercilessly when he was young, always referring to him as the "little one." Philip was seven years younger than the next sibling ahead of him. He always felt as though he didn't do as well as they did, was never good enough, and could never measure up to their standards.

A particularly traumatic event took place when Philip was about six years old. His father became very ill and entered the hospital. The entire family went to visit him there one day. His mother and sisters were soft-spoken around their ailing father, but Philip burst into tears and became uncontrollably upset because he adored his dad and was so afraid of losing him. His screaming, intense crying, and clinging to the bed caused the family to literally drag Philip out of the hospital. After they arrived home, his sisters never let him forget what a baby he was, how he had messed up their visit, and how his outburst may have upset their father and worsened his condition. This awful burden, placed on such a young child, heavily bore down upon him.

When Philip was in the Army and saw his comrades die in front of him, the same buttons of shame and fear were pressed again. Just as when he was six years old, he felt frightened, overwhelmed, and completely devastated, screaming hysterically. Again he felt inept, not man enough, not mature enough, and not good enough.

By using the 7 Steps of Rebirth, the adult Philip began to heal the little six-year-old so that the origin of the trauma could be addressed. As part of "Step 3: Acknowledge—'Whoops, There I Go Again,'" Philip was able to see that his impatience with his children and his shortness with his wife was a repetition of his sisters' intolerance of his behavior as a frightened six-year-old.

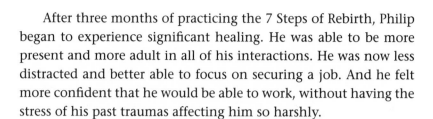

After three months of practicing the 7 Steps of Rebirth, Philip began to experience significant healing. He was able to be more present and more adult in all of his interactions. He was now less distracted and better able to focus on securing a job. And he felt more confident that he would be able to work, without having the stress of his past traumas affecting him so harshly.

Universal Laws, Holistic Healing, and Health

While most of us have heard that stress is bad for our health, too often we may not realize just how devastating its effects can be.

Back in the 1950s, a radio disc jockey named Brian experimented with staying awake as long as he could while on the air, just to see how far he could push himself. Monitored by a physician, he seemed to be able to handle the lack of sleep at first, but by the end of the third day, he was experiencing hallucinations. He continued to stay awake on the air for about a week, which completely threw his system out of balance. His ability to focus was gone, and eventually he lost his job as a result (and his wife left him as well).

What Brian, and his physician, didn't realize is that sleep is an absolutely crucial antidote for stress. Because Brian wasn't sleeping, his brain waves couldn't slow down and enter the REM, or rapid eye movement, cycle—the level of consciousness at which dreaming occurs. He also didn't slip into other important cycles, such as theta or delta (a state in which one sleeps very deeply). Instead, for an entire week, Brian was continuously in a beta state, an alert and active level of consciousness. He hallucinated because his brain needed to dream, so it forced him to do so while awake. The experience was so unnerving and disruptive to his system that even after the week was over and he had gotten plenty of rest and medication, he never fully regained normalcy in his life.

Like Brian, we all must learn to work with and respect the universal law of the wave. We can't continue to push ourselves forward relentlessly without rest. We must balance our forward movement with breaks for rejuvenation.

Fifty years ago, when this disc jockey learned the dangers of going without sleep for a long stretch, we in the West knew little about breathing techniques, supplements, or holistic-healing approaches to addressing stress and health issues. We also knew little about the functioning of the brain and its processes. Today, with our increased knowledge, we might be able to help someone like Brian return to normal functioning after such an experience.

Stress is continually compounded because we don't go down to baseline after each stressful occurrence. Eventually, because we remain stuck in our fight-or-flight response, our internal systems begin to break down. Our parasympathetic nervous system is unable to take over and repair the damage to our cells caused by the response to stress. Before we had electricity—and with it the ability to stay awake in the light for 24 hours—we were forced to experience long stretches of darkness in the wintertime. With no illumination to aid us in the usual activities, we slept for many hours each night. Nowadays, we have so much to do that we force ourselves to cut short our sleep, keep ourselves awake with caffeine and other stimulants, and try to fit in as many activities as we can before we collapse from exhaustion each day.

Not taking enough time for rest and never coming down to baseline is the perfect prescription for the breakdown of internal organs. Understanding the universal law of the wave and the importance of bringing ourselves back from a high level of stress to baseline, we can use one specific breath—Step 2 of the 7 Steps of Rebirth—to counteract the stress response. (Again, to do Step 2, inhale deeply through the nose, hold the breath to a count of four seconds, and exhale slowly through the mouth, making sure the exhale always lasts a little longer than the inhale did.)

This breath slows down your brain waves and heart rate, reduces your blood pressure, and expands your blood vessels instantly. This leads to improved circulation and a lower heart rate since the heart doesn't have to pump as hard to send the blood throughout your whole system. With this one specific breath, you can switch from being in the sympathetic to the parasympathetic mode, from being in the stress mode to being in the repair mode.

When you apply the universal law of the wave and give your body a chance to heal itself, you stop living in an extreme state and being stuck in a stress response. You may say, "Oh, I'm so stressed-out—I've got to quit my job," but quitting your job or removing other stressors from your routine isn't a cure-all, because there will always be sources of pressure in life. Everything we do, every job we have, and every relationship we are in produces stress—it's essential and inevitable, just like the principle of repetition.

There is no such thing in life as no stress. If we don't have it, we don't have the wave. If we don't have the wave, we have a straight, flat line; we have death. *Nothing is static in God's world.* It may move very slowly, very quickly, or in different directions, but nothing is static.

The most important way to address stress isn't to aim to avoid it completely, but instead to learn to handle it differently. However, it does make sense to leave stressful situations if you can't manage your responses to them. For instance, if the level of stress you experience at work is such that you really have no means of managing it effectively, you should leave the job, lest you become very ill. If a very volatile relationship is toxic for you, you have to move away from that as well. Yes, you need to heal the connection with that soul sooner or later, but perhaps you won't be able to do it in the current lifetime.

Remember—to use the metaphor of the university from the last chapter—there will always be another chance to take the course again. So if a relationship or situation is causing you extreme stress, be gentle with yourself, apply the universal law of the wave, and give yourself a chance to rest and reconnect with your adult self, using the 7 Steps of Rebirth. You'll make better decisions in this lifetime, and know that your repetitions will be gentler. Working with the universal laws will help you feel less overwhelmed.

Before I began jogging in 1979, I'd never exercised a day in my life. Although I was healthy and trim, I couldn't run a whole block without stopping because I'd begin to shake and was in terrible pain. However, I was determined to prevail. I would run a very short block, walk a few steps, run another block, walk a few

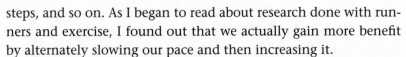

steps, and so on. As I began to read about research done with runners and exercise, I found out that we actually gain more benefit by alternately slowing our pace and then increasing it.

Exercising in this fashion burns more calories and is much more beneficial to our entire body and its systems than trying to work out an increasing amount each day. Thus, I was reenacting the shape of the wave without ever realizing it consciously at the time. Whenever we model the shape of the wave, alternating rest with activity, we'll be in harmony with the hum of the universe all the way down to the level of our cells.

In addition to governing our response to stress and affecting our health, the enactment of the wave or pendulum also applies to issues that crop up in our professional lives, a theme that will be explored in the next chapter.

CHAPTER SIX

WORK-RELATED ISSUES

We repeat the stories of our current and relevant previous lives, choosing certain jobs and professions not only because they match our education, skills, and interests, but because they offer us an opportunity to heal from past traumas. Repetition also influences our work style and decisions about employment, which is why we'll often wonder, *Is it me, or is this workplace just as dysfunctional as the last one I was in?* Unconsciously, we decide to get involved in situations where our history, anxiety, depression, and low self-esteem will cause us enough suffering that even if we're avoiding difficult emotions in our personal life, we'll be forced to face them in our professional one.

Christina's Story (revisited)

When I was working with Christina, whose story was introduced in Chapter 4, she discovered a relevant lifetime that shed light on her work situation. We'd already found that she was repeating past-life themes of betrayal, depression, and suicide in her current life and had chosen to be born to a father who had multiple affairs and a mother who responded by becoming depressed and suicidal. Christina had come to me in order to learn how to break her own pattern of having affairs with married men, and in our conversations, I learned that she was caught in another pattern of repetition: She was a workaholic like her father was. I suspected that a past-life regression would help her feel the pain that was causing her to be addicted to her job.

Christina repeatedly referred to a sense of urgency with respect to working hard and being successful. If she didn't succeed, she said that "it would be unthinkable and disastrous." I found this a strangely intense way of describing failure. It was far different from saying, "Work is important." To understand her perception of urgency and doom related to her work life, she did a past-life regression to a lifetime in China when she was six years old:

> *A poor, brown-eyed, scrawny little girl, Lu-Tan lives with her mother and siblings in one of the shacks overlooking the city of Shanghai. Her mother, sick and fragile, always seems to have a baby at her breast. One day, weak and preoccupied with caring for her brood, her mother sends Lu-Tan down to the market to find any small job to earn a few coins so that her family might eat that night.*
>
> *Lu-Tan dutifully follows her mother's instructions and does her best to find work, but to no avail. The sun is setting, and Lu-Tan hasn't scraped up a single yuan. As she shuffles home, head bowed low and shoulders drooping, she feels miserable about facing her mother empty-handed. Barely able to see the path home through her tears, Lu-Tan prays, as she has done many times before, for Quan Yin, the mother goddess of compassion, to help save her.*
>
> *As Lu-Tan comes closer to the little shack where she and her family live, she sees smoke and flames. Her tiny heart beating hard and fast in her chest, she knows that her mother and siblings are in danger. When she arrives on the scene, everyone in the village is screaming and running around trying to douse the flames with buckets and washtubs filled with water.*

As Lu-Tan stands, paralyzed by grief, staring at her ram-shackle home as it goes up in flames, she begins to sob hysterically. She thinks that if she had only found work and brought home a little money, her mother and siblings would have all been out buying rice and vegetables. They would still be alive instead of dead inside the inferno before her.

A neighbor holds Lu-Tan close to her chest, comforting her, but the little girl is inconsolable. Squirming free of her grasp, Lu-Tan rushes into the flames to join her mother and siblings and is consumed by the fire.

Lu-Tan's guilt had caused her to instantly punish herself by joining the people she loved, ending her own life. She felt that her family had died because of her, and thus *she* didn't deserve to live.

Christina finally understood why work took on such an urgency for her. The fire that had destroyed her family in her lifetime in China had been an accident; she hadn't been responsible for it. But at six years old, she didn't know that. In her childish mind, she felt she was at fault—that if she'd worked harder, her loved ones' lives would have been saved. Only with adult awareness could she see that this was an irrational interpretation of events.

After accessing and making sense of the events of this past life, Christina used the 7 Steps of Rebirth to heal six-year-old Lu-Tan of her guilt and anguish. In the safe space that Christina created for her child self, she assured Lu-Tan that the fire wasn't her fault, that she wasn't responsible for her family's well-being, and that she deserved to play and be free of adult responsibilities. The 7 Steps allowed Christina to stop feeling compelled to work so many hours and freed her up to enjoy life.

Brenda's Story

Frustrated and upset, wiping her tearstained face, Brenda—an African-American woman working as a data-entry clerk in a bank—explained to me that she desperately needed my help. She was experiencing a great deal of anxiety. Her main source of stress was her new boss's threat to lay her off because she didn't have her general equivalency diploma (GED), which the bank was now requiring of all its clerks.

She had worked very hard all of her life to get to this point, and she couldn't bear to lose her job now. How would she support her kids? How long would it take her to find another job, never mind if she'd like it as much as this one? What was she going to do? Deeply worried and overwhelmed, she was finding it increasingly hard to focus on her work. Her biggest fear was that despite how well she'd performed on the job, the boss would decide she wasn't qualified to keep it—in short, she was afraid that she wasn't "good enough," and this fear, I would learn, was rooted in her childhood.

I asked Brenda about her past, and she told me that she was the middle child of five. Her biological father was an abusive alcoholic who had left home when she was six. Brenda became pregnant at 16, dropped out of school, broke up with her baby's father, and moved in with a man named Fred who was 20 years her senior. A year later, Fred lost his factory job and started drinking heavily. He was violent toward Brenda and toward her baby as well. She nevertheless got pregnant again and ended up having two children with him while supporting the family by cleaning houses.

A few years later, she finally decided that she had withstood enough abuse. Moreover, the physical toll from her work as a housekeeper was becoming too much for her to handle. She decided it was time to make a change in her life.

Brenda finally landed the job at the bank doing data-entry work. She loved her job, and everyone at work loved *her*. She was very hardworking, dependable, and conscientious. After she'd been there for four years, the bank was bought out by another company. The employment requirements changed, stipulating that completion of high school was required for all employees.

Very alarmed that she might lose her job, Brenda decided to work toward earning her GED. She went to school and studied at night in the hopes of creating a different future for herself and her three children. Meanwhile, Fred's abuse toward her and the children worsened. He was resentful that she was working on her education, and he continually put her down. Finally, one day she got so sick and tired of his abuse that she kicked him out of the house.

After a few months, Fred asked to return home, claiming that he was now sober. Brenda was unsure what she should do and started having anxiety attacks at work. The bank sent her to me because she was such a good worker, and they were pleased that she was making the effort to get her GED in order to keep her job.

Brenda was anxious about not passing her GED test and even more anxious about the possibility of losing her job if she didn't. Without Fred's income, she was afraid that she wouldn't be able to support her children or pay for their day care. At the same time, she was worried about her boyfriend's possible return. Fred, as well as Brenda's mother and father, had always told her that she was stupid and that she would never amount to anything. How was she going to manage? Her anxiety was getting in the way of her studies and her job. She was terrified that she would lose everything.

One of the key repetitions in Brenda's current lifetime was clear: As the daughter of an alcoholic, she was drawn to an alcoholic partner. In therapy, she also revealed that her mother had never protected her from a violent father and a sexually abusive uncle. Brenda, too, didn't step in and effectively protect her own children from Fred's physical abuse—another repetition in her life.

I had Brenda use breathing techniques to release anxiety, but clearly, she had deeper issues to address as well, so I felt that she should work with the 7 Steps of Rebirth immediately. Brenda had no difficulty with Steps 1 and 2, but got stuck on "Step 3: Acknowledge—'Whoops, There I Go Again!'" Understandably, Brenda saw herself as a good person who was the victim of an abusive and unreliable partner. In her mind, if she accepted responsibility for her choices in life, she would have to feel guilty and bad about herself. I reassured her that it was pointless and unfair to judge herself for decisions she'd made unconsciously, and that by taking Step 3, she could begin to move away from her victim mentality

and toward a sense of her own power to create a healthier reality for herself.

Initially, she said, "It's my bastard father's fault I'm in this situation," or "If it weren't for my bastard boyfriend . . . the bosses and management . . . Everyone wants to do me in." After several sessions, her victim mentality began to be replaced with an empowering attitude. She would say, "Okay, I can do this. I'm responsible for my actions. I know I can reach my goals and keep my anxiety under control. I'm going to make it."

Although Brenda was able to consciously identify a dramatic event that occurred when she was six years old—namely, her father's abandonment of the family—and recalled being sexually abused by an uncle when she was ten, "Step 4: Get a Number" revealed a long-repressed memory of another principal trauma that had deeply wounded her.

After I'd gotten Brenda to relax and work through the first three steps, I quickly said, "Give me a number," and she immediately responded, "Four." With my gentle coaxing, she returned to the time when she was four, and remembered that her biological father had abused her on several occasions when she was that age.

I encouraged Brenda to begin "Step 5: Meet the Child" and create a magical nature scene where she could get in touch with and reassure her four-year-old self. She met little Brenda, who was crying inconsolably. Her adult self put her arms around the girl and suddenly became aware that her father had not only abused her as a four-year-old, but he'd also threatened to kill the entire family if she told her mother.

No wonder the child Brenda was sobbing and wailing: She felt responsible for her whole family, at an age when she was far too young to take on such a burden—and on top of that, her father's uncontrollable rages terrified her. The four-year-old Brenda was so overwhelmed by this trauma that her mind chose to hide it from her consciousness in order to protect her from the pain and terror of the memory.

Brenda reassured her four-year-old self that she was safe, and promised that she would continue visiting her, bringing her comfort, support, and love. (Later, she would repeat the 7 Steps of Rebirth and reassure the six- and ten-year-old selves who had also been abused.) Then, once Brenda was able to affirm herself in the present reality as the mature, capable adult she was, she could more fully take on life and handle the obstacles she was facing without giving in to crippling anxiety.

I explained to her that the unhealed child self had taken over her life. It was this child self who was insisting that Brenda was responsible for everyone and that nobody else could be trusted to help her care for her children. It was this child self who was drawn to men who would be likely to create a scenario reminiscent of the abuse in her childhood.

Once she began working with the 7 Steps of Rebirth, Brenda started to heal swiftly. Within three months, she was able to let go of her anxiety enough to absorb and process the material she was learning for her GED. She had decided not to allow Fred to return to her home and felt no ambivalence about that decision. She felt empowered, more comfortable, and safe. She was beginning to take steps to ensure her employment, as well as the betterment and protection of her children and herself.

Brenda continued to use the 7 Steps of Rebirth daily, because the results were immediate. After completing her GED, she signed up for classes at a community college to further secure her employment and to improve her prospects at the bank. She was now able to focus and study; and her feelings of not being "good enough" to deserve an education, a decent job, and a loving partner had been replaced by feelings that she was *entitled* to them.

Because of her sense of empowerment, Brenda now functioned very much from the adult perspective. She was healthy and strong. No matter what happened, she had the strength to face her boss, boyfriend, and children. She could stand tall and sure on her own two feet, because she had created a shift in her understanding and awareness. However, I explained to her that she would need to continue using the 7 Steps of Rebirth with regularity for the effects of her progress to be maintained.

Roland's Story

Racing down the hospital corridor, speed-walking in and out of the rooms to check that all the equipment was in good working order, Roland was abruptly interrupted by his new female boss. He was expecting the usual praise, but the "rug was pulled out" from under him when he instead heard the words: "Roland, you're laid off. You need to pack up your things and leave immediately."

Roland was in a state of shock. Just two months earlier, he had been promoted to a supervisory position in the maintenance department. He had always received positive feedback about his work and got along well with co-workers and the hospital staff. No explanation for the layoff was offered to him, and nothing more was said. He left the hospital feeling completely bewildered and dejected.

Roland was 49 years old and unemployed when he came to see me approximately a year after he'd been laid off. He saw himself as a complete failure and was still in a state of shock over having been dismissed. I asked him, "When have you felt this way before?"

At first, Roland said, "Never. I've never been laid off before this."

Knowing that the repetitions we create are not necessarily literal, I asked him again, "When was the rug pulled out from under you—just like that? When did you feel shocked and like a failure?"

Roland immediately remembered: Years before, his bride had told him on their wedding day that she wanted to leave, and he convinced her it was just the jitters, so she went ahead with the ceremony in front of hundreds of guests. Eight weeks later, she told him that she'd made a big mistake and demanded he grant her a divorce immediately. Two weeks later, she moved to New York City, and Roland never heard from her again. The resulting dissolution of the marriage was handled through attorneys.

The repetition of this trauma that seemed to come out of the blue occurred when Roland was laid off. The same emotions of hurt and anger that he'd felt toward his ex-wife were very much repeated in the situation at work. Roland withdrew and suffered from deep depression that lasted for almost a year after the wedding, and again after the layoff.

Eventually, Roland married a woman who was agreeable and supportive. However, he and his new wife didn't share a deep, intimate connection. Badly hurt by his previous experience of marriage, Roland avoided being in such a vulnerable position again and assured himself that he was "safe" in this relationship. Indeed, his second wife didn't leave him, but unconsciously, he knew that he had to experience an unexplained and sudden abandonment again. This time, the pattern played out at his place of employment. It was a job he felt safe in, one that didn't challenge him. He felt complete security. After all, businesses always need maintenance workers, so he didn't think there was any chance he'd lose his job.

While soul mates and family members will often be the ones who provide us with the opportunity to reexperience the painful emotions associated with our past traumas, a workplace can also serve as a classroom for learning our lessons and healing ourselves at last. The boss who reminds us of our father, the co-worker who acts as a stand-in for our sister, and the client who reminds us of our demanding ex-spouse all serve to push our buttons and cause us to engage in repetition again.

While Roland was very hesitant to look at his story and accept responsibility for his part in creating his work situation, he told me that he was willing to engage in the 7 Steps of Rebirth if it would help him feel less depressed and stressed. Roland easily visualized the stop sign in Step 1, and he experienced immediate relief in Step 2 due to the dramatic change in hormones that occurs with deep breathing. But as so often happens with people, "Step 3: Acknowledge—'Whoops, There I Go Again!'" was difficult for him.

He felt victimized by the cruel behavior of his ex-wife as well as by his female boss, who had been extremely harsh in suddenly laying him off with no explanation. Sometimes we need

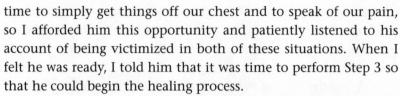

time to simply get things off our chest and to speak of our pain, so I afforded him this opportunity and patiently listened to his account of being victimized in both of these situations. When I felt he was ready, I told him that it was time to perform Step 3 so that he could begin the healing process.

The closer the repetition is to the original event in terms of emotions, the more effectively the buttons get pressed: Roland didn't become attracted to a woman with intimacy issues, but to one who was capable of abandoning him suddenly. Later, he was drawn to a job that seemed secure on the surface but would be taken away from him with no warning. The repetition shocked him on a conscious level, but his unconscious knew it was just the situation he needed to experience in order to be jolted into the healing process.

In Roland's case, as so often happens, when we reached "Step 4: Get a Number," the first number that popped up corresponded with how old he was when he was traumatized as an adult. The number was 28, his age at the time his first wife left him, two months after their wedding. However, the origin of a recent trauma invariably goes back to early experiences in childhood. Since events are imprinted on the brain much more dramatically at this stage of development, their effects become an integral part of our life patterns and the blueprint for the later trauma. I asked Roland to think of a number between 0 and 10, and the first to come to his mind was 3. He was in a suggestible, trancelike state; and I guided him to remember any painful and dramatic experiences that occurred when he was three years old.

Roland remembered that his mother left the family abruptly and without explanation when he was at that tender age and was gone for an entire year while he was sent to live with a relative. To have "the rug pulled out" from under him in this way traumatized him. This was the trauma that had drawn Roland to his first wife and later to a job where he was very likely to be unceremoniously let go.

Roland's mother had been affectionate and loving, so after she left, he was terrified and frightened. His father became emotionally withdrawn and so severely depressed that eventually he gave custody of his son to Roland's stern aunt. Although Roland's mother returned a year later and his immediate family was reunited, the trauma of that experience had deeply affected him. To avoid the pain of remembering that time, his mind repressed the memory. This made it easier for him to function at the time, but it set the stage for him to re-create that trauma in the future.

From the vantage point of the adult, Roland was now able to use the 7 Steps of Rebirth throughout his daily life in order to exit the paralyzing effects of his depression and heal himself of the wound of sudden abandonment. He was curious about the subject of past lives and wanted to explore some of his own to deepen his understanding of the current life and its repetitive patterns and to help him heal at an even deeper level.

In the first relevant past lifetime Roland accessed, he was a South American woman named Paula:

Paula, 18 years old, has long black hair and a rather plain face. She is happily flitting about, reviewing all the necessary preparations—it is now her wedding day. Her four siblings are playing around her, and her mother is fussing with her dress and hair. The setting is 1825 in Bolivia.

Paula is extremely excited and eager to marry the dashing young man who came from Argentina and persuaded her father to let him marry her. It hadn't taken much persuasion to secure Paula's consent, for she immediately fell in love with the handsome, tall adventurer. Paula isn't a great beauty, and in the three years since she became eligible for marriage, no other man had expressed an interest in her. Thus, her father, a wealthy landowner and cattle rancher, was intent upon marrying off his oldest daughter to this promising young groom. Although it had never been very clear what this man or his family did in Argentina, her father didn't ask a lot of questions.

Paula is increasingly excited and flustered as the time of the wedding ceremony draws near. She's dressed in a beautiful satin gown with a lace mantilla over her thick black curls. Today she

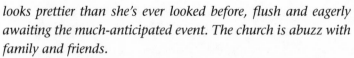

looks prettier than she's ever looked before, flush and eagerly awaiting the much-anticipated event. The church is abuzz with family and friends.

As she begins to walk down the long aisle on her father's arm, she looks up toward the altar. To her amazement, she doesn't see her fiancé standing there. Startled and frightened, she looks over at her father, who motions her to continue walking toward the front of the church. Her father stops before the altar and quickly turns to one of Paula's sisters, 12-year-old Isabella. He whispers to the girl that she must see if the young man is still getting ready in one of the side rooms.

Isabella hurries off to the back of the church, then rushes from room to room, looking everywhere for her sister's intended. She talks with the priest and anyone who is around, asking if they have seen him. She discovers that he was last seen about 30 minutes earlier, elegantly dressed in his wedding suit while embracing Paula's other sister, Marisa, as they rode off on his horse. Sadly, Isabella relays this shocking news to their father, who whispers it to Paula. Devastated, she faints on the spot.

Jilted at the altar and profoundly humiliated that her fiancé has run off with her younger, more attractive sister, Paula flees the church as soon as she comes to. She runs home, rips off her beautiful dress, and withdraws into her bedroom for many months. She falls into a deep depression that lasts well over a year, and no one can console her.

Paula never marries, remaining a spinster to the end of her days and becoming increasingly bitter and resentful. Always daydreaming, she spends her time sewing and embroidering, and she rarely interacts with those she loves. All attempts by her family and friends to help her fail miserably. Bitter and brokenhearted, she dies at the age of 56.

While undergoing this regression, Roland cried intensely, experiencing Paula's pain of being left at the altar. He understood the repetition that was created in this lifetime when his wife abandoned him two months after the wedding, when his mother suddenly disappeared, and when he was abruptly dismissed from his maintenance job at the hospital. This past life in Bolivia clarified his repetitions and made him aware of the basis for his feelings of despair, abandonment, and betrayal. The lesson he needed to learn from that previous lifetime in South America was to acknowledge the pain of the loss, yet be able to move beyond it enough to derive pleasure or comfort from other experiences in life.

Roland continued to use the 7 Steps of Rebirth regularly and conscientiously every time he experienced resentment or anxiety and accompanying depression, and he began understanding the patterns in his life. He could now see clearly why he had such trouble making commitments to friends and family alike: He'd been unconsciously choosing situations that would allow him to avoid the pain of sudden abandonment.

As he healed, Roland opened himself up to greater intimacy, because his deep-rooted fear of having those he loved suddenly disappear and reject him was eased. His relationship with his wife improved significantly as he found the courage to risk reaching out to her, expressing his love, and allowing himself to be vulnerable.

Because Roland was very much in the child mode and was deeply depressed prior to therapy, he'd been unable to secure a job during the year following his layoff. As he began to work on healing himself and was more frequently in the adult mode, he was able to search for employment systematically and effectively, and he no longer let his resentment and fear prevent him from applying for a job. At last, he was able to find a position that was much more to his liking and appropriate to his skill level than his old one had been.

Lisa's Story

Morning rush at the restaurant had come to an end. Exhausted, 41-year-old Lisa, one of the waitresses, stomped her feet in frustration, screaming at her co-workers—and one waitress in particular—for not having given her more help with the horde of customers.

Storming into her boss's office and slamming the door behind her, the enraged Lisa stuttered and sputtered about what had just happened and impulsively announced that she was quitting.

Lisa came to see me after walking out on her ninth job. She'd been having recurring problems with co-workers as well as bosses, kept changing jobs, and could never seem to settle into any kind of profession or stable work situation. She felt depressed, anxious, frustrated, and angry; and she told me she was now having temper tantrums regularly. She recognized that she had to address her anger-management problem and low tolerance for frustration if she was to be steadily employed in work she enjoyed.

Lisa told me she was the middle child in a family of seven kids and was the product of a mother who rejected her family emotionally. Her mom was critical, cold, and distant; and like her siblings, Lisa experienced this as rejection. Her father was a serious alcoholic who was raging drunk nearly every day. Lisa's parents finally divorced when she was six years old.

Bright, creative, and highly emotional, Lisa grew up with a great deal of fear and anger that she was never able to express. She was also constantly tormented by her oldest sister, who would hit her, pull her hair, pinch her, and ridicule her because of a slight speech impediment. Her sister's relentless torment exacerbated Lisa's stutter, particularly when she was angry and felt helpless.

Eventually, Lisa married an alcoholic and had two daughters with him. He encouraged her to drink with him; soon she, too, became an alcoholic. During seven years of excessive drinking, Lisa and her husband were arrested several times for drunken driving and had explosive fights, many of which resulted in physical harm to both parties.

After an exceptionally brutal altercation one night, Lisa and her husband decided that for their own sake as well as that of their children, they would have to become sober, so they both joined Alcoholics Anonymous. However, after they'd achieved sobriety for a stretch, their depression, which had been masked by their alcohol use, became painfully evident to them. Both were dissatisfied with their lives and their marriage, and were unable to work out their mutual issues. They divorced three years later.

Because of Lisa's alternating rages and deep depression, she was having problems at home and work and felt completely overwhelmed and incapacitated.

Like Lisa, all of us must face and acknowledge our anger. It's a necessary emotion; however, we need to work on it so that we can move past it. If we avoid and deny it, it will just sit inside us, turning into depression. When our rage does get expressed, it can be exceptionally harsh and destructive. Knowing its power, we'll often try to repress it, but this isn't healthy. We all experience anger and ugliness, and at times we do harm to others. Pretending that this emotion doesn't exist only allows it to fester.

Accessing anger, and allowing ourselves to experience it, is a necessary and integral part of the process of forgiveness. When we transcend a situation without understanding, owning, and acknowledging the whole story—without permitting ourselves to feel the force of our anger—we prevent ourselves from knowing our painful truth, and we will unconsciously re-create situations that cause us to feel enraged or depressed. If, however, we admit to the intensity of our anger and acknowledge its source and how it has affected us, we can work through our feelings and consciously choose friends, family members, and work situations that *don't* cause us to feel angry or depressed.

In order to aid Lisa's healing and recovery, we decided to explore her relevant past lives using regression hypnotherapy. Lisa was Henrietta in a former lifetime in the Deep South:

> *Henrietta is orphaned at the age of eight when she loses her immediate family in the Civil War. Her parents and siblings are dragged off their land in Alabama, beaten, and killed by Union soldiers. She survives by hiding high up in a tree. After the dust settles, a neighbor takes her to the home of her uncle, a wealthy plantation owner. He and his wife have four children, the youngest being a daughter who is three years older than Henrietta.*
>
> *When Henrietta arrives, instead of being welcomed as a member of the family, her uncle makes it clear that she is*

expected to work as a maid in the house. She takes care of every-one's needs, particularly those of Sybil, the youngest daughter, who torments Henrietta relentlessly, often hitting her, pulling her hair, and making fun of her. Henrietta's uncle is an alco-holic who beats her and berates her while her aunt looks the other way.

Although she is bright and curious, Henrietta isn't allowed to learn to read and write and has never gone to school, but she secretly teaches herself how to read using the books in her uncle's library. She begins to dream of becoming free and inde-pendent, having her own life, and being able to pursue different interests that go beyond the day-to-day drudgery of a maid.

As an adult, Henrietta makes her way to New York City, where she is able to procure a job as a maid for a family living in a tawny-colored townhouse in Manhattan. While the couple is educated, kind, and cultured, their oldest daughter, Myrna, is overweight, plain, mean, and physically abusive to Henrietta. Myrna hates the other girl, is jealous of her because she's so pretty and polite, and never gives her a moment's peace.

Henrietta tolerates Myrna, works hard, and indulges her love of reading whenever she can. Five years later, she persuades the local librarian to give her a job organizing the books and cleaning the library every night. She leaves the townhouse and rents a tiny room in a boardinghouse. Henrietta is thrilled with the changes in her life and is finally happy. Soon, however, three of her co-workers begin to resent her. One in particular puts her down constantly, making fun of her accent, saying she talks like an "uneducated little Southerner."

Once again, Henrietta feels tormented and picked on by her peers. The repetition in her life becomes evident as she goes from one situation to another, feeling alone, abandoned, mis-treated, and unheard. She is always at the mercy of a female who taunts her, and she feels bereft and without emotional sup-port as a result.

One spring morning, after an especially difficult week in which she is the target of extreme and brutal harassment at the library, Henrietta slits her wrists with a knife, committing suicide.

When Lisa accessed this lifetime, she cried intensely as she relived Henrietta's anguish and torment. She was coming to understand that the themes she'd been experiencing, such as alcoholism and suicide, were already present in this troubled 19th-century life. In addition, her pattern of being stuck in jobs below her skill level and dealing with peers who were abusive to her were repeating in lifetime after lifetime.

In the incarnation as Henrietta, she committed suicide out of sheer despair. In her present life, Lisa had attempted suicide while she was in an abusive marriage and drinking heavily. Experiencing and realizing these repetitive patterns in her past lifetimes as well as her current one, she now understood the importance of changing her reactions and learning ways to deal differently with her depression. This is how she would transcend her past, affirming self and life.

By using the 7 Steps of Rebirth to reassure her child self in a way her mother had never done, Lisa affirmed her power to be in control of her life and to handle trauma. She began to feel lighter and freer and less anxious and enraged. Soon, Lisa found a job that was more stimulating both intellectually and personally. She was now more compassionate toward her own children and less bothered by the behavior of her co-workers. She eventually took courses at a community college, becoming an early-childhood-education teacher's aide. Lisa had worked so hard on developing patience and accepting the child within herself that she was now able to impart that knowledge and guidance to her own biological children and to those she worked with at the school.

When therapy was terminated, Lisa reported feeling a new-found sense of clarity and happiness. She was now dating a divorced co-worker, an art teacher with whom she was able to laugh, share many stories, and feel safe. He was gentle and supportive and truly listened to her. In keeping with Lisa's pattern, he was an alcoholic, but he'd been sober for more than 15 years—an example of the fact that as we heal, our repetitions play out in a much gentler way.

The 7 Steps of Rebirth was the primary, most effective vehicle for enabling Lisa to transform her life. Lively and vibrant—and now calmer and clearer—Lisa was able to keep her emotions and temper more modulated and balanced. By extension, her speech became slower and her stutter barely perceptible. Finally, Lisa was able to keep a job, pursue a career that she loved, and deal with her co-workers in an adult way.

Like Christina, Brenda, and Roland, Lisa came to therapy because of a work-related issue but later realized that work was just one of the many areas of her life where repetition was taking place. In this way, she was presented with the choice of healing herself of her tendency to continue in the same old pattern.

Although we often play out our repetitions at work, we're even more likely to do so in our sexual relationships, because sex has the potential to generate strong emotions, both good and bad. What's more, sexual traumas—which are deeply disturbing both to the person who experiences them as well as to the one who inflicts them on another—can only be healed by reexperiencing the abuse again in some form, as you'll see in the chapter that follows.

CHAPTER SEVEN

SEXUAL ISSUES

The Divine created two genders not simply to propagate the species but also to allow human beings to feel a sense of oneness. When a male and a female have this experience at the point of orgasm, it is a reenactment, at a deeper and more profound level, of being at one with God, Who has both masculine and feminine aspects.

Male and female bodies respond differently to sexuality. In the female brain, the area stimulated by orgasm is the neocortex, the structure associated with relationships, but in the male brain, the stimulated area is the one associated with motor functions. This is why it's much easier for a man to experience sex as a purely physical activity, disconnected from love and relationships. Yet, when a man and woman experience orgasm together, it's a very powerful event that reminds them of coming home and gives them the feeling of ecstasy and unity with the Divine.

Spirituality and Sex

In *The Practical Kabbalah Guidebook,* C. J. M. Hopking writes: "*Yesod* corresponds to the expression of sexual energies, which is one of the most powerful energies on the planet: poets and mystics have long since recognized that the ecstasy experienced at the height of the sexual act can be likened to spiritual experience."

High-level meditators such as Buddhist monks experience ecstasy when they are in deep meditation. The brain functions in the exact same manner as it does at the point of orgasm: Both sides are in harmony, with brain waves in sync. Usually, our right hemisphere processes one kind of brain wave and our left hemisphere another, but they come into synchronization at the point of orgasm and during deep meditation.

The intent of coming together at the point of orgasm is to be "at one"—at one with each other, at one with ecstasy, at one with God. When a man and a woman share the experience of orgasm, they're experiencing union and transcending their differences. Spiritually, this mirrors our yearning to transcend our differences with others and reflects our desire for wholeness, completeness, and union with the Divine. When we come together as man and woman in that moment, we remind ourselves that no matter how dissimilar we are, no matter how separate we are, we can still experience oneness as we feel our connection with our Creator.

The significance of the separate parts of male and female uniting is also intrinsic to many religious traditions, including Kabbalah, Christianity, and Taoism. In Kabbalah, the male aspect, or *hesed,* is purported to be the benevolent side of God. The female aspect, or *shekhinah,* is the powerful fire—the passion and the compassion. In Christianity, Mother Mary represents the female aspect of the Divine, and in Taoism, this unity between masculine and feminine forces is represented by the symbol of yin and yang.

The Divine, in wanting to connect with us, provides the vehicle that affords the expression of compassionate union through love and sexuality. This is the essence of spirituality.

Hidden Sexual Issues

Sexuality is a powerful drive, one that's very useful for pushing us into repeating the issues in our lives and for creating situations that will give us the opportunity to make different choices so that we can heal. We're sexually attracted to people who will allow us to engage in repetition. If that magical spark is present, it's because the other person shares our issues, and unconsciously we're making a deal to work through them together, as partners.

During my initial interview with my clients, I ask them standard questions dealing with their sexual history, such as: *Are you sexually active? Who are your sexual partners? Are you having an affair? How frequently do you have sex? Who initiates sex, and how often?* Then I pose other questions: *Do you enjoy sex? Is it pleasurable? Do you have orgasms? How often do you have them?*

In other words, I get the whole picture of their sex lives after asking only a few questions. For instance, if a client's reply is: "I have sex seven times a week, and my partner always initiates it," that tells me that this person is always in a reactive stance, going along with what others want but not feeling enough desire to ask for what he or she wants.

If the client is female and married, and she replies, "I really prefer to be with women rather than with my husband or other men," a huge part of the story is revealed. Rarely will clients announce, "I'm married, but I'm a lesbian." However, I know that if I ask specific questions, I'll learn what their sexual predilections are.

Sex is often the elephant in the room, the topic that therapists and clients avoid, thinking that it's separate from all the other issues a person may have—but this isn't the case. I know that what someone tells me about their sexual desires and behaviors can reveal a great deal about their patterns in all areas of life, including in work and relationships.

Ann's Story

Ann, 45, came to see me because she was becoming increasingly depressed. Married, she'd been a stay-at-home mom for the first ten years of her marriage while she raised her three children, who were now teenagers.

Ann told me that she'd been on antidepressants for the last year and a half, and while the medication seemed to help her a little in the beginning, it didn't ease her anxiety at all. Ann also took an occasional over-the-counter sleeping remedy, but this was rare. My questioning revealed no signs of drug abuse in her or her family.

She firmly stated that she didn't want to talk about her childhood or anything except how to "get rid of" her current depression. I told her that we don't just "get rid of" depression or anxiety. Both are responses to traumas, and to heal, we must be aware of the reasons underlying them, as well as what can be done to minimize their effects. Otherwise, these conditions are only a monster around the corner that may reappear at any moment.

Research performed in an experimental setting has shown that when a person cries, Area 25 in the brain is stimulated. Overactive in those with a long, chronic history of depression, Area 25 jumps into action the moment someone experiences a trigger, creating the same old feelings of sadness, fear, and worry. To cure depression, we must retrain the brain to stop activating Area 25, and the only way to do so is to play detective and discover what originally overstimulated it through powerful feelings of depression. To alleviate Ann's profound sadness and hopelessness, I explained, we would have to dig beneath the surface.

I asked Ann my usual questions about sexuality, and she told me that she and her husband, Nick, had only had sex three times over the last ten years. I inquired, "Since Nick is healthy, do you know if he masturbates? Do you know if he's gay?" Ann assured me that he wasn't gay, and I took her answer at face value for the moment.

I then posed the most obvious question: "Is your husband having an affair?" Ann began to tear up. She said that she didn't know and had never asked him. I inquired, "What else is he doing with his sexual energy? What might be going on? Is he on blood-pressure medication or antidepressants? Because they can reduce sexual desire." Ann replied that none of these was the case, and she wasn't sure what was happening with his sexual drive. She'd never asked Nick about their lack of a sex life, nor had she tried to figure out why he was so uninterested in having one.

We then delved into Ann's personal history. After the last of her children started kindergarten and she had more time for herself, she decided to continue her education and eventually became a lawyer. Her husband was also 45 years old; was physically active, going to the gym every morning; and was very fit and healthy. He owned a small manufacturing company and often worked late. Ann and Nick frequently entertained clients and business associates in their home or at restaurants. Although they were socially active, the couple drank very little other than an occasional glass of wine. They lived a clean and healthy lifestyle.

Ann told me that she enjoyed a good relationship with Nick, and they usually got along very well. All their friends thought they were beautifully matched and a lot of fun. Also, she and her husband thoroughly enjoyed parenting. They attended soccer games, swim meets, and violin recitals, participating very actively and enthusiastically in the raising of their kids. Their children did well academically, although both parents were somewhat concerned that their middle child might have a learning disability; however, they'd recently enrolled him in a yoga class that was making a huge difference in his ability to focus on his schoolwork. In other words, the nature of Ann's problem didn't reside in troubled children, poverty, drugs, or alcohol. What was it, then?

Ann wanted to reestablish a sexual relationship with her husband. Years ago when they'd been sexually active, Nick was always the initiator, but when he stopped, she never understood why. Ann was too self-conscious to even broach the subject. Since Nick wasn't interested in sex anymore, she felt that he must no longer

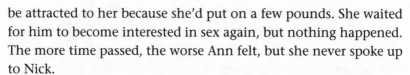

be attracted to her because she'd put on a few pounds. She waited for him to become interested in sex again, but nothing happened. The more time passed, the worse Ann felt, but she never spoke up to Nick.

As sexual behavior begins to change, secrecy and avoidance become very common. Our discomfort with sexuality, and its importance to us, makes it difficult to admit when there's a problem. Silence and denial become the order of the day.

One Saturday evening, Ann tried to rekindle her husband's romantic and sexual interest in her. She sent the children to her sister's home for the weekend. She prepared Nick's favorite meal: linguini with white clam sauce and a crisp salad of spring greens. Uncorking a lovely bottle of pinot grigio, they dined by candlelight.

After the meal, Ann invited Nick to join her in the hot tub under the stars. Upon hearing this suggestion, he quickly informed her that he had to finish a project and was going back to the office for a while. Not wanting to give up, Ann pushed aside her feelings of rejection and offered to "keep the fires burning" until he came back. However, when Nick returned at midnight, they were both tired, and Ann didn't feel like attempting once more to excite her husband. She never tried this approach again, and she felt extremely hurt and rejected.

Ann's depression and anxiety increased after that. Although she could talk to Nick about anything else, sex was the one subject she didn't feel confident or secure enough to bring up. However, one evening Ann and Nick were watching television and a Viagra commercial came on. She suggested that maybe he should see a doctor. This really upset him—he said he was fine. Ann still had no idea why her husband was so disinterested sexually, because they enjoyed each other in every other way.

Ann accepted the fact that it might help to review her childhood history at this point, and when I asked her to immediately give me a number, she answered, "12." I inquired what had happened when she was that age.

Ann remembered that her mother had gone through a very difficult time right around then. For a year, she had been depressed

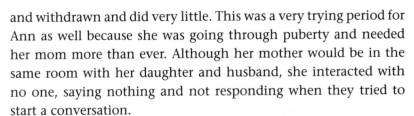

and withdrawn and did very little. This was a very trying period for Ann as well because she was going through puberty and needed her mom more than ever. Although her mother would be in the same room with her daughter and husband, she interacted with no one, saying nothing and not responding when they tried to start a conversation.

Since her mother was neither mentally nor emotionally present, Ann learned about wearing a bra and makeup from her girlfriends and *their* mothers. They taught her about menstruation as well: what was happening to her body, what to do, and what to purchase. Ann experienced a sense of abandonment, and in her childish mind, she assumed that her mother was ignoring her because she wasn't attractive or worthy enough of her attention. Eventually, her mother became more interactive with her daughter, but her withdrawal when Ann needed her the most left a deep imprint on the young girl.

The year before her mother fell into depression and withdrawal had been one of the worst in Ann's life. Her parents fought all the time, constantly screaming at each other. Her mother had accused her father of never being around. She also had accused him of having an affair with the neighbor across the street, a woman her mother referred to as "the hussy." The fights had been so frequent that Ann's father moved out of the house for six months.

Her mother was devastated. Ann's grandmother had to help take care of the children and the home each day. The grandmother then called Ann's father and told him that he was desperately needed at home. Her father moved back, but only because of the children. However, when he did return, he slept in his own bedroom, which he'd established two years earlier. His wife's depression continued to worsen, and by the time Ann was 12, her mother had become completely withdrawn.

Part of the childhood trauma that Ann experienced was the fear of losing her father. When he did come back, she feared being abandoned by her mother altogether—because her mother might as well have been absent for that whole year. The threat of losing one parent and then another caused tremendous stress for Ann.

At the heart of her parents' fights and the consequent depression, anxiety, and withdrawal of her mother was sexuality. Ann could see how she was engaging in repetition in her own life with her husband, responding just as her mother did when her father became sexually absent.

Ann was extremely capable of managing every aspect of her life other than her sexual relationship with Nick. She was a very skilled and successful litigator. However, she couldn't face her husband and discuss their sex life and negotiate a better situation. Ann couldn't understand why there was such a gap in her abilities, but I explained that when she was working as an attorney, she was acting out the role of the adult. When she was with her husband, she was in the role of the frightened child and the self-conscious preteen. She couldn't possibly have the confidence needed to talk about such a painful subject.

I then asked Ann to give me a smaller number, something between 0 and 10. The number 4 popped into her awareness. Ann remembered that when she was four years old, her younger brother had been born with a congenital stomach disorder. Several surgeries were performed to restructure the stomach and develop a proper digestive tract. Her parents took him to the Mayo Clinic and Johns Hopkins, as well as a number of other centers. At the age of four, for all intents and purposes, Ann had lost both her parents. Her grandmother, who was very strict, took care of her while her mom and dad were gone with the baby for weeks at a time. The trauma created issues of abandonment and isolation.

Parents who have a child with severe physical problems are either brought closer together or, if the condition is protracted, are pulled apart, going in different directions. In fact, parents who have lost a child will very often divorce. They become overwhelmed with grief and feel guilty or blame the other parent for the loss, even if their rational minds tell them that no one was responsible. They'll frequently deal with their sorrow differently and feel that their partner isn't grieving properly or that he or she doesn't care as much as they do. The parents will continually ask themselves, *Who is doing enough, who is not, and who is to blame?*

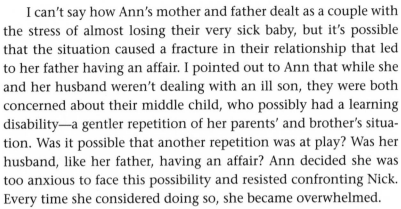

I can't say how Ann's mother and father dealt as a couple with the stress of almost losing their very sick baby, but it's possible that the situation caused a fracture in their relationship that led to her father having an affair. I pointed out to Ann that while she and her husband weren't dealing with an ill son, they were both concerned about their middle child, who possibly had a learning disability—a gentler repetition of her parents' and brother's situation. Was it possible that another repetition was at play? Was her husband, like her father, having an affair? Ann decided she was too anxious to face this possibility and resisted confronting Nick. Every time she considered doing so, she became overwhelmed.

I had Ann practice the 7 Steps of Rebirth, and she found that her anxiety immediately began to diminish, especially when she worked with the specific breathing technique. Having identified the origins of her depression and anxiety, she met and nurtured the 4-year-old, and later, the 12-year-old. She practiced the 7 Steps of Rebirth at least three, and up to as many as seven, times a day. Within six weeks, she was much better able to manage her feelings.

Ann used the 7 Steps of Rebirth most often when she was alone, waiting for Nick to come home for dinner. When he would call her and say that he was working late again, she felt saddened and overwhelmed. She wanted to have sex with him, and here she couldn't even get him to sit down and have dinner with her! However, since Ann had identified why she felt anxious, she now knew how to deal with it. She set aside the child self and handled the situation accordingly, as the adult. She was on her healing journey after only six weeks of using the 7 Steps of Rebirth.

At last, Ann decided to confront Nick. She invited him to meet her for dinner at their favorite Italian restaurant and prepared herself mentally and emotionally to discuss their sex life—or lack thereof. Right before he entered the restaurant, Ann used the 7 Steps of Rebirth in order to remind herself that she was now a capable, intelligent, and courageous adult.

After ordering a glass of Chianti, Ann came right out and asked Nick if he'd been having an affair. He initially denied it and was shocked that she even brought up the subject. After she explained her feelings and concerns and told him that she was prepared to leave him, his eyes began to well up with tears. He admitted to the other relationship, which had begun at the time he stopped having sex with Ann—he'd been having a difficult time at work, and the affair had made him feel important and empowered. Now, however, he was willing to end it, and he begged Ann to stay. He declared that he loved her and the children so much that he couldn't bear to lose them. He promised to stop seeing his lover because, as he said, his wife and children were his whole life. At this point, Ann suggested they go to couples therapy, and he readily agreed.

After an intensive weekend of counseling, they began to rekindle their relationship. They talked about how they'd met, what initially attracted them to each other, what they really liked about each other, when they fell in love, and how they'd felt at the time. They then reminisced about their wedding day and honeymoon. Tearfully, they recalled when their daughter, their oldest child, was born, as well as how much they loved *all* their children. They spoke of their fears and insecurities and were encouraged to own their personal history and the baggage they brought into the marriage.

At the end of that weekend of rediscovery and reconnection, they continued discussing all the wonderful and painful aspects of their life together: their children, accomplishments, joys, and sorrows. They engaged in verbal and emotional sharing, creating an intimacy that became the groundwork for reconnecting sexually. Before long, Ann and Nick were enjoying romantic, sexual evenings; and their relationship grew deeper and stronger. They were in the process of being healed.

Elizabeth's Story

Elizabeth, 36, was concerned because she and her husband, Jack, only had sex once every few months, and over the past three years, she'd become increasingly depressed. She and Jack had been having sex about three times a week, but suddenly it had dropped off. Elizabeth thought perhaps the problem was that she was often tired out by taking care of their four children and by working so hard at her job as an administrative assistant.

What's more, Elizabeth was worried because her depression and anxiety were now diminishing her capacity to take care of her children as well as handle her job. She had trouble getting up in the morning and sleeping at night—all of the classic symptoms of depression and restlessness. This necessitated reaching out to her mother and Jack's parents for help with the house and the kids. She got along well with her in-laws, and Jack liked her mother. She really loved her job, but the primary focus in her life was her husband, children, and extended family.

Elizabeth was strongly opposed to taking medication for depression or anxiety because her brother had gone on antidepressants after he had been disabled in a car accident, and Elizabeth firmly believed that the effects of the medication were even more damaging to him than his confinement to a wheelchair. Therefore, she was determined not to go this route and hoped that therapy would help her overcome her depression.

Three years previously, Jack had been laid off from his job and was unemployed for six months. He'd claimed he was feeling fine, but Elizabeth felt certain that he was at least somewhat depressed and upset. After all, soon after Jack lost his job, their sex life almost completely disappeared.

When Elizabeth told me that Jack had been constantly on the computer after that, looking for job possibilities and sending out résumés, I was immediately suspicious. I asked her if she'd ever bothered to take a look at the résumés he was e-mailing to computer employment sites. Elizabeth said she trusted Jack, felt he was highly responsible, and thought that he was really working hard at his job search. However, she couldn't understand why it took him so long to find work because at that time the economy was flourishing.

Eventually, Jack found a position, and Elizabeth never felt any need to check into his activities on the computer. Yet, their sexual relationship hadn't resumed, and she was becoming more bewildered and depressed. Jack was still sitting at the computer every night after dinner. Elizabeth noticed that whenever she would enter the room, especially in the evening, he would always react with a start, press a key, and whatever was on the screen would change. She only caught a fleeting glance at the flickering monitor. She asked him a couple of times what he was doing. He said that he needed to get more information that he was unable to access during the day in order to secure his job. Elizabeth felt confident and assured of his sense of responsibility. She felt it best to encourage him.

Initially, Jack had told her that he was on the computer constantly because he was looking for a job. Then, while working at his new position, he was on it every evening in order to "get more work done." So, like a good little girl, Elizabeth was obedient and said, "Okay. That's fine."

Most of us are too frightened to see what might be brewing beneath the surface and slip into denial. While we may have faith in the other person, there's nothing wrong with questioning a spouse. Doing so doesn't mean we're mistrustful, but it *does* mean we're being a discerning, capable, and intelligent adult who's able to see clearly and reason logically. We must be honest and ask questions if we want to change the situation, undo the patterns, and begin to heal.

Since Jack had found a job but their sex life hadn't resumed, I suggested that Elizabeth browse through the computer's history. She came back the next week shaken and upset. She had accessed Jack's online activity over the past several months, and the majority of the sites he'd visited were pornographic. She hunted further and found charges amounting to thousands of dollars, all for porn Websites, on one of their seldom-used credit cards. Jack had requested that the bills be sent to his brother's house, which infuriated her. She was angry that her husband's brother had participated in what she felt was a cover-up of his behavior. She felt betrayed, and hurt as well.

My first question was: "Do any of the sites Jack visited involve children? Because if they do, I would have to report your husband to the authorities on ethical grounds." Elizabeth told me that the same thought had also crossed her mind—after all, she was concerned about her four children. She looked carefully throughout the entire history of Jack's Internet activities, but to her relief, she found no evidence that he'd ever been to a site featuring children. However, the ones he did visit showed pictures and videos of just about everything else: women with women, women with men, single and group sex, sex between black actors, sex between white ones, and sadomasochism.

Elizabeth was shocked that she had been lied to and felt betrayed—not only because of the money Jack had secretly spent, but also because he'd shown a lack of interest in her sexually while getting aroused by pornography. She was also stunned because they were both staunch Catholics and attended church regularly. Jack's secret pastime was totally outside the realm of his behavior as she knew it. There had never been any hint before of any activities she considered to be abnormal.

She felt as if she'd been swept up in a sudden tornado. Once she found out the truth, she spent most of the week sleeping and completely skipped work for three days. She totally withdrew, not knowing what to do. The notion of divorce wasn't out of the question, since her parents were also Catholic and they'd gotten divorced.

I assuaged her panic and assured her of how common her situation really is. The relationship doesn't have to end in divorce because one partner is having an affair or has a sexual addiction. There are couples counselors who specialize in sex therapy who can be very helpful in such situations. I strongly advised Elizabeth not to make a decision about leaving her marriage at this time, and I recommended that she and her husband seek therapy together.

First, she needed to confront Jack, sit down, and discuss the situation to see if he really wanted to stop this behavior. Second, once he ended it (assuming he wanted to), she would have to act like a detective and check the computer periodically when he wasn't home to make sure he was keeping his word. I told her that after confronting her husband, she should block all of the sites immediately using a software program. I also said that if he was truly addicted to them, he would need help overcoming his problem. Elizabeth believed Jack *was* addicted because of the huge amount of money he'd spent on his secret hobby. I then recommended a support group called Sex and Love Addicts Anonymous (SLAA). I explained that just like alcoholism or drug abuse, sex addiction is a problem that deserves treatment, not punishment. Elizabeth began to educate herself about this topic, and she continued to work with me.

Elizabeth's repetition was that just as her mother had immediately decided to divorce her philandering husband after discovering his infidelity, Elizabeth was ready to leave her own husband without giving him a chance to work on their relationship. The consequences of her parents' divorce were very difficult for Elizabeth and her two siblings. She could see that she was setting up her own family for the same situation. Although Jack wasn't having physical affairs with women, he was sexually interacting with characters and images on the computer. The sexual betrayal was a repetition of what had happened between Elizabeth's parents.

Elizabeth revealed that Jack had brought home a couple of pornographic movies a few years earlier and asked her to watch them with him. She was totally turned off by them and wouldn't continue to watch them or allow Jack to bring any more home. She asked me if she should have given in to his request, considering his current addiction.

I said, "It's unwise to agree to something just to please him when you're so strongly opposed to it. You and Jack need to reach some kind of agreement about pornography. You might try watching those movies again once or twice, but if you're still turned off by them, then Jack needs to agree that pornographic videos won't be a part of your sex life together. Maybe you can decide to do something very much in the context of sexuality with a lot of sensuality and romance. Get playful and act out fantasy roles, try different positions, experiment with sex toys, and look at some sex guides to get ideas—but you must both agree on what you will do together sexually."

I persuaded Elizabeth to confront Jack. She decided to have at least another month of intense therapy in order to feel stronger and more confident in facing what lay ahead. She practiced the 7 Steps of Rebirth at least three times a day, using the specific breathing technique to remain calm. While doing so, she began setting aside her eight-year-old self (her age at the time her parents divorced) in the magical nature scene.

There was also a four-year-old who popped up and needed love and nurturing. A memory came forth: When Elizabeth was four, her parents had gotten into a huge fight. They thought that she and her sister and brother were asleep upstairs. The fighting was so loud and intense that her mother became hysterical and started throwing dishes. This memory was particularly traumatic to Elizabeth because her father had walked out of the house and was gone for an entire month. She had blocked from her consciousness all memory of this experience.

The sense of the child feeling powerless and unable to speak up on her own behalf returned to her when she started having problems with her husband. Elizabeth's child self didn't insist on knowing why the sex had stopped and what was going on with her husband. She was an adult in other areas of her life, but when it came to sex, she was in a frightened-child mode. It was very important that she learn to put aside this child.

We worked twice a week for a month before Elizabeth felt that she was operating in an adult mode. We used role-playing to explore in an emotionally safe way what would happen to Elizabeth if Jack were to deny his pornography habit or brush off her concerns. We covered all the possible reactions and objections he might have. I also suggested some statements she could make during the actual confrontation, such as, "I know that you're doing this. It's unacceptable to me, and hurtful to me and our marriage."

Elizabeth was now ready to confront her husband. At first, he denied the computer pornography and then became enraged that she'd dared look through his online history. She stood her ground, having prepared herself for this reaction. Finally, when Elizabeth told him flat out that she wouldn't live like this anymore, Jack

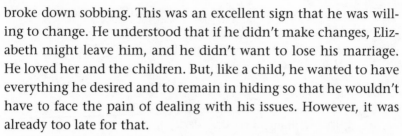

broke down sobbing. This was an excellent sign that he was willing to change. He understood that if he didn't make changes, Elizabeth might leave him, and he didn't want to lose his marriage. He loved her and the children. But, like a child, he wanted to have everything he desired and to remain in hiding so that he wouldn't have to face the pain of dealing with his issues. However, it was already too late for that.

Elizabeth and Jack started marital counseling and found a support group for sex addicts and their partners. Like Ann and Nick, they attended an intense weekend workshop for couples that was transformative for both of them. They explored the origins of the problem in their history and got in touch with the reasons why they got married. They loved each other. Except for their differing views on pornography, their values were almost identical. They cherished their families and were churchgoers.

Elizabeth now understood what her repetition was, but she didn't know what pattern Jack was repeating in his life. She encouraged him to see me, which he did twice.

On the first visit, I asked him about how he'd become addicted to pornography. He explained that in the course of his job search, he accidentally came across a pornographic site and was excited by it. Before he knew it, he was accessing these sites more and more often, lying to his wife, and secretly spending thousands of dollars on his hobby. I asked him if he had any painful memories about sex, dating back to his childhood. He thought about it for a moment and then told me about something that had happened when he was nine years old.

Jack and a couple of his buddies from school were having a pissing contest in the garage. There was no sexual intent; it was merely a competition to see who could urinate the farthest. His mother came into the garage and saw the three boys holding their own penises. She felt that their behavior was dreadfully sinful and threatened punishment when her husband came home. That night, Jack was whipped mercilessly by his father. From then on, he was prevented from ever having anything to do with his best friends.

This experience was so traumatic to little Jack that it was a defining event leading to secrecy surrounding sex. The repetition was that he was surreptitiously viewing sexual material on his computer, making sure that nobody saw what he was doing, and hoping to get away with it.

Jack's second and last visit with me involved learning the 7 Steps of Rebirth. While he practiced them, he met his nine-year-old self who'd been severely punished for an act that his mother had considered sexual. He loved, nurtured, and assured the little one that no one would ever hurt him again. When Jack separated from the child self, he was the adult who was ready to tackle the years of work that would be needed to cure his addiction.

Jack continued to see a sex therapist, but I knew that this therapist wouldn't deal with the whole notion of repetition and the 7 Steps of Rebirth. However, I felt that both of these approaches were necessary if he was to overcome his addiction.

After being in marital therapy for about six months, Elizabeth and Jack discontinued weekly counseling but went for follow-up visits every six weeks for the next year. The purpose of the occasional monitoring was to help support Jack in his new behavior. He also continued going to the sex addicts' support group for three years.

The reason why Jack, and many people, need extensive therapy to deal with sexual problems is that our sexual behavior doesn't change very quickly. The drive for sex is extremely powerful, second only to our will to survive. Every time we fulfill a sexual desire, the relief and physiological reaction of having an orgasm is so deliciously satisfying, lovely, and wonderful that the behaviors that led to that fulfillment can easily become addictive. Since such an addiction is so powerful, it's necessary to address it with much support, love, gentle firmness, and diversion.

Within a month and a half of the start of Elizabeth's therapy with me, after she and Jack had acknowledged their problem and begun trying other therapies as well, he began to be more responsive to her sexual overtures. She took the computer away for three months in order to give them more time together and with their family.

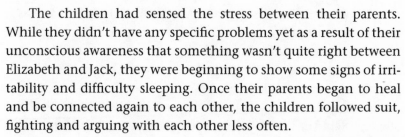

The children had sensed the stress between their parents. While they didn't have any specific problems yet as a result of their unconscious awareness that something wasn't quite right between Elizabeth and Jack, they were beginning to show some signs of irritability and difficulty sleeping. Once their parents began to heal and be connected again to each other, the children followed suit, fighting and arguing with each other less often.

The key to the family's healing was Jack's willingness to acknowledge and work on his sexual addiction, despite the painful feelings it stirred in him.

By practicing the 7 Steps of Rebirth, sexual addiction can be treated at the core. Also, by working with support groups and in therapy, people can reinforce new behaviors again and again and recommit to their relationships. In my experience, if there's no involvement in a multifaceted treatment program, stopping a sexual addiction doesn't work. People don't quit on their own, because the desire to repeat the sexual behavior is too great, and too rooted in our basic physiology, including the urges of our primitive brain.

Meeting people on the computer often leads to an affair—if not an actual sexual betrayal of the spouse, then an emotional one—and this has become common. In a chat room, you may begin communicating with someone a few states away. Pretty soon, without realizing it, you're opening your heart and thoughts to that person, saying things like, "My wife doesn't understand me. It's so wonderful to talk to you. You're so sensitive and beautiful." Before you know it, a full-fledged affair has begun. You get together, talk, explore, and are intimate with one another while on the computer. You may even arrange to physically meet.

Computer affairs have been known to destroy families and relationships. Imagine the convenience of getting involved with someone without having to take the other person out for a drink or dinner. No money needs to be spent, and you can carry on your behavior right in your home, under your own roof. If you're married or currently in a committed partnership, be aware of the consequences of a computer affair, because they can be painful, far-reaching, and very destructive to existing relationships.

The temptation can be great, because pornography has become much more readily available. We should experience sex as being joyous, pleasurable, and uplifting—an expression of love and connection. Otherwise, we become so caught up in the sex act for all the wrong reasons that we avoid building intimacy, which isn't good for us or for the people around us.

Sexuality and Sexual Orientation

Over the course of my professional life, I've come to discover that homosexual men and women often have different issues that play out in their repetitions. Commonly, male homosexuals have suffered some form of sexual abuse or trauma at the hands of another male, in this or a past life, while female homosexuals sometimes have suffered sexual abuse or trauma and sometimes have suffered a trauma in their relationship with their mother—again, these situations may have occurred in this life, a past life, or both.

Heterosexual men and women will often have sexual problems in a relationship because sexual experiences in the past led to painful affairs, breakups, or other negative consequences. The trauma of being shamed for having sexual feelings or exploring one's sexuality as a child will be re-created later, in adult sexual relationships. Suffering the fallout from a parent's affair also can cause trauma in a child that leads to sexual problems and repetition later. However, the very worst sexual traumas that are suffered by men, such as rape and sexual abuse, often result in the victim unconsciously choosing homosexuality in this lifetime or the next.

Men who were molested by another male in their childhood or adolescence may not consciously recall the abuse. It might appear in their dreams or remain buried deep in their unconscious. Sexual abuse is deeply damaging, causing an imprint on the soul and creating the need for repetition.

As a therapist, I look to explain behavior and not judge it. There's nothing "wrong" with being homosexual any more than it's "wrong" to have issues regarding abandonment, betrayal, or alcohol abuse. Every one of us has issues that cause us to follow patterns of repetition.

In almost every civilization throughout history, it has been very difficult to be homosexual, with the notable exceptions of ancient Greece and certain Native American cultures. Having gay or lesbian relationships or sex is often judged as sinful, causing homosexuals to feel ashamed or guilty about their natural desires and inclinations. In some societies, they are persecuted, tortured, and killed.

A soul who chooses to reincarnate as a homosexual is almost sure to struggle with rejection, guilt, and abuse, all of which are terrible from our perspective as human beings. Yet, from the perspective of the soul, all of the situations that generate such painful emotions offer excellent opportunities for healing. If we can set aside our judgments of ourselves and others and look at our sexual interactions and those of our partners as having been created for the purpose of healing, then it's easier for us to exit patterns of betrayal, guilt, abuse, and shame.

Dan's Story

Sexual behavior that's motivated by the desire for power can be exploitative and abusive. As a society, we're becoming increasingly aware of how sex can be used as a weapon, but in ancient times in many cultures, sexual domination of people who were weaker was commonplace and accepted. I'm not surprised that often my clients who are dealing with sexual issues are able to reclaim a memory of a sexual trauma from a past life that was absolutely brutal. It can take many lifetimes to recover from such horrendous abuse.

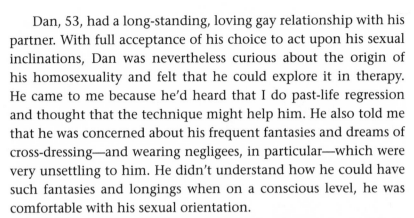
Dan, 53, had a long-standing, loving gay relationship with his partner. With full acceptance of his choice to act upon his sexual inclinations, Dan was nevertheless curious about the origin of his homosexuality and felt that he could explore it in therapy. He came to me because he'd heard that I do past-life regression and thought that the technique might help him. He also told me that he was concerned about his frequent fantasies and dreams of cross-dressing—and wearing negligees, in particular—which were very unsettling to him. He didn't understand how he could have such fantasies and longings when on a conscious level, he was comfortable with his sexual orientation.

When we discussed his history in this lifetime, Dan told me that from the time he was very young up through the age of 15, he'd slept in his mother's bed—at her request. There was neither sexual intent nor abuse or molestation on her part, but she was creating a situation of *emotional* incest. Dan's mother would have nothing to do with his father (likewise, his dad had nothing to do with either one of them). He was strictly an ancillary figure in the home and slept in a separate room. Dan's mother loved and supported her son wholeheartedly, but by keeping him in her bed all those years, she implicitly gave him the message: "My partner, your father, is out of my bed and life experiences, and I want you to take his place. I love you. I trust you. I lean on you—and I don't love, trust, or lean on him. You're precious to me."

Since his mother was so dependent on him, the extent of the emotional incest was severe. Dan had no siblings and his father ignored him, so he was emotionally reliant on his mother. She was the authority figure as well as the only one who loved and cared for him, but she had poor boundaries. In addition to having her son sleep in her bed, she would talk to him as if he were a mate or partner, confiding in him about troubles or asking him to be a part of her decisions. Being in bed with his mother aroused anxiety in Dan, but as a child, he was unaware of its significance and potential repercussions.

Dan started to have an attraction to men when he was a teenager but didn't act on these impulses until his first sexual experience, with a man, when he was 22. As an adult, Dan was very troubled about whether it was "right" or "wrong" to be close to a woman. Was he betraying his sexual orientation by becoming emotionally close to women?

Although he had female friends, he assiduously avoided any physical intimacy with them. Years before while he was sexually fantasizing, he suddenly had flashes of being in bed with his nightgown-clad mother. Although he felt certain his mom had never actually molested him, he found this image so disturbing that he avoided women in his fantasies altogether. He indulged in his homosexual fantasies and urges, however, because they didn't cause him to feel deeply uncomfortable.

Although Dan had maintained a very happy relationship with a man for more than 20 years and was at peace with his choice, he always wondered why the possibility of experiencing arousal in response to a female produced such anxiety and fear in him. He also wanted to understand the origin of his fantasy of cross-dressing, one that he'd never acted on but which still disturbed and confused him.

Dan's fantasy was, in essence, repeating part of his trauma in his current lifetime—that is, it was a repetition of his experience in bed with his mother. He couldn't reenact the situation of incest exactly; thus, the repetition took on a safer form. Now, instead of seeing himself in bed with his mother in his dream—an image that was too disturbing for him to accept—Dan fantasized about wearing a negligee himself, which wasn't as upsetting for him. Nevertheless, this image of the negligee held a strong emotional charge for him. He was haunted by the vision of his mother and wouldn't share his cross-dressing fantasy with his partner because he felt too ashamed.

I worked with Dan to access a relevant past life, knowing that it was likely he would recall a story of sexual abuse, which he did:

Deep in the heart of the Casbah in Morocco, in a dingy, dimly lit den that is cloudy with the smoke of hashish lingering in the air, Mansour is curled in a tight fetal position, his back hugging a corner of the room. His fragile, naked body is bloody and scarred from continual whippings and blows. Mansour, a lost child of 11, is a sex slave to a horrendously large and barbaric man. During an exceptionally brutal sexual encounter late one night, Mansour dies.

Because Mansour's soul left the physical world at a time of extreme intensity, the script that was set was powerfully charged, and his soul made the decision to return to the physical world immediately and deal with issues of sexuality.

Once Dan understood the connection between his dreams and fantasy and his current story, as well as their link to his past life, he was relieved. First, he was glad that everything he experienced made sense. Second, he realized that it was okay not to act on his fantasies or dreams, and that he didn't have to judge himself negatively just because his fantasy contradicted the feelings and beliefs he held at a conscious level. Using the 7 Steps of Rebirth, he was able to heal the boy who had shared a bed with Mother and was able to be an adult in the present. His fantasies about his mom, and urges to dress in women's clothing, diminished considerably. Also, by revealing his secret to me and then to his partner, Dan took the emotional charge out of it and felt freed from anxiety and guilt.

At the end of our work, Dan expressed a sense of satisfaction with his life choices. He said, "I'm perfectly happy and content continuing on with my male lover. In fact, I made the decision that I'm going to share my fantasies with him, because I don't need those secrets anymore, and I don't have to feel bad about them. There had always been this part of me that I was hiding. Now I can be fully open. I can be 100 percent present in our relationship."

He continued by saying, "Dr. Doris, we'll meet in another life, perhaps, and I'll tell you how the rest of *this* life unfolds. Maybe in a future lifetime, I'll make different choices, and that will be another time and another place." He really understood the notion of repetition. He was now able to experience his relationship with a full heart and lead a richer, happier, and more open life with his partner.

I don't believe that sexual orientation is determined completely or definitively in our cells, in our genes, or *in utero*. Rather, it's largely based on our history in this life and in past ones. We choose the bodies and families to be born into based on what we're likely to encounter, and then we can repeat the stories of our current and previous lives, giving us new opportunities to heal from past trauma. How is an adult male going to work through the trauma of having been molested by another male when he was a child if he doesn't experience it again now, in the present? Simply to talk about sexual abuse with no emotional charge attached won't bring about significant healing, so our unconscious mind chooses to put us in situations where we're likely to reexperience the very same painful feelings of abuse and then decide to change our reactions and exit our old patterns.

In our culture, people can be very judgmental about homosexual acts, and this is what drives that behavior underground. I've had clients who were happily married men with children who secretly had anonymous homosexual sex and couldn't understand the compulsion. Inevitably, the source of such behavior is sexual trauma. One client in particular, Lloyd, had been molested as a child by a baseball coach who, he learned, also had abused Lloyd's three brothers. As men, all four brothers were married but carrying on secret homosexual encounters.

Lloyd believed that this childhood sexual trauma was at the heart of his own behavior, and he wanted to know if his was a common experience. Out of curiosity, one night he asked all the men in a gay bar he frequented whether they'd ever been sexually molested as children, and every single man said yes. In fact, I have yet to counsel a homosexual man who didn't experience a sexual trauma in this lifetime, let alone previous ones.

So, let's be accepting of each other and not judge each other, but let's also explore the origin and the truth of our story and of our repetitions. If we understand our reasons and motivations, we can more fully accept and embrace our relationships with clarity and with an open, loving heart.

Gabriella's Story

Gabriella, a 34-year-old social worker who was well educated and articulate, came to me for help with some very serious problems in her relationship with her lesbian partner, Sandy. Gabriella revealed to me that she had been with Sandy for three years, and when they got along, they both were loving and respectful. However, when there was conflict, Sandy inflicted extreme physical abuse on Gabriella. In fact, when she first came to see me, Gabriella had a black eye and bruises on her back, arms, and neck.

Gabriella and Sandy had been in couples counseling a year before. The tools and techniques they'd been taught were somewhat helpful, but the violence only subsided to a point: It was a little less frequent, but the intensity of the fights had escalated. The last time Sandy beat her up, Gabriella had feared for her own life.

We began by discussing Gabriella's childhood. She was the second of six children: The oldest was a girl, and the four youngest were boys. Her father preferred Gabriella's sister and was always very close to her. Her mother was obese and had low self-esteem, which was exacerbated by her husband's many open affairs with women who were very attractive and slender. This depressed and infuriated her because she couldn't keep her husband in line. Every time she looked at Gabriella, she projected her self-hatred onto her daughter. So, while she was physically abusive to all the children to some extent, hitting them upon the slightest provocation, she was exceptionally hard on Gabriella. She beat, berated, and belittled her. Conversely, the father wasn't at all abusive to any of the children.

While Gabriella's mother tormented her, her brothers relentlessly teased her, calling her "fatso," "shorty," "ugly duckling," "four eyes," and—because she was cross-eyed until she had an operation as a teenager to correct this condition—"the cross-eyed monster." When she complained to her father, he always dismissed her. No matter what she did, she could never get her parents' support and love. However, her extreme sadness came from constantly feeling rejected by her mother. She yearned for maternal love, compassion, and attention.

Gabriella didn't date at all in high school. When she went to college, she made friends with a couple of young men. One in particular was interested in her because he loved her sharp mind. She lost weight and started feeling better about herself. The young man soon asked her out. On their first date, he began kissing and touching her. She became so uncomfortable and frightened that she jumped up and left, never to go out with him again.

Gabriella started socializing a little and joined a sorority but left within six months. Being in such close quarters with the sorority girls became difficult for her because she realized that she was sexually attracted to a number of them. The intense emotional closeness and physical proximity was tempting, and she was afraid she might act on her feelings, so she moved out.

Gabriella reflected more and realized that when she was in high school, she had been attracted to the other girls in gym class, particularly the swimmers. The girls were very beautiful and had long, fluid limbs. She would admire their shape, especially their breasts. Her feelings made her very uncomfortable and fed into her self-concept of being different, strange, unattractive, undesirable, and out of place. At age 13, she'd started looking at girls, and she thought that her attraction was bizarre. When she went off to college and became exposed to more liberal social attitudes in the academic environment, she began to think that maybe she could explore the possibility of a relationship with a female.

One of the girls in her psychology class, Carole, reached out to Gabriella, and they spent a great deal of time studying together. She became Gabriella's first lover in their senior year. She was tall, blonde, and somewhat plain, but Gabriella felt that her girlfriend was prettier and more desirable than she was.

Within three months, Carole became verbally harsh toward Gabriella. Even so, after graduation they moved in together. Carole's behavior worsened as she started to become physically abusive. Soon, Gabriella was hospitalized for a broken nose, a fractured kneecap, and a dislocated shoulder. When her doctor said that he would report the abuse, she became so frightened that she finally ended that relationship.

After a few years of work and travel, Gabriella settled into a career as a social worker, helping battered women. She began dating her current partner, Sandy, after discovering that they had many interests in common and were both very artistic. They also shared similar childhood experiences: Sandy had come from a family where her mother had been physically abusive toward her and verbally cruel. When not picking on her daughter, Sandy's mother was unavailable and withdrawn, suffering from chronic depression. Sandy was physically abused by her father as well.

For the first year and a half, Gabriella and Sandy's relationship was unusually kind and loving. However, Sandy became increasingly jealous of Gabriella and any female contacts she made. If Gabriella ever talked about working with a female client, boss, or colleague who was kind, Sandy would become enraged and the beatings began.

During therapy, I asked Gabriella why she was staying with Sandy. She replied, "Because I love her." This is the classic statement of the so-called victim talking about the perpetrator.

I would never label Gabriella a masochist. The word *masochist,* like *sadist,* should be removed from the English language. We never *want* to hurt ourselves or others. When our behavior is self-debasing or we continue selecting abusive partners, whether consciously or unconsciously, this results in physical and emotional suffering. Our intention, however, isn't to seek pain for pain's sake but to heal from past trauma.

Masochism is the mirror image of sadism. Anger and rage at having been abused as a child can cause us to want to hurt, damage, or injure others. But deep down, we're never out to harm anyone; rather, we're repeating these patterns because this is the only way we can experience today what we felt during the original trauma of abuse, whether that happened 10 years ago, 30 years ago, or many lifetimes ago.

Gabriella really wanted to understand what was going on in her life and why. As a social worker, she always felt ashamed when she helped people who were ailing or abused, wondering, *What about me? How much abuse am I going to continue to take? How can I be so hypocritical as to tell Mrs. Jones that she has to press charges against her husband or urge Ms. Smith to report her boyfriend's abuse to the police when I'm letting Sandy beat me so often and so much?* Gabriella got tired of explaining to everyone why she was so bruised. She'd told them so many stories of falling or clumsily bumping into something that no one believed her excuses anymore.

Gabriella longed to understand why was she tolerating one abusive relationship after another. Also, because her family had disowned her, she was feeling very lonely and isolated.

Although she understood that her mother had rejected her, when she was using the 7 Steps of Rebirth, she found it very difficult to do "Step 3: Acknowledge—'Whoops, There I Go Again!'" In all of her therapy, both for herself and others, she wrestled with the concept of victimization. She felt victimized because she was the least-preferred child and was totally left out of the family circle. She felt victimized by her abusers who were her current and past partners. By the same token, she experienced guilt because she realized that she'd actually tolerated them. She initially believed that it was only her "bad luck" that she'd ended up with those abusive women.

As Gabriella started to understand the dynamics of her relationships, she began to take ownership of them. She was slowly realizing that at an unconscious level, she'd played a part in the selection of those partners. It was a struggle for her to perceive that unknowingly she had *chosen* to participate in situations in which she was abused. I told her that she mustn't think of herself as a masochist. Her choices were made by her powerful unconscious for the purpose of bringing about her healing. This was very different from wanting to hurt herself.

Three weeks after she'd begun practicing the 7 Steps of Rebirth, Gabriella began to feel calmer and more empowered. At least with this new tool, she could do something about her anguish and not feel so troubled and victimized.

Gabriella hadn't dealt with tapping the unconscious in her work with abused women and children. Her whole focus was to help her clients, rescue them, and get them to leave the perpetrators of the abuse. By practicing the 7 Steps of Rebirth, the whole notion of the unconscious and her responsibility for her life story was awakened.

Gabriella began to work even more with the 7 Steps of Rebirth. She met herself at ages one, two, and three, because those are the numbers that came up for her in "Step 4: Get a Number." In the beautiful, magical nature scene, she held herself as a baby, bathed the infant, and put lotion and talcum powder on her before reassuring her, separating, and returning to the present as the adult.

Gabriella began to see, and acknowledge, the connection between her relationship with her mother and her selection of abusive partners. She also knew what to do about it.

At our next session, and with my support, Gabriella brought Sandy with her in order to confront her. Gabriella told the other woman, "Now I understand why I've picked my partners who have been so abusive to me."

She then laid down the law gently yet firmly. She said, "I love you, Sandy. I want us to continue having a relationship. However, if you ever lay one finger on me again or call me a name, you're out of my house. I want you to hear this in the presence of my therapist. This is not a threat. This is a decision that I've made as an adult."

After hearing this, Sandy started bullying Gabriella and shouting, "How dare you threaten me!"

Gabriella responded firmly, "Stop it, and stop it *now*. Otherwise, I'm going to get a restraining order against you and have you put out of my house. Remember, I know how to do these things because I'm always helping my clients."

Suddenly, Sandy burst into tears and said, "I'm so sorry. Please don't throw me out."

I told Sandy that I hoped she would stay with these feelings of pain and sorrow that she was expressing now, rather than running to her anger as a defense against the discomfort or giving in to depression and refusing to go to work.

Anger is very empowering and energizing. We release more adrenaline when we're angry. When we're very down and start feeling mad, it's an indicator that the depression is beginning to lift, because anger is the flip side of depression. It propels us out of our paralysis and lethargy and into action.

I urged Sandy to get into therapy (not with me, as that would be a conflict of interest). She took my advice and began counseling. Gabriella continued to work with the tools I gave her. Also, Sandy began to feel calmer and to improve significantly when she started using the 7 Steps of Rebirth, which Gabriella had shared with her. Both earnestly worked on healing their relationship, which gradually became much healthier and more loving, and the violence stopped.

It's important to note that healing herself didn't mean Gabriella lost her sexual attraction to women. Lesbianism would stay with her in this lifetime and, perhaps, in future ones as well, but her repetitions of the mother trauma and the seeking of nurturing at another woman's breast would be much gentler than they had been in this life.

Gabriella realized the origins of her sexuality and accepted them without judgment. She was no longer anxious. She didn't feel guilty or hypocritical when she advised her clients to leave their abusers (of whom she was also less judgmental). To help her clients further, she began teaching them about the 7 Steps of Rebirth, emphasizing how helpful it is for stress management. She called me many months after she'd terminated her therapy and said that at least two of her clients were beginning to realize—without guilt and without judgment—that they'd played a part in their own stories, and were starting to change their reactions in order to exit the patterns and heal.

In my experience, the origin of female homosexuality, or lesbianism, isn't the same as that of male homosexuality, so the healing process is different as well. With the latter, there's always a history of being sexually abused or molested by a male in the current life or in relevant past lives. Healing then occurs through repetition involving relationships with men. The precedents are different with females, however. Some women who were horribly sexually abused or molested by men will engage in a very literal repetition and become involved with another male abuser. Some, however, will turn to a female in order to feel a sense of comfort and safety, and this is especially likely if the woman was molested by a man and was rejected by her mother when she sought comfort.

In other words, when a woman is a lesbian, it's the little girl inside her who is running to another female to feel safe. But because she's an adult with sexual feelings, her attraction to this mother figure then turns sexual.

Seeking comfort at the breast of a woman becomes the repetition of having been rejected at the breast of a mother who wouldn't or couldn't nurture her daughter. Not having been protected or affectionately cared for by her female parent, and instead having been rejected harshly or abused, causes her to seek out repetition and to experience it more intensely with a woman in the present. After all, where can she again feel the sharp, mordant pain of having been rejected or abused by a mother figure? It is literally at the breast of another woman.

The little girl within the woman is still yearning for Mother's love and nurturing, so she searches for it elsewhere. Can an adult woman receive maternal nurturing from someone of the same gender without the relationship becoming sexual? Of course. But because the child seeking nurturing is living in an adult body, she expresses this yearning sexually. However, even if her sexual longings are satisfied, it doesn't alleviate her feelings of lack and loss. These painful emotions can only be healed by healing the child who suffered trauma.

Twenty-five years ago, statistics indicated that one out of six females were sexually abused. A few years later, the statistics indicated the number had risen to one out of four, and now it's one out of two who experience sexual abuse or molestation. This cuts across racial, economic, educational, religious, and social

lines—across the board. In a short time, we also have gone from the "taboo of incest" to open and even public discussion of this form of abuse.

The more people talk about it, the easier it is for those who have been abused—both male and female—to acknowledge it, explore it, and ultimately, heal from it. Fortunately, the unconscious is more likely to allow the conscious mind to recall such a traumatic event (or events) because we're now better able to handle the horror of it than we were when no one discussed it.

The 7 Steps of Rebirth are a powerful core technique for healing ourselves of repetitions, but writing and rewriting our stories and practicing the 4 Steps of Joy are also extremely helpful tools for exiting repetition. Each of them (presented in Part III), like the 7 Steps, works by building a bridge between the conscious and unconscious mind, accessing hidden wisdom and awareness that must come to the surface if we are to heal.

PART III

YOUR STORY

CHAPTER EIGHT

WRITING
YOUR STORY

A story is the way we describe the facts and events of life. When we tell *ours,* it's as though we've written a script for a play or movie. We organize the events and cast the individuals in our lives as particular characters in this drama, creating an emotional narrative. This is very different from a flat or linguistic description of people and events. History—"his story"—is our collective story, the one we agree upon. Just as different people may have very different ways of telling the story of our collective experiences, there are many ways in which we can tell our own story. We can vary the descriptions of the characters and events. We can also come up with a different beginning, middle, and end and rewrite our past, present, and projection of what will happen in the future. The way we tell our story—our interpretation of what happened—will determine what emotions we feel.

Our stories are so amazingly rich that nothing can compare to them, including soap operas on television! Most often we believe them to be our reality and carved in stone, but they are ongoing and changeable. Writing our own individual story is an opportunity to exercise our God-given gift of free choice. Basically, we can choose to perceive the circumstances of our lives differently. Having done so, we can then begin to rewrite our story, acting in a new way, getting involved with different people, and experiencing new events (a process I'll discuss in detail in the next chapter). We'll find ourselves making different decisions than we did before, because our unconscious mind won't continually overrule our conscious one.

When we write our story in the third person, as if describing someone else, we're less likely to color it with strong emotions that cause us to judge ourselves and others so harshly that we miss the lessons contained therein. By constructing a third-person narrative, we gain perspective and a sense of empowerment that will allow us to operate from the vantage point of the adult.

On the other hand, when we tell the story while in a child mode, we perceive that we have no power over our circumstances. Often we see ourselves as victims. As a result, in the present we let other people in our lives take over and manipulate and exert control over us. Our story—of being a misunderstood outcast, a lonely and shy person, or an unappreciated workaholic who never takes a break from trying to help others—becomes our reality. The past becomes the present . . . and the future.

This kind of life story is very limiting and makes it difficult for us to come to clear and healthy decisions. The narrative we weave around the facts prevents us from seeing how we can act in ways that don't cause us to feel powerless, betrayed, abandoned, unappreciated, and so on.

Once we own our life stories and take responsibility for them— letting go of the childlike perspective that we are powerless victims of circumstance—we begin to see that we are their *creators* and are able to change them at any time. We can begin to exit our patterns of repetition at last.

Writing Your Story

Many of us are fascinated by soap operas. They're popular in numerous countries, and some of us plan our lives around

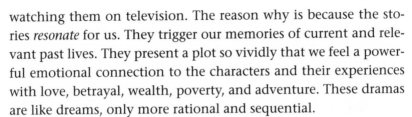

watching them on television. The reason why is because the stories *resonate* for us. They trigger our memories of current and relevant past lives. They present a plot so vividly that we feel a powerful emotional connection to the characters and their experiences with love, betrayal, wealth, poverty, and adventure. These dramas are like dreams, only more rational and sequential.

Every one of us has the most amazing soap opera in our head, heart, and life. Claim it. It's *your* story. And if you don't like it, change it.

To do so, you must start by writing the story of your life, allowing your unconscious to inform you with key memories that flesh out your tale. Then you must examine it, letting go of any judgments that cause you pain, such as: *This is the story of someone who didn't live up to his potential,* or *This is the story of a victim of bad parenting.* Only when you let go of these judgments can you see your story clearly, understand it, recognize your repetitions, and own the fact that you are—and always have been—the storyteller. This process of writing out your story, putting it on paper (or into a computer document), and owning it is an extremely powerful tool that enhances the healing you do when using the 7 Steps of Rebirth.

As you reveal the elements of your story and how you think and feel about them, you'll start to get a perspective that you don't have when you're caught up in the events. For example, describing yourself and your life in the third person, you might find yourself writing: *Once upon a time there was a little girl named Dolores. She had pretty blonde hair and blue eyes. She was sweet and so lively. Yet, there was a sadness in her because no one knew the secrets in her home. She was often afraid.*

Writing in the third person is an important part of gaining perspective. When we use the pronoun *I*, we're focused on our own experience and point of view. When we use *he* or *she* to tell our story, it's as if we take a step off the stage and into the back row of seats in the theater, recognizing that while we're the actor in our story, we are also the writer and director. We're able to see a larger picture and limit the distorting effects of strong emotions that we create when we tell the narrative in the first person. Instead of being pulled into the old story of being a victim—and feeling angry and hurt—we choose not to write: "*I* had no friends as a child," but rather, "*He* had no friends as a child."

Because writing is a creative process, once you begin to describe your story, more of it comes forward, and eventually, the truth that's hidden in your unconscious will be revealed. By writing down your memories and life events, you're behaving as the proactive adult. You're the storyteller taking charge of your story.

This process, combined with practicing the 7 Steps of Rebirth, will gradually open the doors to your unconscious, and knowledge and wisdom will slowly and gently become more present in your conscious reality. Images may come to you in dreams, nudging you to acknowledge and examine what your unconscious knows. You may start to become aware of symbols in your waking life, realizing that your back only seems to hurt or "give out" when you've been asked to take on responsibilities that frighten and worry you, and that you tend to describe yourself or others as "spineless" or "not having a backbone." These symbols, just like those in your dreams, are the result of the unconscious speaking to you. As you notice them, add them to your story.

A helpful approach to writing your story is to think of yourself as the actor, director, producer, and writer of a play that's going to be performed in a theater. Imagine you're facing the stage and watching your play unfold. You're now witnessing and observing your own story from the perspective of the scenes' creator. Having stepped back, you're able to watch every aspect of your life and relationships from the vantage point of the adult who's in charge instead of that of the child who's on the stage playing a character in an unsatisfying story, feeling powerless to choose his or her own lines of dialogue and actions. What does the adult observe from the back row of the theater?

While writing your story, jot down the information as it comes to you and without judgment. By viewing your story as a play—that is, doing so with perspective and *without judgment*—you are in a much better position to see the whole picture and understand

what's going on and why. Only then can you take control of the play and change it.

Shakespeare once wrote: "All the world's a stage, / and all the men and women merely players." In my view, this statement produces a sense of hopelessness. The truth of the statement is: "All the world's a stage, and we are all Shakespeares"! *You* are in the audience watching. *You* are the author of your life story. *You* are Shakespeare, creating amazing tales.

If you own your power as Shakespeare and you don't like what's happening onstage, remember that you can always change it. If the character on the right-hand side of the stage is really getting out of hand, you can write him out of the play. You can hire and dismiss as many actors as you wish, because it's your production and you're in charge of the finances; you are the *producer.* You can move the actors around on the stage as often as you wish, because you are also the *director.* When the curtain comes down, you're signaling the end of this story in the current lifetime. You may choose to write another at another time, in another place. By incarnating again, in a different lifetime, your soul will write, direct, and produce a new theatrical piece.

Sometimes playwrights will feel so frustrated by the play that they give up hope of being able to change it in a satisfactory way. They'll say, "This is so awful. I can't stand it anymore!" and walk out of the theater, leaving the actors in midsentence, confused and unsure of what to do next. They haven't been paid, the curtain hasn't come down, and the money hasn't been returned to the investors. No one knows what to do.

This is what happens when people commit suicide. They are in such tremendous pain that they give up, not realizing that they're destined to find themselves in the identical position again, being the writer, director, and playwright in another theater, wrestling with the same troubles they had in their previous production. We must listen to the call of our unconscious mind, return to our role as the creator of a play, and try again.

Writing your story and then rewriting it are tools for healing because they help you become conscious of your role as storyteller, director, and producer. Instead of avoiding the truth—that you're in charge of this story—you own your role and begin to make changes in your patterns of repetition.

How to Write Your Story

Before you begin to write your story, create a comfortable and relaxing atmosphere. Don't answer the phone or turn on the television. These intrusions will interrupt your process. The goal is to create an environment that will allow your energy and the information from your unconscious mind to flow easily and effortlessly. Take up to 15 minutes to prepare for this important work: Put on your favorite relaxing, instrumental music, if you like. If you prefer to begin with a prayer, do so. If you want to light incense or a candle, then go ahead. Provide yourself with a setting that will help you focus on this activity and feel that you're doing something important and sacred, because *you* are important and sacred. You're God's precious child.

Settle into a comfortable, seated position, then take three deep breaths. Inhale through the nose, hold your breath to a count of four (or four seconds), and exhale slowly through the mouth, remembering that the exhalation always lasts longer than the inhalation. This specific breath will transport you from a stressful mode to a state of relaxation. You'll be able to view writing your story as a pleasurable event. If you look upon this process as a duty, you'll be blocked from accessing the knowledge and awareness deep in your unconscious. You'll react to the exercise with the same resistance, nonacceptance, blind obedience, or passivity with which you may have handled other experiences in your life; and you won't be able to do the work properly.

You want to greet this process with a sense of the sacred—with an open heart and positive anticipation—so that writing your story is a pleasure and a joy. Let go of any thoughts about doing the exercise correctly or writing in a way that would meet the standards of your English teachers in school. If you feel anxious about this, use the 7 Steps of Rebirth technique and reassure your child self that he or she is safe and loved no matter what.

Again, it's very important to write in the third person—describing yourself as if you were discussing another person, saying, "He did this" or "She did that." By taking on the role of the observer or witness, you'll facilitate the expression and flow of your tale.

Begin by writing down the basics: where you were born, how many brothers and sisters you have, and how you used to feel when you were a child. For example: *Once upon a time, there was a little girl called Tal. She was born in Tel Aviv and was a curious little kid. She always got into her older sister's things and was scolded for it.*

Avoid being too analytical as you write, assessing and critiquing what happened. The point isn't to assign blame or judge, saying, "It's too bad that no one understood the girl's curiosity" or "The parents should have given her more attention." These sorts of assessments come from the conscious mind, and your aim is to open up to the wisdom of the *un*conscious mind. Remaining in your conscious mind will block you from accessing it.

The writing process shouldn't be so difficult or laborious that it becomes overwhelming. *Keep it simple.* This is very important!

Write for as long as an hour, and cover a five- to ten-year period in your writing session. For example, begin by writing about your life from birth to age five.

Describe your parents. What was your mother like? *She was an artist and very sweet. Everybody loved her, but she was always very fearful and passive.* What was your father like? *He was loving and a good man, but boy, did he have a temper! He was so intense that the little girl was frightened of him most of the time.*

You may not have conscious memory of the first two, three, or four years of your life, but write down whatever comes to you. If you have a recollection that others in your family deny happened, go ahead and write it down exactly as you remember it. You, and no one else, are the storyteller.

You may want to open up old family albums and look at photos of yourself from the past to jog your memory. Pictures are

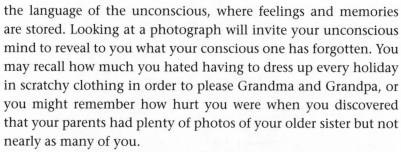

the language of the unconscious, where feelings and memories are stored. Looking at a photograph will invite your unconscious mind to reveal to you what your conscious one has forgotten. You may recall how much you hated having to dress up every holiday in scratchy clothing in order to please Grandma and Grandpa, or you might remember how hurt you were when you discovered that your parents had plenty of photos of your older sister but not nearly as many of you.

You may also find it helpful to try to remember what you were doing in kindergarten, first grade, second grade, and so on, calculating how old you were at the time. Often we associate our childhood memories with the class we were in, our teacher, and our schoolmates.

You shouldn't show your story to anyone, no matter how close, at this time. In fact, it's better not to share your writing with anyone until you've finished the whole project—and even then, don't feel that you must do so. Nobody will be checking your writing or spelling or judging what it sounds like. The goal isn't to become a published author, but to take the time to reflect on your life and write about it.

Again, tackle each five-year interval at a separate session, and give yourself a few days between sessions. Otherwise, trying to write your whole story from beginning to the present would be an overwhelming task. Accessing your memories and feelings in small increments allows you to experience your emotions without becoming consumed by them or feeling so frightened of their intensity that you decide to stop writing your story. Also, because you've had a wealth of experience each decade of your life, you would be unable to describe it all in a couple of sessions. Too much would be overlooked. Take your time and allow your memories to bubble up as you're writing, and also between sessions.

After you take a break, return to the adventure of writing and self-discovery by telling the story of the next five years of your life. It's a good idea to set a goal of completing your story over the course of two or three months so that you don't get distracted and leave your work unfinished. You might schedule your sessions into your calendar to ensure that you do your writing.

Accessing Memories

Every one of us experiences and expresses defenses that may block memories from difficult periods in our lives. Maybe all you were able to recall is: *Once upon a time, there was a little boy named Tommy. Tommy was born in Kansas and had three siblings. He was the oldest and always had to take care of everyone. He remembers summers being especially hot. There were many storms, too. The lightning was like a light show to the little boy. The thunder was deafening. He remembers one time when there was a storm that caused terrible flooding.*

If that's all that comes up, so be it. Set it aside. Also, don't write any longer than 30 to 60 minutes per session. Stay focused on recording whatever you recall or know about that five- to ten-year period. Don't go back to it the next day. Give yourself some time to process what you've remembered and written, then return to the writing in a few days.

Another important aspect of this exercise is to record events exactly as you remember them instead of trying to write a "happier" story. Accept your memories as they are without trying to alter them, and don't feel that you have to be careful not to create a story that might offend others or contradict their version of events.

For example, my clients often say to me, "Well, it's really not fair. I'm just telling you the bad stuff that my parents did. But they were really good people, and they did their best. I don't want you to have the wrong idea about them."

And I always reply, "I'm not sitting in judgment of you or your parents. It doesn't matter. You don't have to give me a balanced view at this time. Your memories are what they are. But eventually, as we continue in our work, I *will* help you balance your story, and you'll feel more comfortable about the way you describe your family."

For now, write down whatever memories come to mind and *don't whitewash anything.* You don't have to show what you've written to your siblings, who might exclaim, "Oh, you don't remember things right! I don't know what childhood *you're* talking about;

mine was wonderful." No one has to agree with your version of events. By not showing your story to your children, your spouse, your friends, or in fact anyone at all, you take away the pressure of writing it in such a way as to please your readers. That's not the purpose of this exercise.

You may have some memories of a past life that come to you. If so, you might want to write down the details you recall, no matter how trivial they may seem, and then consider whether any of these elements are somehow repeated in your current lifetime. Do you recall going on a journey holding a spear over your left shoulder and now experience mysterious, recurring pain in that area of your body? Do you recall being at a banquet where a killing spree took place, and now you're a therapist who helps people with eating disorders heal their negative feelings about food? Sometimes unexplained interests and hobbies can be clues to past lives.

For example, Mary Lou, my client from Chapter 1 who had been the Native American warrior Lightning Feather in a past life, had always loved horses—especially roan ones—and had always been drawn to Native American art and music.

Phobias and unexplained sources of anxiety and discomfort are often rooted in a past lifetime, too. Pay attention to the seasons during which incidents in your past life took place, and notice whether there are times of the year that you, in your current life, dread or feel negatively about. Notice what age you were when significant events took place. By examining the seemingly unimportant details of this life, or a past one, you may well uncover repetitions that have been buried in your unconscious.

As you delve further into this process, eventually painful issues will begin to seep out of your unconscious and into your conscious awareness. By writing in small increments of time, you'll gradually become more in touch with your history, feelings, and life experiences. By the same token, the message you're giving your unconscious and your brain is: *I'm getting ready to take a long and deep look at who I am and what went on in my life.*

Your unconscious wants you to be as aware as possible. It will begin to reveal its wisdom to you, usually in small increments, providing flashes of memories and images that appear in dreams. You'll probably find that you're dreaming more, and that the content is more memorable and intense, because your unconscious is eager to share its knowledge with you and this is one of the most effective ways in which it can communicate with you.

Dreams are like today's newspaper: They deal with current events, commentaries about the past, and recommendations for the future (just like the editorial page does). Yours will address whatever is going on with you right now, including your decision to write your story. It's important to record your nocturnal visions in a journal kept near your bed. Write down the details immediately upon awakening, and focus on remembering what happened—the images, sensations, and emotions you experienced—rather than getting stuck on analyzing any particular part of your dream. The analysis can come later, when you've finished noting the details.

The more you bring the unconscious into your conscious reality, the more you'll be aware not only of your story but of your emotions and the connections between your current and relevant past lives.

Mary Lou, who grew up in the West Virginia hills in this life and was a surgical-turned-visiting nurse, had a dream that was so upsetting for her that she came back to therapy. In fact, it was telling her that she still had issues to work on.

The dream began with her as a little girl, five or six years old, coming out of the woods into a village of wigwams and calling for her mother. Then, suddenly, she was an adult, holding her baby daughter (Mary Lou had several children in her current waking life) in the home where she grew up. She was trying to get her mother's attention, saying, "Mama, I've come to show you my beautiful daughter—look at her," but her mom was preoccupied with taking care of Mary Lou's younger brother (which was an issue in her real life when she was a child).

Her feelings were hurt, so she left the house and began walking down the mountain. The skies began to grow dark, and Mary Lou was afraid of being caught in a thunderstorm and falling down on the muddy path. She was terrified of dropping the baby. The fear was so intense that upon waking, she was crying and shaking.

The themes of Mary Lou's past life—of being responsible for the death of an innocent, and of being abandoned and alone—were clear in this dream. So were the themes of her current life, including feeling responsible for children who were in danger (she worked as a visiting nurse, checking up on kids in unsafe circumstances), anxiety, and feeling unheard. Fear of dropping the baby represented, among other things, not wanting to lose the gains she had made in giving birth to a new self. Fortunately, Mary Lou was so affected by the urgency and intensity of her dream that she came back into therapy to continue her progress.

So don't be surprised if *you* start having memorable and even upsetting dreams as you write your story. Pay attention to these messages from your unconscious and compare them to your conscious memories, which you've committed to paper.

Lakesha Writes Her Story

When you begin your own story, your writing may sound simple and basic. One of my clients, Lakesha, a 37-year-old African-American woman, started off her story in this way:

> *Once upon a time, there was a little girl called Lakesha. She had a miserable childhood. Now, Lakesha is better, but she's still unhappy with the guy she's living with.*

This description is very brief, and that's fine. Lakesha went on to write:

> *Lakesha and her family lived with her grandmother. Her grandmother was very strict.*

At that, Lakesha ended her writing session because nothing else came to mind. When she returned to her story a few days

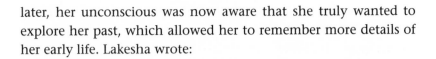

later, her unconscious was now aware that she truly wanted to explore her past, which allowed her to remember more details of her early life. Lakesha wrote:

> *She had a neighbor, Mrs. Jones, who used to bring over some greens every Friday night. They were delicious, and Lakesha loved them. Mrs. Jones was just so nice.*

Lakesha noticed that things she hadn't remembered—namely, the detail about Mrs. Jones and the greens—were now beginning to come to the surface. This memory was benign and didn't shed any great light on Lakesha's difficulties or painful emotions, but that's okay; it was a beginning. She had started the process of observing who she was and what she had experienced. Up until this point, she'd only been *reacting* to her life, not reflecting on what had happened to her and how she felt about those experiences.

You, too, might think that the details you start to remember are trivial and not worth recording—but they *are*. Don't judge what you remember. Simply allow the memories to come forth, and continue to write them down.

When Lakesha revisited her story at the next session, she remembered how she used to love it when Mrs. Jones would visit, but another memory—a more painful one—came through:

> *Her mom would come home every Friday drunk because that's when she'd get paid. So Mrs. Jones brought over collard greens and ham hocks so the kids would have something to eat. Lakesha's grandmother was away working, so she wasn't able to feed the children. Mrs. Jones was always so kind, bringing them food on Fridays.*

Lakesha was beginning to get a sense of her overall childhood environment—what was lovely and what was painful.

Lakesha also remembered that when she was five years old, her father, a drug dealer, was killed in a shoot-out. She didn't recall how she'd heard the news or whether she went to the funeral, but she remembered how she felt.

This isn't uncommon. Often people will block certain memories and be left with only general feelings or impressions. The memories you do recall may seem like trivial ones, but don't judge them. Write them down. They may have symbolic meanings that you'll recognize later.

If you remember one thing and not another, that's okay. If you continually have difficulty recalling the past, keep in mind that leaving some time in between writing sessions creates a sacred space during which the unconscious can begin to reveal its wisdom to you, and memories will start bubbling up to the surface. At times, you'll feel inspired and may be surprised by the number of memories that flow forth.

While writing your story, you may slip into using the first person. If this happens, go back and change it to the third person. If you start writing "I," resistance will jump in with a vengeance. Your old habits will creep back, and you'll lose perspective and start judging yourself and others, portraying someone as a victim and someone as a persecutor. By writing in the third person, you retain your distance as a witness or observer of the events.

As you work on your story, pay attention to how you feel—not just when you're writing, but between sessions, too. Are there any changes in your emotional state? Are you fighting more often with your partner, or perhaps less often? How many times do you think about your mother in a day? You might think that you rarely engage in a behavior, but when you add up every instance of it, you realize that you're obsessing.

Lakesha counted up how many times she thought about her daughter in a day and recognized that she was worrying constantly: wondering whether Sierra had done her chores, what she and her friends were up to, whether she was doing poorly in school and hiding it, and so on. How many times do *you* think about your children or your spouse in a day?

Regardless of how carefully you observe yourself, you can never be truly objective about your life. However, you can detach enough in order to continue being the witness. Observe with an open heart, and take notes as if you were a nonjudgmental reporter. Use facts and data, even if the facts make you feel uncomfortable.

As Lakesha wrote her story, she began to access memories from when she was a toddler:

> *Before he died, Lakesha's biological father came over to the apartment every Saturday night to visit her and her siblings. There were huge fights, and there was violence. That's why she hated Saturday evenings. She preferred to just go to sleep.*

The witness perspective she was developing was giving her information gently, slowly, and without lambasting her, without judging her. This is representative of the manner in which the Divine sees us and loves us. Just as the writing exercise gave Lakesha the information gradually, without assigning blame, so does God want us to grow and change gently and not feel judged.

Again, when we write our story, it's very important to maintain an attitude of nonjudgment. Since we've all experienced blame, loss, pain, blocking, or abuse, being compassionate with ourselves is of paramount importance. Even if we don't experience gentleness anywhere in our lives, we can at least be gentle with *ourselves*. What better way to experience gentleness than in writing our own story? We do this safely, privately, comfortably, and confidentially.

One of the most important services a therapist can provide to clients is the opportunity for them to tell their story and to have someone listen attentively and genuinely hear them. My clients commonly complain to me, "No one ever paid any attention to me. No one heard me. If I spoke of pain, if I spoke of abuse, if I spoke of problems, if I spoke of delight—if I spoke of nothing at all—no one heard me. It's wonderful that someone is now listening to me."

All of us yearn to be heard. In the absence of having a therapist, you can begin to feel heard by engaging in the simple process of writing your own story—or even dictating it into a tape recorder if you're uncomfortable with using a pen or a computer.

Once you're in the process, you might be surprised by the positive memories that come back to you in a flash.

While driving one day, Lakesha suddenly remembered an assignment from a particularly wonderful English teacher she'd had in the tenth grade. The teacher had been talking about Shakespeare's *King Lear* and the fact that he had three daughters and was betrayed by two of them. All the kids were bored because they didn't relate to the play. But when the teacher began to tell a story that had been in the newspaper that paralleled the plot of *King Lear*—a story about a person in the students' own African-American community—the class began to show an interest in what she was saying. Once they could imagine themselves or someone they knew in the story, it became tangible and fascinating.

Their homework was to write a story of their choosing, and Lakesha wrote a tale in which a father betrayed his three children. She had turned the story of *King Lear* around, writing about a father who was abusive to his daughters, violating their trust in him. That, in fact, was her own personal story.

Lakesha had been writing for about three months when she recalled that class and how much her teacher had inspired her—and how wonderful it had felt when she'd read Lakesha's story aloud to the class because she thought so highly of it. Lakesha hadn't reflected on this incident since, but it was a lovely memory to relive.

It might seem that we would consciously choose to remember the good times and forget the bad, but the fact is that we often push aside the positive memories, events, and feelings along with the painful ones. It's as if our recollections are objects in a room, and those that are painful are so toxic that we can't bear to stay surrounded by everything long enough to discern which items we feel comfortable looking at and touching and which we want to run away from. We simply shut the door and cut off our access to *all* memories, pleasant and unpleasant.

Even when you don't actually forget the good times, they may not be as readily available in your awareness. When you allow a successful experience to enter your consciousness, you're bringing in the associated positive emotions along with it, generating endorphins. Your body actually creates these healing hormones when you perform the simple act of remembering a success you experienced. Your spirits will be lifted and your self-esteem raised, so be proud of what you accomplished, and be happy.

You might think, *Oh, I did that then, but it was a long time ago and not very important—it has nothing to do with the present.* Oh yes it does! Reliving these memories is very good for you. Why not feel better today because of the remembrance of something that took place 20 years ago? As you savor the thought of the past, you retrain your mind to believe that you can be successful.

Remember, though, that you don't have to show your story to anyone or get their approval for this exercise.

Proud of what she'd written, Lakesha eagerly shared what she'd done and discovered with a couple of her sisters and her best friends. Unfortunately, their reaction was to say, "Are you *still* writing that story? Quit it already!" Feeling the pressure from her peers, Lakesha put aside her writing for a time, but when she had that flash of a positive high-school memory while driving, she reawakened to the excitement and pleasure of writing and picked up her pen again.

It took quite some time and many writing sessions for Lakesha's awareness to deepen and increase. Sometimes she would wake up with tears in her eyes because she'd been writing about some period in her life that had been particularly difficult, and her dreams became a review of her experiences at that time. When she got to the point where she was describing her mother's death, Lakesha got in touch with a lot of pain, even though her mom had been neglectful and even abusive.

She found this confusing, but so often when people die—particularly a parent—we cry not only about what was, but also about what could have been. Once they're gone, any hope that they could change, or that our relationship with them could be repaired, dissolves. Even if we believe in an afterlife and that the souls will communicate and reconnect in heaven, we'll never see or touch them again on Earth, and we can't help mourning the loss of the future we'd hoped to share with these individuals. Again, by writing in the third person, you can remain the observer and avoid the temptation to judge yourself as foolish or sentimental for feeling sad about the death of someone who didn't treat you well.

How Writing Your Story Can Heal Your Life

In the process of writing, you bring to the surface memories and feelings that have been hidden from you. Once these memories are in the light, you can begin to examine them, make connections, and get insight into your life today.

Several weeks into the exercise of writing her story, Lakesha dreamed that she was 15 again and her mother had just died, and in her dream she expressed her grief—which she hadn't done in real life. As she thought about this, it occurred to her that her own child, Sierra, was now 15 years old. Mother and daughter hadn't been getting along, and Lakesha began to wonder what the connection to the dream was. What was the repetition? Was she afraid that, like her mother, she would pass away and leave behind a vulnerable teenage daughter?

Lakesha was young and in relatively good health, so it was unlikely that she would die, but she asked herself, *Is Sierra unconsciously picking up the message from me that I'm afraid I'm going to die and leave her an orphan?* In fact, the fear of being separated from her daughter was causing Lakesha to be anxious and overly controlling, and Sierra was reacting by being rebellious. Only by making the connection between her own loss at age 15 and her fear of repetition could Lakesha emotionally handle the harsh truth that she was creating conflict with her daughter out of a sense of fear. Now that she was conscious of this, she could choose to be in the adult mode and heal their relationship.

As Lakesha continued to write her story, she got in touch with the sense of loss and the distress she'd felt when her mother died. Although she didn't share her feelings with Sierra, within a few weeks her daughter began to calm down and the two of them were getting along better. From what Lakesha could see, she hadn't changed her behavior toward Sierra, and there was no particular reason why the teenager should be less rebellious or defensive. Somehow, she felt, the process of writing had changed the energy between them. Sierra even came to her mother and asked her to attend a school function with her.

In fact, Lakesha's behavior *had* changed, but the changes were so subtle that neither she nor Sierra consciously picked up on them. Lakesha's tone of voice, body language, and facial expressions revealed that on the inside, she'd let go of her obsessions and fears about Sierra, which signaled to her daughter that she, too, could relax.

Sierra suddenly remembered the *King Lear*–like story her mother had written in the tenth grade, because Lakesha had read it to her when the girl was seven years old. She said, "Mom, remember that story you wrote in high school? Can I read it? Because we're studying Shakespeare now." Sierra was making the connection from the past to the present and was actually seeking to create in herself her mother's strengths, intelligence, and success.

Lakesha was thrilled as she handed Sierra a copy of the story. She realized that the two of them had forged a conscious bridge between them, and that she wasn't just passing along a few handwritten pages to her daughter, she was handing her a sense of self-esteem and the message: "You, too, can write a story of power—your own story—and I will support you."

Lakesha and Sierra were hearing each other and were able to communicate in a new way. As my client was changing her energy and her reactions, positive changes were occurring in and around her daughter. By writing her story, Lakesha projected a different set of expectations for Sierra, both consciously and unconsciously. Sierra then made a conscious adjustment in her perception of her mother. She was freed up from many of her fears, the worst being the death of her mom—a fear Lakesha had suspected her daughter had and which Sierra revealed to her one night when they were talking about longevity. Released from the pressure of her mother's anxiety, Sierra was able to react to Lakesha from the vantage point of her own person.

Throughout all of this, Lakesha never did show Sierra what she'd written, so don't think that you must share your story with others in order to resolve problems in your relationship and get them to understand your point of view or listen to you. As you use this process, you'll begin healing yourself, and your repetitions will be gentler and less painful. You'll become conscious of your role of storyteller and be in your proactive, adult mode more often. This will greatly affect the people around you and the situations you're in. There's no need to expose yourself to possible criticism as you work with this healing tool of writing your story. Follow through with this exercise until it's complete; afterward, when you've finished, if you want to share certain events with others, then by all means do so . . . but if you don't, then keep it confidential.

Remember, it's crucial to be honest and forthcoming as you write your story. If you hold back, telling yourself, *Things weren't really so bad after all,* you won't get to the bottom of what's bothering you or blocking you.

For example, you might say, "I know stomach cancer runs in my family, and I have some problems with my stomach, but it's no big deal," which may not be truthful. If you fear that your stomach problems will turn into cancer, acknowledge that. If you look honestly at your and your family's troubles in this physical area, you'll start to see the symbolic meaning of stomach problems, as well as the repetition in your life. You'll make a connection and say, "We all had to digest so much abuse. No wonder I, like everyone in my family, have had stomachaches. I don't want to take in all that stress, and there was so much of it growing up!"

Then, once you're conscious of the cause of your stomachaches, you can be the adult and consciously work at healing your emotional traumas. In this way, your body won't have to create a stomachache in order to get your attention. You can stop "swallowing" your pride and "taking it in" and "stomaching" abuse . . . and taking antacids.

While writing, you may find it more difficult to maintain the role of the observer as you come closer to events in the present. The pain of your recent memories is much closer to the surface, and it may be a struggle to retain a sense of perspective. Once you get to the last ten years of your story, write about only one or two years during any particular session in order to minimize the pain of remembering the job you loved but lost, the romantic partner who betrayed you, or the failure you experienced when you took a risk. Keep writing in the third person, and be kind to yourself.

Once you've completed your story, set it aside. Every 40 days or so, take an hour or two to read it to yourself from the beginning. This will give you a sense of the fullness of your story and a long, historical view of your life. You'll remind yourself in a very powerful way that *you* are the storyteller. As you read about growing up and what it was like when you started having boy- or girlfriends, you'll reexperience your feelings and start to recognize your patterns of repetition, from the point of view of the observer.

When Lakesha started writing, her memories wouldn't come to her, but by the end of the process, she had her entire life story on the page. She was able to read about the painful experiences without creating feelings of anger, sadness, resentment, or fear. In addition, she was able to make connections that she couldn't make previously because examining the events of her life had felt too traumatic before she began this process.

She told me, "Sometimes, I think, *Look at me. Look at how far I've come.* My first boyfriend used to hit me. My mother hit me, too. My grandmother was so strict, she would beat me with an electrical cord. I didn't think about it because that's how it was. Everybody I knew used to get beaten.

"My mother used to get drunk, and we didn't have enough to eat. My father would visit Saturday nights and be drunk. My parents would have wild fights. My first boyfriend used to get drunk and high. My first husband was a drunk and beat me.

"I can see the repetition in all this, but I *can* say that I don't hit my daughter or anyone else, and I don't get drunk or high. Whatever repetitions I'm still experiencing, they're nothing like what they were."

Lakesha began to notice the repetition in her jobs as well. When she worked at the corner grocery store, her boss was a woman who used to pick on her and never listened to her. When she was employed at a large home-improvement store, her female supervisor was always impatient and critical and made Lakesha feel stupid. She realized that her female superiors always gave her a hard time, just like her mother had. Her mom was forever putting her down, and her grandmother whipped her mercilessly.

Lakesha could now see her repetitions in every aspect of her life. She was also able to admit that with her own daughter, she'd been harsh—verbally, not physically—and she hadn't listened as well as she could have. She could accept this about herself without judgment now that she saw that it was a gentler repetition of patterns established in her childhood. She could also take pride in knowing that she was healing the traumas that had caused her unconscious mind to re-create the patterns.

As you consider the repetitions in your own life, keep in mind that you shouldn't take them too literally. If you say, "My father was an alcoholic, and I never felt close to him, but I don't even drink, and I've never been involved with an alcoholic man," you may miss the fact that you're addicted to working long hours and use your job as an excuse to avoid intimacy with your husband. If you make literal comparisons, you'll deny the existence of the repetition and overlook the connections between various experiences.

By writing in the third person, keeping your perspective, and never analyzing or judging, you'll allow memories and information to surface a little at a time. You'll notice that your parents divorced when you were ten, just as your mother's father died when *she* was that age. You'll remember that your mom told you she hated eating around the dining-room table with her family, and you'll realize that your own dinner table is constantly covered with clutter, and the one in your kitchen is too small for you and your family to eat at together. Then you'll hear your business partner say, "This customer is one big headache," and remember that as a child, you resented having to make dinner whenever your mother took to her bed with a migraine.

You may think all of these connections are amazing, but they're not unusual. In fact, they're everywhere. You just don't see them until you begin the process of opening up to what your unconscious can tell you.

If you tend to say, "I don't know why I always make such bad choices!" let go of your judgment and realize that you came to the best possible decisions in order to create the necessary repetitions. Ultimately, they were good decisions for your soul. Creating the repetitions gives you an opportunity to experience the past so that you can change your reactions. Deep down, your soul knows that this is the *only* way to begin to exit those patterns and heal.

Guidelines for Writing Your Story

Setting:

- Create a comfortable, relaxed environment, free of interruptions.

- View your writing with a sense of discovery, adventure, anticipation, and joy.

Time Allotment:

- Write for no more than 30 to 60 minutes per session, leaving a three- to five-day interval between sessions.

- At each session, write down the experiences and feelings you had over a five- to ten-year period of your life. As you get closer to the present, cover only one or two years per session.

- The writing process may take several months.

Guidelines for Writing Your Story
(cont'd.)

Process:

- Write in the third person at all times—be the observer or witness.

- Don't analyze or judge what you write.

- Write candidly and truthfully, without sparing anyone's feelings.

- Don't share what you've written until you're finished, and only do so then if you so choose.

- If experiences pop into your memory randomly, write them down. Record everything that comes into your mind, no matter where you are in your writing process at the time. (For example, if you're writing about ages 10 to 15 and you suddenly remember something that happened when you were 25, write that down and revisit it later, when you're working on the years 20 to 25.)

Completion:

- Read your entire story to yourself.

- Reread it every 40 days or so to appreciate its fullness and your history.

- Get a sense of how you would have liked your story to unfold.

CHAPTER NINE

REWRITING YOUR STORY

Now begins the second part of the writing process: rewriting your story.

Writing your story involved discovery, knowing, reacquainting yourself with who you are, and a sense of adventure and amazement. *Rewriting* it allows you to make the impossible . . . possible. It's like entering a nightmare with a conscious awareness that you're in charge of what happens and telling the monster, "Begone!" comforting yourself, and righting the situation easily and confidently.

Just as you can control a dream, you can rewrite your life story in any way you like. When you do, you activate your adult awareness and make conscious choices to act differently. You don't have to just react to life, and operate like a frightened child. You can exit your patterns of repetition at last.

As you rewrite your story, just as when you wrote it initially, don't try to tackle the entire project in one sitting. Start with the first five years of your life. What was your mother like? Your father? Now, how would you prefer to rewrite the story? What do you want your early childhood to be like? What, ideally,

would your teenage years have looked like? Allow your imagination to flow.

In the process of rewriting your story, it may seem as if you're indulging in a foolish fantasy, but you aren't. You can't change the past, but you *can* change the present. By using your imagination to create the experience of a happy childhood and a triumphant personal history, you affect your energy right down to the cellular level and begin to feel and believe in the possibilities of joy and transformation.

Everything that might have been—and could be—can now be incorporated into your new story. You're making all of it real, if only on paper. The gentler, more fulfilling life you would have liked to live becomes true in your mind as you use your imagination and experience feeling loved, cherished, and listened to by your mother and father and appreciated and nourished by your siblings, teachers, neighbors, and friends. The positive energy you create in yourself as you feel the emotions that naturally accompany this new story will reverberate throughout all areas of your life.

As you're going along, you can change the facts as you wish. When you put pen to paper and rewrite the facts, you don't have to work within the boundaries of reality. If you choose to describe how you were born into a family that had wealth and financial stability, you embrace the conviction that wealth and financial stability are your birthright. This belief directly affects your feelings, perceptions, and actions regarding money. It isn't a matter of being ashamed of being from a poor family. Instead, it's all about believing that you can feel and be financially secure and comfortable with money in your present life.

Profound consequences take place as you rewrite your story. The more you begin to believe it, the more it will affect you at all levels. You may think that you're just writing a fantasy, but the more you "live" your new story, the stronger the message you send to your unconscious will be. You can do whatever you want. You can become a marvelous singer or athlete, or the president of a company. You just have to work for it and let go of your limited beliefs. For example, you may not become a celebrated musical artist who performs in large venues in front of thousands of adoring fans, but you can sing with tremendous passion and beauty and touch the hearts of the people who *do* listen to you.

It's important to express your conscious desires again and again. When you do so, you can go from living in a *film noir* to living in Technicolor, because you're creating the energy of being a marvelous singer, a wealthy person whose financial situation is secure, and so on.

You may choose to write an ending to your story, allowing yourself to live happily ever after, or you might opt not to have an ending at all and simply be open to the possibilities life presents you with. Consciously, from the point of view of an adult, you are in charge of writing a story that works for you.

Lakesha Rewrites Her Story

As Lakesha rewrote her story, she changed some of the facts. She began:

> *Once upon a time, there was a little girl called Janet. She had pretty wavy black hair. Her parents were wealthy. Her father was the best family doctor in town and the pride of the local African-American community.*

In the process of rewriting her story, Lakesha found that her relationship with her daughter improved dramatically. In addition, she truly began to believe that she could be rich. With this belief giving her courage and inspiration, she started watching Suze Orman, the successful financial advisor, on television. She began looking into the stock market and invested a small amount of money. Soon Lakesha realized that she had an interest in investing and a knack for numbers. When her friends found out about her success, they began to participate in some of the investments with her, five dollars at a time.

Lakesha grew more enthusiastic and encouraged as time went on. She decided to take some courses at night at the local

community college in order to formally educate herself about finance and investing. Within a year, she had made several thousand dollars. Lakesha had gone from being continually poor—and perceiving that poverty was a way of life for her—to a perception, belief, and reality of greater abundance. This was the beginning of making the impossible, possible!

Rewriting Our Stories Changes Our World

All of us are energy beings, and all of us are connected. By healing ourselves, we heal the people around us. Lakesha discovered this in the process of writing her story—she affected her daughter, Sierra, energetically, without having to "do" something differently. It wasn't that she consciously chose to interact with Sierra in a new way; rather, it was that she changed *her* energy, and that affected her daughter's. It's just like the clerk in the post office who is so full of happiness that he makes an ordinary transaction into a joyous exchange of energy and causes you to walk away from the window feeling uplifted.

When we make a conscious decision coming from our adult self, we exercise our free will instead of being led around by the child self, who doesn't have the wisdom and skills to make good choices. We can resolve to make better ones than those we've made in the past that led to trauma.

It's not always easy to see, but when we make sound, adult decisions, we generate healing energy that radiates outward from us in all directions, affecting not just our family, but our peers, our friends, and even strangers. We actually have the power to participate in healing the world by impacting others with this shift in our own energy.

Most of us wish we could make the world a better place, but we say, "I know I can change myself, but why do *I* have to change when that other person is mean and won't do anything differently? Why do I have to be the 'bigger person'?" The answer is, *because we have no control over other people.* The only way to help them heal is by changing ourselves and letting *our* healing affect them energetically. The positive energy will then influence others.

It will even touch those who have died and crossed over, helping to break the energetic chains that continue to bind them to us and allowing them to move along on their journey. We continue to carry our feelings and attachments in our hearts and in our minds, even though the people involved are long since gone and physically not present. Although it may seem wonderful to retain this connection after loved ones die, we may prevent them from moving forward.

One of my clients is still enraged at his father, who died 25 years ago, because his dad was abusive to him. This unhealed trauma continues to affect them both karmically. Once my client begins to heal, he will help his father's soul do the same.

It may seem hard to believe these connections still exist after a person dies, but they do. When we access another lifetime, whether it took place 500 or 5,000 years ago, we do so vividly and palpably. No physical cells and no body have survived from that lifetime that the energy of consciousness could cling to—there's nothing of that physical reality that has remained at all. Yet, the experience of accessing and entering that past life is so real and emotionally charged that we live it and feel it as if it were in the present—because it *is* real. The energy of feelings and emotions transcends time and space.

As we change our own behavior and our own reactions, we change our energy . . . and our world.

Guidelines for Rewriting Your Story

Setting:

- Create a comfortable, relaxed environment, free of interruptions.

- View your writing with a sense of discovery, adventure, anticipation, and joy.

Time Allotment:

- Write for no more than 30 to 60 minutes per session, leaving a three- to five-day interval between sessions.

- At each session, write down your imagined experiences and feelings over a five- to ten-year period of your life. As you get closer to the present, cover only one or two years per session.

- The writing process may take several months.

Process:

- Embark on the process of creating a "fantasy" of what you would have wanted to look like, what you would have preferred your family and home life to be like, what you wish you could have become, and so forth. Remember, you're now making the impossible, possible!

Completion:

- Read your rewritten story whenever you need a pick-me-up and a reminder of all the possibilities your life presents you with as it continues to unfold.

CHAPTER TEN

RECONNECTING WITH JOY

When we experience joy, we're instantly connected to God and His unconditional caring for each of us. Our Creator loves us with *compassion,* a word that means "with passion." Passion is an intense feeling of love, and God's love is tremendously powerful and healing.

Pure joy allows us to experience that powerful, healing Divine love and to have hope and faith. This feeling is one that each of us can easily access at any time and in any place when we practice the 4 Steps of Joy. As with the 7 Steps of Rebirth, this technique was inspired by my Angels and Spirit Guides. It will help you access joy and make it readily available, as if it were in a protected vial, ready to be opened up and used whenever you wish.

As you read about the 4 Steps of Joy, keep in mind that this tool isn't to be used in lieu of the 7 Steps of Rebirth, but rather in combination with them. I usually recommend that my clients go through the 7 Steps of Rebirth and then follow up by doing the 4 Steps of Joy a few minutes later. If your adult self is able to reassure the child self and separate from it, then it can be present to experience the 4 Steps of Joy. Regardless of what's happening in your life, you can generate joy at any time using this technique, retraining yourself to experience pure happiness.

The 4 Steps of Joy are especially beneficial for those who have difficulty expressing or labeling emotions of any kind. What *is* joy? What about fear? Anger? Sadness? Disappointment? Delight? For those who are uncomfortable with the world of feelings, the labeling of emotions is similar to learning a new language. For example, you might remark, "I *feel* that I want to leave now," which is a statement of action rather than a true feeling. We say such things when we're out of touch with our emotions.

If we want to heal ourselves, we must understand that joy is a crucial emotion. When we feel it, we're able to fully experience God's creation and become aware of the Divine's presence in our lives, and this gives us the strength to continue in our human existence as we face the inevitable traumas that we're confronted with.

But we can't really "pursue" happiness or joy. If we do, it will prove to be very elusive. What we *can* strive to do is actively, consciously choose to create this powerful emotion. The 4 Steps of Joy allow us to do so and step into the feeling fully, awakening our spirit and improving our physiological well-being.

Debbie's story shows just how important joy is if we want to begin to heal.

Debbie's Story

Debbie, 58, worked with chemicals as a laboratory technician for a large corporation. She had been an exemplary employee and an asset to the company. However, when she came to see me, her husband had recently left her, and she'd become depressed and found it increasingly difficult to concentrate on the job. When she started making mistakes, her bosses insisted she take time off, go on disability, and get help; otherwise, they were going to have to let her go.

Debbie came to my office depressed and devoid of any emotion. Her personality was flat, as were her voice and appearance.

She told me that she loved her job and just wanted me to help her enough so that she could soon return to work, nothing more.

Debbie's life had always been joyless. Her mother had suffered from severe depression: She would sit on the sofa day in and day out with the curtains drawn, and she wasn't emotionally present for her children. One afternoon when Debbie was five and her brother was six, they were laughing and harmlessly playing "I'll show you mine if you show me yours." Their mother heard their giggles, got up to see what was going on, and flew into a rage at the sight of the children touching each other's genitals. She beat them mercilessly. This was the only time she ever hit them. After that traumatic event, they weren't allowed to be alone in the same room again. They never played or laughed together or felt safe enough to express joy or spontaneity after that. Both children shut down emotionally.

The message her mother gave Debbie and her brother was: "Never touch each other, and physical contact of any kind will result in trauma." It's no wonder that when Debbie got married and had sex, she closed her eyes and totally dissociated, never experiencing an orgasm. The intimacy was too terrifying for her. She had completely dulled herself emotionally in the rest of her life as well. In the family she created with her husband, there was no closeness, no joy, no sharing of meals or confidences. At work, she performed her tasks in isolation. She had no close friends and had only a superficial relationship with her two adult children.

Although I was able to give Debbie tools and techniques to improve her concentration so that she could function and eventually return to work, I felt that she had to heal her fear of emotion and experience joy. Happiness is vitalizing. It not only heals depression; it actually helps our bodies to generate new, healthy cells and operate more efficiently. While the 7 Steps of Rebirth and the techniques of writing and rewriting her story would prove helpful to her, Debbie had to learn to create joy in her life. She also needed to access her creativity.

When we experience creativity, we're reminded of our connection to the Creator, and we feel strength and hope. This is why

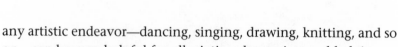

any artistic endeavor—dancing, singing, drawing, knitting, and so on—can be very helpful for alleviating depression and helping us access joy.

I told Debbie that if she didn't deal with some of the patterns in her life, she would repeat them unconsciously. But it was very hard for her to accept any notion of the unconscious influencing her behavior. After all, she had a scientific background and believed that life, like chemistry, follows simple formulas: $A + B = A + B$. If you start getting C, then there's a very tangible reason for this result that's observable. She had never reflected on why she behaved the way she did and couldn't imagine that there might be memories or feelings buried deep inside her that were affecting her.

Depression is a numbing of feeling, a turning down of the volume on all emotions—from joy to sadness, gratitude to anger. As with memories, the mind will shut down all feelings in an attempt to protect us from experiencing the most painful ones. Debbie's were almost nonexistent, even when she talked about her divorce. I asked her, "When have you, even for a moment, felt wonderful?"

She said, "I've never felt *wonderful*."

"You're a walker," I reminded her. "Haven't you ever taken a stroll outside in nature?"

She replied, "Oh yes, in the summer."

I asked her to pick any experience that was "unusually agreeable." (I even had to watch the intensity of my words, since she couldn't relate to the idea of something being a *wonderful* or *joyous* event.)

Debbie told me that she once went for a walk on the beach after work. It was evening, and the sun was setting over the lake. She was so moved by the beauty and the intense colors of the sunset that she stopped in her tracks and just stared out at the horizon. The next thing she knew, it was 20 minutes later, and she'd had no idea that so much time had elapsed. In order to appreciate the beauty of nature and its magic, she unconsciously went into a trance, almost like being asleep. Her conscious reality was devoid of this awareness because she had shut down her feelings so effectively.

Debbie described the experience of standing on the shore. There was a gentle, cool breeze. The lake was very calm. The colors of the sky were brilliant. As time passed, she removed her shoes and didn't remember having done so. The sand felt cool and refreshing between her toes. It soothed her, and she'd never felt that way before. It was like magic. I suggested that Debbie go home and develop that scene with all her senses, deepening her awareness of the colors, sounds, sensations, and smells.

I told her that as she created her joyous nature scene, she should really *see* the colors of the sunset. Simply saying that it was colorful and beautiful wasn't enough. I told her, "See the shades—orange, fuchsia, yellow, red, and purple—and how they layer, swirl, and interconnect with each other. What about the reflection on the water? The light glitters and sparkles like diamonds on its surface."

All of a sudden, this woman who had been so tense, uptight, flat, and unemotional began to describe the sunset using words that were metaphorical and amazingly evocative. She identified the colors and became aware of the distinct smells and sounds of nature: the gentle lapping of the waves on the shore, the calling of the gulls, the sensation of the cool breeze against her skin, and the gritty yet soft feel of sand between her toes. I told her to take the time to enter the scene as fully as possible, experiencing it with all her senses. Then I asked her how she felt.

She replied, "It really feels good."

At this point, I began to teach Debbie the 4 Steps of Joy so that she could draw upon the experience of the beauty of the sunset easily and swiftly to create joy.

The 4 Steps of Joy

The 4 Steps of Joy are precise and specific. The first three steps are identical to those of the 7 Steps of Rebirth (for a review of these initial steps, see the summary at the end of this chapter). Once again, the simplicity of the technique belies its effectiveness.

When you feel miserable . . .

Step 1: Stop.
Step 2: Breathe.
Step 3: Acknowledge—"Whoops, there I go again!"
Step 4: Reconnect with joy.

Remember, it's not your boss giving you a hard time; and the world, the government, your brother, your wife, your husband, or anyone else isn't causing the repetition and your painful feelings. You're the storyteller, and you can change the story anytime you like. When you perform the final step, develop a nature scene, as Debbie did, and bring it into your awareness and experience a few moments of joy with all of your senses.

It's imperative that this experience of joy relate strictly to nature. Don't seek to re-create one that involves a relationship, because relationships change, and your mind will point that out to you. For example, if you say, "A moment of joy for me was when I looked at the beautiful face of my baby," your mind will rush in with the not-very-joyous thought: *And now my baby is 16 years old, and she's driving me crazy. She crashed the car. She doesn't want to go along with my rules, and she's* <u>*impossible!*</u> Relationships are complex, emotionally laden, and multidimensional. Only in nature can we experience the purity and awe of joy.

Most of us have had at least one such uplifting experience. If, however, you've been housebound and unable to experience the outdoors firsthand, then watch a nature video. Pause at the scene that most uplifts you and enter into it. Absorb it with all of your senses. Feel what it would be like to be standing in the middle of the scene. Memorize the colors, imagine the smells and sounds, and visualize being there. When you select a joyous experience with nature that stimulates your senses, it's easier to recall it at will.

To find joy is to experience a brief, exquisite moment without any expectations or demands placed on us, one in which we feel touched by Divine love and compassion. Nature provides us with a continual reminder of the grandeur of creation and the presence of the Divine, which is why it's so easy to feel pure joy while experiencing the trees, birds, flowers, sky, and rivers. We get so lost in subways, cars, highways, laptops, and iPods. It would behoove us to take a walk every day and absorb the natural beauty that surrounds us, whether outside in nature or in our own imagination. Nature is everywhere, even in the heart of the city, and it can be breathtakingly beautiful and uplifting.

A very short description of your nature scene can serve as a code that will allow you to instantly access it. Most of us have visited an ATM (automatic teller machine) to extract money from the bank using a PIN (personal identification number) that immediately connects us to our account. Recalling the experience of joy as discussed in the 4 Steps of Joy is similar to using an ATM card. Metaphorically speaking, our "ATM"—*A Touch of Magic*—card instantly cues us and allows us to access our joyous experience.

For example, the code for Debbie's beautiful sunset over the lake could simply be "sunset on the lake." Yours might be "majestic Rockies," "blue sea," "doe in the moonlight," "crystalline snowflakes at dawn," and so on. When you repeatedly use your code, you condition your mind to generate a feeling of joy. Through repetition, the brain will now respond instantly by releasing the "happy" hormones: dopamine, norepinephrine, and serotonin. It's just like the bank releasing money from your account when you insert your card and enter your code.

As soon as you use the 4 Steps of Joy technique, you swiftly extract a joyous experience from your brain's memory bank. But unlike a real checking or savings account, your brain's memory bank has no shortage of funds. You can access joy again and again and your account will never be depleted. In fact, each time you use the code to do so, your experience is enhanced, intensified, and richer. Just as the more you practice typing, the more skilled you'll become and the faster you'll achieve the results you desire, the more you practice the 4 Steps of Joy, the easier it will be for you to quickly access deep feelings of joy. You can actually reprogram your brain to create this powerful emotion on command.

It's as if you wanted to withdraw $100 and the bank machine quickly gave you that $100 plus an extra $20; hence, the magic!

Using the 4 Steps of Joy

The cells in the brain have receptors, which receive stimuli and respond by releasing the hormones that are appropriate to the triggering event or emotion. The cells that receive stimuli most often will replicate the most. If we feel anger again and again, we're creating anger neuropeptides (because all emotions are neuropeptides), and the cells that respond to them are stimulated over and over. They replicate more quickly than other cells that respond to different emotions, so soon the brain is hardwired to very easily experience anger and allow it to affect the body. The system is perfectly set up to deal with this familiar emotion.

The opposite is also true: If the receptors for joy have barely been used, they won't replicate quickly and won't be replaced when they die off. As a result, we'll be unaccustomed to experiencing joy and having it affect us throughout our physical being.

Luckily, we're able to retrain our amazing brain at any age. We do so by choosing to experience joy again and again, stimulating our brain to make more and more receptors for joy. By repeatedly recalling experiences of this emotion fully and with all of our senses, we awaken those receptors in our brain and get them operating. The brain knows what to do—after all, we're not asking it to develop something from nothing, like wings on a human being! It's just a little "out of shape." It rewires itself when it remembers what it did naturally before we began giving in to anger so often. The receptors for joy will always be there—and always have been. Every baby enters the world with brain cells ready to receive and experience joy.

In Debbie's case, dullness and lack of expressiveness prevailed throughout her life. My client needed to repeatedly experience joy in order for her brain to wake up and use those forgotten receptors.

In addition, she had to feel pain so that the receptors that had been covered up by dullness, almost like a curtain, could now be exposed. After all, pain is an important warning bell. Just as physical discomfort wakes us up to the fact that we have a bodily injury, emotional pain wakes us up to the fact that we have a wound in our psyche that must be attended to.

Debbie's mother used to draw the curtains and sit on the sofa in the dark. Debbie needed to pull the curtains aside in order for light to enter so she could bring certain receptors back to life. She was able to train her brain through repetition. In working with the 7 Steps of Rebirth, she became more aware of her sadness and discomfort as she gradually opened herself up to a range of feelings. Using the 4 Steps of Joy over and over again, she was able to generate joy and begin healing herself—something she hadn't imagined she could do.

Often, like Debbie, we think our problem is simply anxiety, depression, an inability to concentrate, or too much stress, but when we explore our repetitions, we start to realize that we have the potential for much deeper healing than merely "fixing" our immediate issues. The 4 Steps of Joy can help us bring about that deeper healing.

Debbie started to feel much better after she began using the 4 Steps of Joy to break out of her numbness. A week later when she came into my office, I saw her smile for the first time. She also mentioned a very serious concern: Not only did she feel joy, but she also felt some pain regarding her husband leaving her. She was wary of continuing to practice the 4 Steps of Joy, because feeling numb was almost preferable—and yet, she didn't want to give up her newfound joy, so she was willing to keep using the tools I'd taught her. Gradually, Debbie was able to return to work, starting part-time and eventually working full days.

We tapered off our sessions. Then, just before the Christmas holidays, she told me that she'd contacted her children and had planned a trip to see her son in California and her daughter in Alaska. They were both a little distant with her on the phone. However, once she saw them in person, they were receptive to her

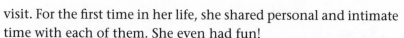
visit. For the first time in her life, she shared personal and intimate time with each of them. She even had fun!

She told me that initially her two children had seemed like strangers, but in both cases, by the end of her visit she felt that she'd forged a new relationship, which she planned to nurture. She said that she felt hopeful about becoming closer to her kids and healing from the pain of her husband leaving her, because now she had family again. She realized at that point how flat her life had been without joy.

The visualization aspect of the 4 Steps of Joy is a key to its power. In fact, positive visualization is far more effective than the popular practice of reciting positive affirmations. Affirmations such as *I am God's child* and *I am wonderful* are valuable, but not sufficient to create joy because they don't have an emotional charge. You can spend hours saying "I feel happy" without actually creating that feeling. When you're depressed or disconnected from your emotions, it's as if your fuses are burned out and you can't create that emotion unless you go deep down into yourself and fix the fuse box—and that's what you do when you use the 4 Steps of Joy.

The 4 Steps of Joy Timeline

When you first start using the 4 Steps of Joy, it's important to take three weeks to develop and connect to the nature scene with all your senses. Do this systematically in order to retrain the cells and receptors in your brain to experience joy. Every day for 21 days, imagine this scene three times—but for a different amount of time, according to this schedule:

Week 1: Expansion. Week 1 is when you expand the length of time you spend on experiencing the joyous nature scene. Every day, relive this experience three times a day, extending the length of time you spend by another two minutes (start with five minutes on Day 1 and go from there).

It's important to step up the amount of time spent to make the experience more vivid. A brief memory—*Oh, I remember when we went to Hawaii and it was beautiful*—may be pleasant, but it doesn't have the power to affect your brain significantly. Engaging the senses—seeing the colors, smelling the scents, hearing the peaceful sounds—creates emotion. Gradually increasing the amount of time you devote to envisioning your joyous nature experience is easier than immediately trying to hold on to these sensations and emotions for a full 17 minutes.

Week 2: Contraction. On Day 1 of Week 2, enter the experience as fully as possible for seven minutes. Each day, reduce the amount of time spent by one minute so that on Day 2 you practice for six minutes, on Day 3 you practice for five, and so on.

Remember that you want to enter this nature scene three times a day. The purpose of this contraction is to reenact the shape of the wave, to work with this principle that's intrinsic to the seasons and to our growth. In doing so, you are connecting with universal energy that we all share and working according to its rhythm.

Week 3: Maintenance. Every day, fully experience the nature scene with all of your senses for one minute, no fewer than three times daily.

After the initial three weeks, be sure that you use the 7 Steps of Rebirth a few minutes before performing the 4 Steps of Joy. In this way, you'll first address your pain and feel it fully instead of rushing to mask it with feelings of joy. You'll also be able to access your adult self, and then, from this mature point of view, you can more easily do the 4 Steps of Joy.

If you only use the 4 Steps of Joy, you'll escape your pain again and again by creating joy, but you won't be able to heal your issues. Leave a little time between the two techniques, or it will be as if you put your entire dinner into a blender: You'll get all the nutrition but won't access the delightful variety of flavors, smells, and textures that you would if you weren't rushing. Your emotions are rich and wonderful and an extremely important part of the human experience. Give yourself time to feel them fully.

Breaking out of numbness and depression will allow you to feel joy, but it will also reconnect you to more painful feelings. Opening up to your emotions means exposing yourself to *all* of them, pleasant and unpleasant. When you allow the Light in, you're opening up to life—which is full of pain and joy, disappointment and achievement, delight and sorrow. You may find yourself hesitant to continue to use the 4 Steps of Joy, because feeling numb might seem almost preferable to experiencing anger, sadness, and the like . . . but believe me, those emotions will decrease in intensity as you use the four techniques for self-healing: the 7 Steps of Rebirth, the 4 Steps of Joy, writing your story, and rewriting your story.

Whenever you feel sadness, anger, or other painful emotions, say "Stop!" and do the rest of the 7 Steps of Rebirth. Then, come back and perform the 4 Steps of Joy.

If you use these techniques to heal your depression or numbness, you may find that once you begin to bring those joy receptors in the brain back to life, positive, joyous memories start to surface. It's as if you regain access to a lost bank account—one full of memories—that you thought was "dead" because you hadn't used it in years. This rich resource will always remain in your name, so you can tap into it again, withdrawing memories and reexperiencing positive emotions.

I also encourage you to get in touch with your creativity, which has healing effects as well. Any creative outlet—an art class at night at the community college; doing painting, writing, or knitting; or just playing with children, who are very imaginative—will help you break out of depression and numbness.

Retraining Your Mind Using the 4 Steps of Joy

Expressing our feelings is important. But if all we express is doom and gloom, we're repeatedly stimulating only those receptors in the brain and allowing the others to fall into disuse. If we only talk about our problems, we keep recycling those same emotions. Initially, we should give voice to them in order to cleanse and clear the system, but then we need to move on to experiencing others.

We can't change the past. However, we *can* change how we feel about it and how it affects us, retraining the mind to create positive emotions instead of automatically generating negative ones—or avoiding emotions altogether. As human beings, we can experience intensity at both ends of the continuum. Our potential for joy is at least as great as it is for pain—in fact, it's even greater because of our connection with the Divine.

I suggest that you have at least four wonderfully joyous experiences on hand from which to draw—four, because while it may seem like an arbitrary number to your conscious mind, your unconscious understands its symbolism. Four is the number of the heart chakra: the seat of our loving feelings and the middle of our seven chakras, the place where we're balanced (between the three energy centers above and the three below). By using four different memories—and four steps—you send a powerful message to your subconscious to awaken your heart chakra and experience feelings of passion, love, and balance.

Holding these memories is like having "liquid" assets in an account that can be readily accessed. If you don't have four joyous past experiences to draw on, you can create them in the present. Take a walk in the outdoors or watch a movie about nature. Do this alone. Even though we're social beings, our spiritual journey is a solitary one, and we can't heal anyone but ourselves—if we try to do so, we get distracted and prevent our own healing. Let your focus be on yourself as you begin to express your God-given gift of free choice and develop and uplift your soul. No one else can do this work for you; you must do it on your own.

The way you learn, transform, grow, and live life is by repetition. You can consciously choose to use repetition to heal instead of having to rely on your unconscious choice to invoke it. You can learn by suffering, or you can learn as you consciously select alternatives that *don't* cause suffering. Using the tools of writing and

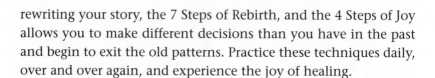

rewriting your story, the 7 Steps of Rebirth, and the 4 Steps of Joy allows you to make different decisions than you have in the past and begin to exit the old patterns. Practice these techniques daily, over and over again, and experience the joy of healing.

Summary of the 4 Steps of Joy

Step 1: Stop. Say "Stop" aloud or silently and visualize a red stop sign.

Step 2: Breathe. Take one deep breath through the nose; hold it to a count of four, or four seconds; and exhale through the mouth, always allowing the exhale to last longer than the inhale. While inhaling, relax your shoulders. While exhaling, drop your jaw and breathe out slowly and evenly with a "Haaaaa" sound.

Step 3: Acknowledge—"Whoops, there I go again!" Simply acknowledge and affirm that this is your story without judgment or criticism.

Step 4: Reconnect with joy. Say your "code" or descriptive phrase silently or aloud. This immediately brings your nature memory into your awareness, allowing you to experience a few moments of joy with all of your senses.

Remember: When practicing the 4 Steps of Joy, use them in combination with the 7 Steps of Rebirth. First go through the 7 Steps of Rebirth, and then, a few minutes later, do the 4 Steps of Joy.

AFTERWORD

As the stories in the Bible show us, even thousands of years ago people were experiencing the same repetitions and interactions that we confront today.

The story of Joseph is an example of someone who truly transcended his history, exited his pattern, and prevailed by making conscious choices:

> *Joseph was a child much loved by his father, Jacob, but his many brothers were very jealous and hated him. Joseph told his father and brothers about a dream he had. He interpreted it to mean that he would have great power and his less-powerful brothers would bow down to him. Hearing about this, his brothers were furious, as it implied that Joseph would someday wield power over them.*
>
> *The brothers conspired to slay Joseph but changed their minds at the last minute and sold him as a slave to a passing caravan. Before handing him over, the brothers took his coat of many colors and dipped it in goat's blood so that they could present it to their father as evidence that an animal had devoured the boy. Jacob, devastated, mourned for days, refusing comfort from any of his children.*
>
> *Meanwhile, Joseph was taken to Egypt and ended up in prison after being falsely accused of a crime. He was released*

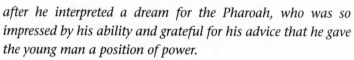

after he interpreted a dream for the Pharoah, who was so impressed by his ability and grateful for his advice that he gave the young man a position of power.

One day, Joseph's brothers came to Egypt to purchase grain. Joseph saw them, but they didn't recognize him now that he was a grown man and dressed in noble garb. He refused to sell them any grain; however, he told them that if they brought him their youngest brother, who hadn't accompanied them, he might consider selling them what they needed. The brothers went home and retrieved Benjamin, who was now the favorite of their father, Jacob. When Joseph saw all his brothers together, he said, "I'll give you grain, but leave your brother Benjamin here."

At that point, one of the brothers, Judah, stood up and said that he wasn't going to allow the youngest to be given to the Egyptians, because it would simply break their father's heart. He said that this had happened once a long time ago, and he wouldn't let it happen again. Judah then offered himself up as a slave and said, "No more. I am the one who caused the heartache of my father, Jacob. I will not cause this heartache again. The price is too great. Don't take my brother. I will be your slave."

Joseph then revealed to his brothers who he really was. He welcomed them with open arms and asked them to return home and bring back his father. They did this, and all were joyously reunited. Jacob was overwhelmed and thrilled at seeing his son, whom he'd thought was lost forever. Joseph expressed his love for all his brothers, showing only kindness and forgiveness.

Judah had an opportunity to repeat the story of selling a brother, but this time he made a different choice and changed his reaction. His soul took an alternative path, and he exited his pattern. Like his brother Judah, Joseph didn't succumb to the repetition of re-creating the identical situation by reacting with jealousy and punishment, as his brothers had done in the past. He could have enslaved Benjamin, just as he had been enslaved, and gotten revenge against his conniving brothers. Had he done so, he would have exchanged the role of victim for that of perpetrator but remained within the pattern of brother abusing brother. Instead, he transcended the situation and offered only love, kindness, and forgiveness to all members of his family.

This ancient story reminds us that no matter how much we've suffered and no matter how much suffering *we* cause, we always have the option to become aware of what we've done, acknowledge it, let go of the judgment that causes us pain and sends us back into denial, and make a new choice. We can't choose for anyone else, but we can always decide that *we* are ready to begin healing. God has given us the great gift of free will, which allows us to unchain ourselves from the past, end the cycle of suffering, move into the future, and open ourselves up to new possibilities.

Exiting Our Patterns
of Repetition and Uplifting Humanity

Repetition has been around as long as human beings have walked the earth, but we don't have to keep repeating the same story again and again. If we consciously choose to exit our patterns, we can uplift humanity and allow all of its members to break free of repetition.

I fervently wish to help create a shift in consciousness within humanity, and I believe that we can begin to make this shift if we stop seeing ourselves as victims and start taking responsibility for our stories.

Spiritually, this is important, because if we constantly think of ourselves as victims and complain about our problems, we focus our attention on negativity, weakness, and darkness. In doing so, we distance ourselves from our faith and the essence of the Light, which is there at all times and in all dimensions. God's love is ever present, but we don't always realize it because we're distracted by our stories.

When we each begin to take responsibility for our own story, we start moving away from being the child or victim who is helpless and powerless, and toward being the empowered adult who is able to make choices. Once we own our story and recognize that we are the storyteller—the writer, director, producer, and actor—we can change any aspect of our narrative and allow the Light to come in. No longer placing our attention on our helplessness and power-lessness, we focus on our openness and realize that we have more power than we thought we had. The Light that is always there will then effortlessly begin to fill us. The more we release our fears and make the impossible possible, the more connected we are with the energies of the Light.

We bring in Light every time we express kindness, no matter how insignificant the act of kindness may seem. Imagine a glass filled with water: When one more spoonful is added, the water overflows. We don't know how much Light is already present, so a single good deed or thought may be the one that creates a criti-cal mass, bringing about enlightenment and a huge shift in the consciousness of humankind. Any simple act of kindness—caring for a pet, gardening with gratitude and love, or even just smiling at a stranger—may be the one that takes us over the top. There-fore, each of us needs to bring Light into the world by doing good whenever we can and trying to exit the patterns that cause us, and others, to suffer.

Healing radiates in all directions: It reaches out to our peers, siblings, and friends; up toward our parents, whether they are alive or have crossed over; and down to our children. If we assume the responsibility of making changes in our own lives, it will affect everyone in our environment and encourage them to make changes, too, and leave behind the patterns of repetition.

If every one of us releases the past, embraces the present, and creates a hopeful and enriching future, we'll produce an important shift in consciousness and play our part, however small, in the transformation of all humanity. It's a goal we can begin to reach for today.

ACKNOWLEDGMENTS

Like the trillions of cells that make up a human body, many people have encouraged and supported me over the last 11 years. Here is a short list:

- Christiane Northrup, M.D., who understood, embraced, and blessed this work from the very beginning. Without her active help and support, this book would not have become a reality. My enduring heartfelt thanks and appreciation will accompany you always.

- Erika Schwartz, M.D., my dear friend, who with wisdom and intuition believed and supported me.

- The Enlightened Sage, the Honorable Rav Itshak Kadouri, who continues to bless me and my work.

- Ned Leavitt, my agent, whose publishing knowledge and expertise supported me in this process.

- Nancy Peske, my gifted editor, whose skillful reorganization and tireless attention to the lyrical flow of the material deeply enriched the spirit of the book.

- Dan Zelling, M.D., for his support and guidance during difficult times when I doubted this book would see the light of day.

- Sheila Pickholtz, my dear longtime friend, whose unwavering support of me and my work has been a blessing in my life.

- Debbie Barnby, Amy Bauer, Evelyn Fisboin, Sandy Giallanza, Joyce Koleno, Judy Mellor, Linda Schiller-Hanna, Nancy Shea, Mark Silber, and Elaine Ujczo, dear friends and supporters, who consistently helped and encouraged me on this long journey.

- Reid Tracy and the staff at Hay House for believing in me and the importance of this message by giving me this opportunity to share it with the world.

- My beloved family for their support, patience, endless encouragement, and love: Esty and Haim, Vivy and Elie, and all the children and little ones who have brought joy, blessings, and warmth to all of us.

ABOUT THE AUTHOR

Doris Eliana Cohen is an internationally trained clinical psychologist with more than 30 years' experience. She holds master of science and Ph.D. degrees in clinical psychology from the University of Miami in Coral Gables, Florida, and graduated summa cum laude with a bachelor of arts in psychology from Agnes Scott College in Decatur, Georgia.

Her private practice in psychology and holistic therapies has helped thousands of clients. She offers consulting and guidance in psychological, life, and relationship issues. Doris is a captivating professional speaker and sought-after expert and instructor in the fields of stress management, personal growth, and healing. Her compassion for her clients, exceptional vision and insight into the human psyche, and intellectual drive have propelled her on a lifelong journey to find the truths and components of self-healing.

Doris's passion for learning and for seeking greater awareness has led her to discover and create complementary methods that combine psychological and alternative-healing modalities. These encompass the hands-on healing practice of Reiki (she is a Usui Reiki Master and teacher), as well as intuitive and spiritually based approaches that include past-life-regression hypnotherapy, psychic readings, dream analysis, and spiritual cleansing. She was formally trained in psychic readings through the Association for Research and Enlightenment (the Edgar Cayce Foundation) and by internationally known metaphysical intuitive Linda Schiller-Hanna.

Doris has given more than 10,000 readings, many of which involved medical intuition. In her work, she places special emphasis on current life patterns and goals and the soul's journey and purpose. In addition, she provides in-depth information and guidance regarding past lives and, more important, their application to the present. She conducts workshops and seminars in the U.S. and internationally on past-life regression, dreams, stress management, and hypnosis.

Doris was born in Cairo, Egypt, and has lived in the Sudan and Israel. She currently resides in Beachwood, Ohio.

NOTES

NOTES

NOTES

NOTES

NOTES

NOTES

NOTES

NOTES

NOTES

We hope you enjoyed this Hay House book. If you'd like to receive a free catalog featuring additional Hay House books and products, or if you'd like information about the Hay Foundation, please contact:

Hay House, Inc.
P.O. Box 5100
Carlsbad, CA 92018-5100

(760) 431-7695 or **(800) 654-5126**
(760) 431-6948 (fax) or **(800) 650-5115 (fax)**
www.hayhouse.com® • **www.hayfoundation.org**

Published and distributed in Australia by: Hay House Australia Pty. Ltd., 18/36 Ralph St., Alexandria NSW 2015 • *Phone:* 612-9669-4299 *Fax:* 612-9669-4144 • www.hayhouse.com.au

Published and distributed in the United Kingdom by: Hay House UK, Ltd., 292B Kensal Rd., London W10 5BE • *Phone:* 44-20-8962-1230 *Fax:* 44-20-8962-1239 • www.hayhouse.co.uk

Published and distributed in the Republic of South Africa by: Hay House SA (Pty), Ltd., P.O. Box 990, Witkoppen 2068 • *Phone/Fax:* 27-11-467-8904 • orders@psdprom.co.za • www.hayhouse.co.za

Published in India by: Hay House Publishers India, Muskaan Complex, Plot No. 3, B-2, Vasant Kunj, New Delhi 110 070 • *Phone:* 91-11-4176-1620 *Fax:* 91-11-4176-1630 • www.hayhouse.co.in

Distributed in Canada by: Raincoast, 9050 Shaughnessy St., Vancouver, B.C. V6P 6E5 • *Phone:* (604) 323-7100 • *Fax:* (604) 323-2600 • www.raincoast.com

Tune in to **HayHouseRadio.com®** for the best in inspirational talk radio featuring top Hay House authors! And, sign up via the Hay House USA Website to receive the Hay House online newsletter and stay informed about what's going on with your favorite authors. You'll receive bimonthly announcements about Discounts and Offers, Special Events, Product Highlights, Free Excerpts, Giveaways, and more!
www.hayhouse.com®